DATE DUE

~~DE 1~~			
~~JE 2 '04~~			

DEMCO 38-296

Kafka,
Love and Courage

Kafka, Love and Courage

The Life of Milena Jesenská

Mary Hockaday

The Overlook Press
Woodstock • New York

First published in the United States in 1997 by
The Overlook Press
Lewis Hollow Road
Woodstock, New York 12498

Library of Congress Cataloging-in-Publication Data

Hockaday, Mary.
    Kafka, love, and courage : the life of Milena Jesenská /
Mary Hockaday.
     p. cm.
1. Milena, 1896-1944. 2. Journalists—Czech Republic—Biography.
3. Kafka, Franz, 1883-1924—Friends and associates. I. Title.
PN5355.C95Z765946 1997   070'.92—dc20
96-29267   CIP
ISBN: 0-87951-751-4

Originally published in Great Britain by André Deutsch Limited
Manufactured in The United States of America
First American Edition
1 3 5 7 9 8 6 4 2

For all my friends in Prague

Contents

Acknowledgments

In Prague my thanks to Eva and Lukáš Kliment, Jana and Vašek Chaloupecký and Ondřej and Marta Ernyei for their wisdom and hospitality; and to Alena Doležalová, Štěpánka Ročková, David Charap, Martin Machovec and Vladimír Alexa for their help with research. Thanks to Hana Klinková at the Museum of Czech Literature at Strahov, Mrs Králová at the National Newspaper and Magazine Archive at Stromovka, and staff at the Museum of the City of Prague for their patience. For their conversation and memories, thanks to Martin Černý, Marie Chaloupecká, Lumír Čivrný, Eduard Goldstücker, Olga Housková, Lenka Reinerová, Zdeněk Urbánek, Libuše Vokrová, and the many others who contributed to my understanding of Milena's life. Special thanks to Marie Jirásková for her deep knowledge and encouragement.

Elsewhere, my thanks to Staša Fleischmann in Paris, Dr Ulrich Wienzerl in Vienna, Gerry Turner in Ireland and my warmest thanks to Steffi Schlamm in Salzburg.

In Britain, my thanks to Fritz Beer, Jonathan Cole, Paul Foote, Stephen Jolley, Bedřich Rohan, Devana Pavlik at the British Library and to all those who helped me in the writing of this book. I would also like to express my gratitude to Sara Menguc and Laura Morris for their unflagging commitment to the book, and to the Society of Authors for a generous research grant from the Authors' Foundation. Thanks also to my parents for their advice and proof-reading and to all my friends for their enthusiasm and support.

Acknowledgments

Schocken Books, published by Pantheon Books, a division of Random House, Inc.

Margarete Buber-Neumann, from *Milena*, first published by Albert Langen-Georg Müller Verlag, Munich, under the title *Milena – Kafkas Freundin*. First published in Great Britain in this translation by Ralph Manheim by Harvill in 1989. Translation copyright © Seaver Books 1988. Reprinted by permission of Henry Holt and Co., Inc.

Alois Jirásek, from *Old Czech Legends*, published by Forest Books, London 1992. Reproduced by kind permission.

For permission to quote from Milena Jesenská's documents and articles and from *Adresát Milena Jesenská* by Jana Černá, thanks to Martin Černý.

For permission to draw on material in the Fond Jaroslava Vondráčková at Strahov and to quote from *Kolem Mileny Jesenské* by Jaroslava Vondráčková, thanks to Marie Jirásková.

Foreword

When I was living in Prague in the early 1990s, like many foreign visitors I read a great deal of Kafka. I had read some of his novels before, but never his correspondence, and *Letters to Milena* was a revelation. But the book revealed more to me about Kafka himself than the person he was writing to. Who was she, this Czech woman who had inspired such passion, such emotional and intellectual engagement from the genius Kafka?

I began to investigate, and it proved an opportune time to do so. After more than forty years of grey Communist rule, Prague was rediscovering its cultural heritage. Kafka, the Jew, could be freely spoken of again, and so could his former lover, the anti-communist Milena. Brief articles appeared about her, and there was a small exhibition devoted to her life. An outline emerged of a rebellious childhood; an early marriage to an older Jewish man; the intimacy with Kafka; a brilliant career as a journalist in a magical Prague; divorce, a second marriage, childbirth, illness and destitution; adoption and then rejection of Communism; a renewed career as a journalist charting the rise of fascism in Central Europe and the German invasion of Czechoslovakia; and eventual arrest and death at the hands of the Germans.

But it was only when I went one step further that she really came alive.

I began to read her articles, climbing the winding staircase of the decrepit pseudo-Gothic castle in Stromovka Park that houses Prague's newspaper archive, sitting at the shabby tables with piles of dusty, leather-bound volumes of pre-Second World War newspapers, and entering the realm of the First Czechoslovak Republic, with all its charm and vitality.

The voice of Milena's articles from this period between the two world wars was startling. Whether she was writing about the latest fashion or the German invasion of Prague in 1939, the tone was fresh, vivid and still pertinent. The more I read, the more the articles (of which there are several hundred) became a window onto both Milena's life and Central Europe before its distortion by Communism. Milena's own writing is the real inspiration behind this book.

Another motivation was a puzzle. As I read and discovered more about Milena I saw photographs of her at different stages of her life. Sometimes it was hard to believe they showed the same person. A photograph from the 1920s reveals a beautiful young woman, of great grace and elegant dress, with bright eyes and a serene expression. A dozen years later her features have become heavy, her eyes are shadowed and her hairstyle and dress are functional rather than becoming. There is something sad but nonetheless defiant about her eyes. I was curious to discover what made the one into the other.

The notes at the end of the book give details on the source material, but I would like to mention at this stage some of the main sources. One is obviously Kafka's *Letters to Milena*, which contains many clues to Milena's life. But we only have one side of the correspondence, and it must also be remembered that the relationship only lasted for a few years.

Then there is an account by Margarete Buber-Neumann, a German democrat who knew Milena when they were both imprisoned in Ravensbrück concentration camp during the war. They had a close friendship and Buber-Neumann's *Milena* is a moving account of life in the camp and a reverent (perhaps too reverent) testament to the woman she admired so much. But Buber-Neumann's version of Milena's life is inevitably partial, in both senses of the word. After the war, she added to the stories Milena had told her through correspondence with other acquaintances. But she was not familiar with Prague and did not speak Czech. Some of *Milena* is, therefore, necessarily incomplete or impressionistic.

There are similar problems with a book by Milena's daughter Jana Černá, *Kafka's Milena*. Jana, always known as Honza, was a child when she last saw her mother; she revered her mother's memory but again her testimony cannot always be relied on. (When her book was published in English, before the collapse of Communism, a reviewer wrote: 'Sadly, but evocatively, this little book completes whatever is to be known of Milena.' Happily, this has proved to be wrong.)

The incompleteness of each of these two books does not mean they should be dismissed. They are powerful and revealing accounts by people who knew Milena personally. But they leave room for something different.

In *Kafka, Love and Courage* I have therefore tried to establish a more objective portrait of Milena. I have drawn on conversations with those still alive who remember her. I am enormously grateful to these men and women who have allowed me to pester them and delve into their sometimes painful memories, especially Lumír Čivrný, Marie Chaloupecká, and Stefanie Schlamm, in her nineties, whom I visited near Salzburg. Stefanie and her husband Willi knew Milena in Prague in the 1930s, and she has given me access to unpublished letters from Milena which offer new insights into the difficult years before the Second World War, and into what Milena's letters to Kafka might have been like.

All those who knew Milena confirmed to me that the charisma I sensed on the pages of the old newspapers was there in real life.

I am also enormously grateful to Marie Jirásková in Prague, who has worked tirelessly to trace material about Milena, and who has allowed me to draw on the private archive of Jaroslava Vondráčková, who knew Milena well. (These papers, which Jirásková has deposited in the Czech Literary Archive, add to Vondráčková's own memoir about Milena, *Kolem Mileny Jesenské (Concerning Milena Jesenská)*.

But my main source, which has not previously been tapped to its full potential, is Milena's own writing. At its best, her journalism is rich, perceptive and committed. Her more personal columns cannot be taken as gospel truth; as a working journalist coining words for a living, she knew how to elaborate on her experiences to make a good story. But the articles are a guide to the people and places she knew, and to her preoccupations. In a wider sense, Milena cannot always be trusted as a source (this is a problem with Buber-Neumann's book, which draws on Milena's camp reminiscences). Her characteristic charm and persuasiveness could shift into more manipulative and mendacious behaviour, as if she was compelled to make her own life compelling. I have therefore tried as far as possible to confirm her accounts from other sources. At other times I have allowed or disallowed her evidence according to my own judgment, given everything else that I know; there must be a place for intuition in any biography. Pure speculation I have always tried to indicate.

A few words on pronunciation and language. For those who are interested, J in Czech is pronounced as Y and a ´ on a vowel serves to lengthen it.

Foreword

Milena's surname is thus pronounced Yesenskar. A ˘ over a consonant serves to soften it (š becomes sh, ž becomes zh etc.). Surnames are feminised for women, by adding á or ová. Thus Jan Jesenský begets Milena Jesenská. Words are generally stressed on the first syllable. I have left place names in Czech except where there is a familiar version in English, for example Wenceslas Square for Václavské náměstí. Czechoslovakia, sometimes referred to as the First Republic, was formed after the First World War out of Slovakia and the Czech lands (which comprise Bohemia and Moravia). Before 1918, when Slovakia and the Czech lands were part of the Austro-Hungarian Empire, the terms German and Austrian can be interchangeable. Prague Germans might also define themselves as Austrian, i.e. citizens of the Empire. After the war German and Austrian signify belonging to Germany or Austria.

Milena – what a rich, heavy name, almost too full to be lifted . . . in colour and form it is marvellously a woman, a woman whom one carries in one's arms out of the world, out of the fire. I don't know which, and she presses herself willingly and trustingly into your arms, only the strong accent on the i is bad, doesn't the name keep leaping away from you? Or is it perhaps only the lucky leap which you yourself make with your burden?

Franz Kafka
Letters to Milena

1

Childhood

Milena was born on 10 August 1896, into the Austro-Hungarian Empire. She was a child of Prague, a city which had declined from being an imperial capital in the fourteenth century to a provincial centre governed from Vienna. But the city had not forgotten its roots. In the decade of Milena's birth, the Czech historian Alois Jirásek published a book of *Old Czech Legends*. It was a contribution to the 'Czech Revival'; like many small nations in the nineteenth century, the Czechs were celebrating their history and culture in an attempt to strengthen national consciousness and justify greater political autonomy. Jirásek wrote of the city's foundation by Old Father Čech; of the visionary queen Libuše; of King Václav (the Wenceslas of the carol) and of the legends of riches and alchemy from Prague's most glorious days. He described the medieval Emperor Charles IV looking down from his castle onto Prague, 'the royal city, with the slanting roofs of its houses, the churches and towers, the reflected gleam of many glass windows, the tree-tops in the numerous gardens and on the islands in the river, all blended in the soft light of the full moon. All was silent. The only sound was that of the water spilling over the dams in the Vltava below.' Milena was able to look down on the same unchanged view and it bound her to the city until the very end of her life.

Milena had an uneasy childhood. Because of her mother's comparatively early death, Milena's father played a much greater part in her life, and from the start her relationship with him was complex and formative. Jan Jesenský came from an 'old but impoverished' Czech family. He was born on 5 March 1870 and named after his father, who was something of a maverick, a man of energy and ideas who nonetheless lost everything in business enterprises. Once, and then again. First Jan Jesenský the elder founded a publishing and printing house, and dreamed of building a small palace for his family in the ancient Malá Strana district where they lived. He wanted also to renovate the quarter's public gardens and plant them with an abundance of flowers. Perhaps it was from her grandfather that Milena inherited her love of flowers. He was good with his hands and admired the arts.

When the print works failed, he acquired a cement works. This must have seemed an astute attempt at recovery since Prague was rapidly expanding. The family had to move, and Mrs Jesenská, Milena's grandmother, now had to raise her eight children, most of them girls, in a smaller apartment at the less charming end of Malá Strana. 'If only just a little something could be certain,' she sighed. But the cement works failed to prosper and Mr Jesenský had to work as an agent for another firm.

Jan Jesenský inwardly scorned his father's misfortunes but in different guise he inherited his father's yearnings. Prague was a city to foster dreams, Malá Strana especially so. The 'lesser side, the small town' was a jumble of small cobbled streets, alleys and archways. Every brick and stone of the quarter, which spread along the river by the fourteenth-century Charles Bridge, told a chapter of Czech history, from the castle of Charles IV, Emperor of half Europe, to the baroque palaces of the ascendant Catholic aristocrats who reclaimed their place in the city after defeating the descendants of the Protestant reformer Jan Hus in the Battle of the White Mountain in 1620.

Jan Jesenský liked to claim his share in the city's history and the long tradition of Czech nationalism and rebellion, declaring that he was descended from Jan Jesenius, the first professor of medicine at Prague's Charles University, who was hanged, drawn and quartered with a score of other Bohemian luminaries in the Old Town Square on 21 June 1621, charged with defying the authority of the Catholic Empire. The claim was spurious, as Jesenius had only daughters. Nonetheless, the story fed the Jesenský family's sense of its destiny.

Jan decided to study medicine and turned to his musical skills to help support himself. After lectures he would serenade the patrons of Prague's restaurants, learning the ways of a world he wished to join. He also gave private tuition and eventually graduated in 1894.

Soon afterwards he married, in a union of convenience as much as true love. Milena Hejzlarová was the daughter of a regional inspector of schools. The family owned a spa near Náchod, in the mountains north-east of Prague; they belonged to the new rich and had a great respect for learning and the arts. Milena Hejzlarová was accomplished and beautiful but, perhaps just as important, she offered a sizeable dowry. This enabled Jan to set up a private practice, and to develop his taste for fine clothes and good living. His dependency on his in-laws did not bring the couple any closer.

Not much is known about Milena Hejzlarová. Her sphere was entirely domestic and her shortened life makes her doubly invisible. Her daughter later talked of her with love, even awe, as a beautiful but shadowy woman. When Milena was near death in Ravensbrück concentration camp, she recalled how her mother would sit of a morning at the mirror in a soft dressing gown, combing her long, wavy chestnut hair. She had green eyes. She may also have been religious, if only in a quiet, dutiful way – Milena always kept a crucifix which had hung over her mother's bed.

Jan Jesenský specialised in orthodontic medicine, and was soon working with some of the most eminent orthodontists of the time. In the first year of his marriage he made an extended visit to Paris to study; whether his wife went with him is unclear. And in the year of Milena's birth he went to Berlin to work with a respected professor of dentistry. So Milena was born to an elusive, ambitious father and an ever-present but frail mother. They lived in an apartment in Prokopovo Square, a small cross-roads in Žižkov, a newish suburb of the spreading city.

Milena was her parents' pride and joy, but in one respect she was not quite good enough for her father. She was a girl. She was made to feel this most acutely when she was about three. Her mother bore a son, who was given his father's name Jan. But Mrs Jesenská was not strong enough to feed the baby, who was a sickly child. Instead of engaging a wet nurse, the scornful Dr Jesenský is said to have declared, 'If my wife can't nurse her babies she shouldn't have them.' Milena, a pale, large-eyed child, watched as her father stormed and her mother fretted until the boy died a few weeks later. Dr Jesenský had his son buried in the family vault. That Milena was left with a sense of guilt and inferiority seems clear from later references to the brother she never had, the son her father never had.

By 1901 the rising young doctor had moved his family to Ferdinand Avenue (now Národní třída) in the town centre, across the river from Malá Strana. The great city of Prague beckoned with treasures for any child. In 1901, when Milena was five, Emperor Franz Josef paid a three-day visit to Prague and was treated with full ceremonial.

There were receptions for the city's dignitaries and a new bridge was opened across the Vltava. Prague was festooned with banners and garlands, and ceremonial arches were constructed along the route taken by the Emperor, with his white gloves and three-cornered hat. Even if Dr Jesenský was one of those Czechs longing for greater autonomy within the Empire, he was at heart a conservative eager for social acceptance, and would have impressed on his little daughter the importance of the visit.

There was more spectacle each year at the Feast of St Mikuláš, or St Nicholas, on 6 December, as important as Christmas itself. A fair filled the Old Town Square, a broad square ringed by baroque facades and towered over by the prickly gothic spires of the Týn church. Milena and Jaroslava Vondráčková, a young friend who would be a life-long acquaintance and was known as Slávka (or occasionally Sláva), would wander from stall to stall with their mothers. Their fathers, who were colleagues, would join them after a drink nearby. Figures roamed through the crowd dressed as St Mikuláš, the Good Angel or the Devil, with their promises of reward or punishment for the well-behaved or naughty child, and the children tasted the treats on offer, sugared almonds, dates and Turkish honey.

Once Drs Jesenský and Vondráček took their daughters to enjoy a new phenomenon. On the square, in a huge canvas tent with a canvas screen, early children's films were shown. Dr Jesenský called it the 'first miracle' for the children. Milena was also taken to a display of wax figures, including sensational evocations of murderers and martyrs. It thrilled and terrified her, kept her awake at night, but drew her back time and time again.

Sometime between 1902 and 1907 the Jesenskýs moved again, to a smart new apartment building in neighbouring Ovocná Street (named after the fruit market nearby). It was a good address, at the bottom of Wenceslas Square (actually a long rectangular avenue). 'In those days there were still beautiful low buildings around there, late baroque, and it all looked like a small provincial town with its neat little square,' Milena later wrote. The move marked Dr Jesenský's rise in an ascendant Prague. The building, with its marble hallway, balconies and carved figures on the balustrade, was self-confident and pleased with itself, an appropriate setting for the residence and surgery of a successful dentist. The spacious sixth-floor apartment was filled with the dark, heavy, mock-Renaissance furniture of the time. Mrs Jesenská was generally considered to have good taste, but Milena was ambivalent about her mother's style. She loved several coloured peasant headscarves which her mother gave her, and later took them on her travels, to add something of her own to hotel rooms. But she also recalled how she cried 'when my mother took away the little pink and blue combs I had brought home from some fair and replaced them with ones made of real tortoiseshell.' Later, Milena also remembered the 'silly, kitsch' picture above her bed, of a big dog sitting mournfully by an empty child's bed.

Milena began to attend the elementary school in the area. Dr Jesenský had placed himself and his family in the thick of things, far from the ghost-filled Malá Strana, at the hub of the fashionable, commercial New Town. As befitted a successful member of the Czech professional classes, Dr Jesenský had joined the political fray. He and Dr Vondráček both supported the party of the Young Czechs, a new grouping determined to see off the 'Old Czechs', whom they accused of subservience to Vienna and a failure to realise Czech national aspirations. They were great admirers of the fifteenth-century Czech reformer Jan Hus (and Milena took him as a hero too). Dr Jesenský attended meetings and read the party paper, *Národní listy*.

The city was growing, changing. Bohemia was the most prosperous part of the Empire, with good land and extensive industry. Prague now had a population of half a million, double that of thirty years before. Industrialisation brought people flocking from the countryside to the city, which was now spreading out from the Old Town Square, bursting through the ancient city walls. The farmland on the hill beyond the far end of Wenceslas Square was gradually being developed. The tangled, overcrowded Jewish quarter between the Old Town Square and the river was knocked down around the turn of the century and a broad new avenue built.

But these changes brought their own tensions. They were partly economic. The growth of an industrial working class created pockets of poverty in and around the city. But it also saw the growth of a labour movement and, with the fluctuations of the industrial economy, conflict between workers and bosses. By the turn of the century the Social Democrats had won some of the best workers' rights in Europe, but not without battles. During Milena's childhood there were periods of unrest, strikes, demonstrations and riots, sometimes in the heart of the city outside Milena's door.

Economic strains exacerbated the other source of conflict in the city, its ethnic mix. Prague was a diverse city where Czechs, Germans and Jews had long lived side by side but, by and large, in their own worlds. The balance of power was a shifting, complex matter. After the defeat of the Protestant Czechs at the Battle of the White Mountain, the Catholic forces of the Empire reasserted their hold on Bohemia, and the pliant nobility aligned itself with Austria. Although the German population, concentrated in Prague and in a crescent around the western tip of the country, was a minority, the German-speaking aristocracy and trading class became dominant politically and culturally. German became the language of power, Czech the language of the countryside. But during the nineteenth century the Czechs, like other nations across Europe, reasserted their national identity and fought (largely in vain) for greater autonomy within the Empire. The lack of political power left energies to be channelled into the cultural sphere: linguists classified the language, the historian František Palacký wrote his huge *History of the Czech Nation* and Czechs regained a sense of themselves as a people with a once glorious past and dreams of a glorious future. Such developments made the Germans uneasy, especially because the Czech population was growing proportionally faster (Germans made up about ten per cent of Prague's population in Milena's day). The failure of Vienna to find a political solution to the increasing agitation between the Germans, loyal to the Austrian Empire, and the restless Czechs, left a fractious, tense situation.

This already volatile mix was further complicated by the presence of a large Jewish community, about five per cent of the population. Their place was never easy, although the Edict of Toleration declared by Emperor Joseph II in 1782 had allowed them to flourish in a way rare in other parts of the Empire. By Milena's day there was a prosperous Jewish business class, which largely chose to identify with the economically more powerful German community, and to speak its language. This was Franz Kafka's Prague, which lived alongside but had no reason to mix with Milena's Prague. His Old Town Square (which he lived on or near for most of his life) and hers might as well have been on other sides of the world. For the Jews were loved neither by the Germans, who regarded them as outsiders, nor by the Czechs, who regarded them as pro-German.

So Milena's childhood was spent in a city where national tension was never far away. As a Czech bourgeoisie developed and demanded greater autonomy, the political battles in the Imperial parliament in Vienna over language and cultural rights were echoed in Prague: in the growth of Czech and German cultural and political groups; in the rivalry of Czech and German newspapers; and sometimes in open conflict on the streets, which became a theatre for national tensions.

At its gentlest, this meant whispers and stares, at its worst, violence. At a young age, Milena was a witness to such conflict. The German-speaking students used to promenade every Sunday on Na příkopě, a broad street that ran into the bottom of Wenceslas Square on one side, while the Czech students walked along Ferdinand Avenue on the other (near Ovocná Street). Most Sundays they sang their national songs, taunted each other and left. Milena would sometimes watch from the window of the apartment. But:

Then came a Sunday which I will never forget as long as I live.... From the Powder Tower came the Austrian students in their coloured caps, not as usual on the pavement, but in the middle of the street. They were singing, marching in formation with ringing, defiant tread. Suddenly a crowd of Czechs appeared from Wenceslas Square; they too were marching in the middle of the street. They walked in silence. My mother and I stood by the window, and she held my hand a little more tightly than was necessary. In the front row of the Czechs walked my father. I recognised him from the window and it gave me great joy, but my mother was pale and tense.... Suddenly a crowd of police came rushing out of Havířská Street and positioned themselves between the two camps, cutting them off from Na příkopě. But both sides continued to advance onwards. And onwards. And onwards. The Czechs reached the police cordon and were ordered to halt. They were told again. And for a third time. I really don't know what happened next. I only know that shots were fired, and that the peaceful crowd was transformed into a howling mob, and that at a stroke Na příkopě was deserted, except for one man in front of the police rifles – my father. Standing quietly, with his arms by his side. Next to him on the pavement lay something horribly strange – I don't know if you've ever seen what someone looks like when they've been shot and they collapse. They're hardly human any more, they look like an old rag. My father stood there for perhaps a minute – for my mother and I it seemed like a year. Then he bent down and began to bandage the human ruins which lay next to him on the pavement. My mother's eyes were half-closed and two big tears were rolling down her cheeks. I still remember how she took me in her arms as if she wanted to crush me.

Milena's father, despite his difficult start, had achieved belonging – in the public world. He did not belong to Milena and her mother.

The distant hero on Na příkopě was hardly ever at home. He rose at dawn, had a cold bath and took his two large dogs for a walk. He worked hard at his practice and his research, and then visited his club. He was a handsome man with a high forehead, broad cheekbones, a cleft chin (which Milena inherited) and arched brows. He sported a slightly old-fashioned frock coat and a low-crowned top hat, and wore a monocle. His garb suggested a man of conservative beliefs but with a touch of eccentricity, vanity and undoubted verve. The position he aspired to was quite compatible with more scurrilous habits, as long as they were carried out in the right places and with panache. He was a keen card-player and gambler, reckless with money now that he had plenty. He is reported to have taken part in one of the last duels in Prague, conducted with sabres, over a literary argument. He was something of a ladies' man, and his ailing wife could not satisfy him. He charmed his colleagues' wives, meeting them for lunchtime walks on Prague's wooded Petřín Hill or escorting them to concerts. In time he took lovers.

At home, Milena learnt to entertain herself. She staged battles between coloured glass marbles and dried beans. She had an expensive, blonde-haired doll, but regarded her as

> a punishment of my childhood. She was kept in the cupboard and I was given her to play with only when I had been especially good – in other words very rarely. But it was as if they punished me for my virtue. The doll was alien, cold, dressed to the nines, and I was forbidden to change her clothes or comb her hair. We sat sadly in the corner, the doll and I, and looked at each other. I felt that I was obliged to be happy and cheerful, and that the adults would be insulted if I did not play, but how to play? When the doll disappeared back into the cupboard I always sighed with relief.

She preferred to invent her own games, to play in freedom, or to read. Her favourite books included the children's classic *Babička* (*Grandmother*), by the nineteenth-century writer Božena Němcová, the story of an old wise woman, beloved by everyone in the village from her grandchildren to the princess in the castle. With its depiction of the traditions and folklore of Czech village life, it was part of the canon of the Czech Revival.

When her father arrived home Milena was expected to kiss his hand and greet him with the polite form of address. He was interested in her doings and could be protective. But there were terrible conflicts too, when Milena's tantrums broke the etiquette between father and daughter. She later told fearful tales about him. How he 'spanked her when she was naughty or obstinate', how he once 'threw her into a big chest full of dirty washing and left the lid closed' as she screamed and screamed. But in these scenes of defiance and rage lies also the bond between them. They were both strong-willed, determined, engaged with each other, if often in battle.

When Dr Jesenský's storms became more than his wife could bear she would sweep Milena up and retreat to her mother's apartment across the river in Malá Strana, on Šeříková Street. It was a peaceful refuge, where they drank tea in the intimate light of oil lamps and where Milena admired the gold musical clock. Her other grandmother lived in Malá Strana too. There were visits here also, into a quite different atmosphere. Her paternal grandmother, used to cooking for a large brood, kneaded dough for dumplings rhythmically and relentlessly. She was a diminutive but surprisingly forthright woman. When Vienna decreed that the whole Empire should move its clocks forward an hour during the summer months, old Mrs Jesenská disparagingly termed the scheme an 'Austrian invention' and continued to follow her sun. 'And when someone said, "It's twelve o'clock", my small, quiet grandmother raged, "Eleven o'clock!" And the words rang out like a royal decree or a sad poem. And really, it was eleven o'clock.'

But there were brighter family times. Milena enjoyed summer holidays in the country or at spa towns, and winter visits with her father to the Hotel Prokop at Špičák in the Šumava mountains in southern Bohemia. She first went there in 1905, and later wrote with love of her visits to the low wooden chalet in the woods with its five windows, 'a golden nest'. It had started life as a way-station for workers building a tunnel through the mountain, run by Old Prokop. When the workers left, he stayed. 'He was tall, like an oak, broad-shouldered ... with a beautiful head, expressive and grey-haired ... a solitary philosopher with a spirit like quartz.' Milena recalled one childhood holiday when they arrived to find the Hotel Prokop sunk in snow up to the chimney: 'The mountains and woods and meadows, silenced by snow, the blue distance, blue like washing blue, which only winter mountain air can create, the air thick with frost and the miraculous, crystalline, white woods were for me a new fairytale, a world full of magic.' In the evening, she sat by the fireside together with pipe-smoking Old Prokop, some Czech skiers with whom the place had become popular, and her father whose face was 'so clear and happy'. 'From that time I went there in summer and winter. My father and I waded criss-cross through the whole landscape, in snow and in rain and in sunshine. I know every tree.' As she grew older, Dr Jesenský encouraged Milena to ski, which was unusual then for a young girl. She became extremely proficient.

At school, Milena was proving to be a bright, quick pupil. She also drew the attention of the teachers with her big blue eyes and long wavy hair. This was a mixed blessing. She later told her daughter how, aged eight or nine, she was chosen to recite a poem and present a bunch of flowers to a visiting member of the board of governors. Her parents were proud of her, and the Jesenskýs' cook even more so. She was determined to prepare the 'little lady' properly. The night before the presentation, she washed Milena's hair and then laboriously dipped each tress in sugar water and rolled it up in paper. When Milena woke up next morning and the papers were removed, her hair stood out in sticky corkscrews, impossible to comb. In her stiff uniform with her stiff curls, Milena slunk into school. The mockery of her fellow pupils was unbearable and she started tearing at her head. The teacher whisked her off to the washroom and rinsed her hair clean. The governor was greeted by a little girl with damp curls and a damp back. Milena later told her daughter she loathed being treated like a 'trained monkey'.

There were other memories of her childhood which she passed on to her daughter, memories of loneliness and memories of the treachery of adults – especially, of course, her parents. She told how once, frightened to return home from school on her own, she stopped a stranger and pretended to be lost until he accompanied her home himself. She described how on an outing to the woods around Prague with her mother and grandmother she suddenly felt abandoned:

> When I was small, my mother took me to the woods and said 'Play here, my dear'. She and grandmother wandered off for a walk and a chat. In one direction I could watch them come and go. But in the other, the path disappeared into undergrowth and suddenly swallowed them up. Time stopped, terrible and suffocating, and all the voices of the wood sang a fearful droning song. The minutes until Mama came round the bend tortured me with the fear of being abandoned; a strange sadness overcame my heart.

Her childhood held treasures too, and there were reasons why Milena may later have chosen to construct a melancholy version of her life to attract her daughter's sympathy. But her distress at the palpable tension and disappointment between her parents seems real enough, judging by the memories she related. She recalled the unusual time Dr Jesenský brought his wife a bunch of violets, only to whisk them away again when a lady friend called. Or the time when she accompanied her mother to a spa for treatment. One day she could not find her mother and hunted for her in the public rooms and eventually in the park. There she saw her in the arms of another man; her mother was not the entirely passive figure sometimes depicted.

Another time, when her mother's frailty had turned to chronic illness and Milena was attending her bedside, she described how she yearned to go outside. She tiptoed out of the room and ran out of the house, sure that no one would miss her for a few minutes. When she crept back to her place, to her relief her mother's eyes were still closed. But softly she heard her mother whisper, 'I don't wonder at you, dear. I'd run away too, at least for a little while, if I only could.' Whether or not these tales are precisely true, they are a map of the childhood that Milena felt herself to have lived, a map which guided her later journeys.

In 1907, when Milena was eleven, she was sent to Prague's prestigious school for girls, the Minerva School. It gave its pupils more than merely an education, though it did that very well. It gave them an identity. Milena became a 'Minerviste'.

Minerva was the first proper gymnasium for girls in Central Europe, the first school dedicated to giving girls as good an education as boys. It was founded in 1890, after a long battle with the Austro-Hungarian authorities in Vienna, by Eliška Krásnohorská, a single-minded writer, feminist and librettist (she wrote operas for Smetana). She started the Minerva Society to promote her idea of a school for girls, and mobilised support from the Prague establishment by exploiting their indignation at the idea that Austria might in any way limit the education and prospects of the daughters of Bohemia. When Vienna eventually acquiesced, the school was run by a series of Heads (for decades, all men), but Eliška Krásnohorská remained deeply involved. At the turn of the century she steered pupils, teachers and parents through a debate about how classical or modern the school should be. She favoured tradition, with all girls learning Latin and Greek, but not all parents were so high-minded. A compromise was found, so that by the time Milena joined the school Latin was still compulsory but not Greek. Krásnohorská, now over sixty and dressed in high-necked dresses with her hair swept back, continued the struggle, and the year after Milena started at Minerva, the school was given the right to conduct matriculation exams which would allow girls to go on to university.

So Milena entered a school with a self-conscious, self-confident identity. Once she had passed the entrance test in dictation and mathematics she joined the elite, the daughters of professionals, businessmen, clerks and craftsmen, from Prague and beyond. Dr Jesenský may have been a conservative in many matters but he wanted the best for his daughter and only child, and the best meant Minerva, radical in its feminism, conservative in its commitment to a traditional education, and appealing in its belief in the development of the Czech nation.

The headmaster in Milena's early years was Josef Grim, nicknamed 'Vladař' ('The Governor'). He was a rather taciturn, deliberate man who liked an orderly school and put much of his energies into improving its finances. But many of the teachers were more sympathetic. They were by and large extremely dedicated men and women, committed to the young school's philosophy of education as the development of the mind, body and sensibility. Milena attended classes in Latin (eight hours a week), Czech, Maths, Physics, Natural Sciences, History, Geography, Religion and probably German. She was a bright if not always disciplined pupil. She also took piano lessons. Classes were from 8 until 1.30 in winter and from 7 until 12.30 in summer. Milena particularly admired her history teacher, Albína Honzáková, a warm, liberal-minded woman whose adoring pupils regarded her as a Raphael Madonna.

The school gave Milena access to a wider education beyond the classroom. Prague was one of the cultural capitals of Europe, attracting the best from East and West. Rodin exhibited there in 1902 and Nijinsky visited in 1912. Minerva organised outings to galleries, concerts and plays. The school rooms were in buildings behind the National Theatre and Milena and her friends would hover on the pavement, looking out for the famous actors and singers who lived in the quarter.

Minerva also arranged cheap tickets for the swimming pools on the River Vltava and the tennis courts on Letná Plain on the other side of the city. On holidays, teachers organised walks and picnics in the

Childhood

Botanical Gardens or on Petřín Hill, and in winter there were skating trips on the frozen river.

Milena was good at sport and her father encouraged her to join the Sokol sporting movement. Sokol (meaning Falcon) had been founded nearly half a century earlier, and beame a nationwide popular movement, based on democracy, fraternal (and sisterly) comradeship, and loyalty to the nation. In the uniform of long drawers, a blue linen skirt which fell below the knee and a long-sleeved blouse, Milena joined in the formation exercises and made her contribution to the building of the Czech nation. At weekends she would accompany her father on long walks, enjoying some of her happiest moments with him. They would walk twenty miles or more, and Milena came to know the hills and woods around Prague well. Sometimes there were just the two of them, sometimes they went with her father's colleagues. She would then retreat into herself. One of Dr Jesenský's friends described her at this time as 'silent, dreaming, shy'.

But at school, among her peers, she made quite another impression. At home her energy and charisma often brought her into conflict with her father, at school it earned her a place of honour. One younger pupil would observe her on those mornings when her father accompanied her to the school steps. Hand in hand, they were a striking pair, he in his smart suit and polished hat, she 'in a grey outfit with a broad, dark velour hat which rose at the front and sloped down at the back trailing a ribbon. It sat so beautifully on her fair wavy hair and set off her delicate profile and luminous skin.' On other days she would walk to school alone or with friends, past the markets and the street traders, Turks and Russians. On Petřín Hill she often noticed the gingerbread man, with 'a black beard and a little, stunted body'. She was too daunted to approach him for his miraculous coloured sweets and biscuits. She loved the markets near her home, the piles of peaches and plums and apples at the Ovocný fruit market, and the way that in spring the Uhelný market was 'scattered with heaps of snowdrops and violets and primroses and pasque flowers, when the whole square shrieked with colours'. The city and Minerva were emerging as the stage for a new life.

In a school atmosphere which fostered intense friendships Milena and her friends stood out, their allegiance even stronger, stranger, more flamboyant than others. She had two particularly close friends. Jarmila Ambrožová was the same age as Milena, the daughter of a middle-class Prague family. She was intense, moody, more secretive, but capable of the same flashes of daring and defiance. Milena was certainly the dominant figure, and where she led Jarmila followed. She even mimicked Milena's ways, adopting her energetic speech pattern and her handwriting. Both girls had long legs, slim waists and exuberant hair. Inevitably they went about in the same clothes, made by Milena's dressmaker, and unwittingly paid for by Dr Jesenský. It was the first sign of Milena's complete disregard for where money came from.

Milena was even closer to Staša Procházková, the daughter of a Prague doctor (whose politics, however, were more liberal than those of the nationalist Dr Jesenský). Staša (no one called her by her full name Stanislava) was an intelligent girl, gifted at languages, musical and full of energy. Although she was two years younger than Milena, she was more her match than Jarmila. Their contemporaries dubbed them the 'Siamese twins' and there were rumours that their closeness went beyond mere friendship. They were certainly, as adolescent girls can be, bound to each other emotionally and excited by each other intellectually.

There were other friends too, but Jarmila and Staša were Milena's closest companions in adolescence. The 'trio' studied together, swam together, played tennis, discussed clothes and boys, bought oranges, cakes and whipped cream, and, on the rare occasions when they were available, bananas. Like good Bohemian maidens they were sentimental about the Czech countryside and Czech poetry.

Milena matured early, physically and mentally. Her battles with her father and the slow vanishing of her mother into illness forced her into early independence and watchfulness. She was not in awe of adults, but at the same time they occupied a different, sometimes confusing world. Her precociousness and her striking looks introduced her to experiences which must have confirmed her powers of attraction, but left her confused about where this might lead. Her father's colleagues could be flattering and attentive, and so too could women. Once on an impulse Milena bought an armful of flowers from a corner flower seller for an actress who was the darling of all Minerva. She rang the bell of the star's apartment and before she knew it, was being welcomed inside and given wine and soda. After a while, the actress turned to Milena's own life and friends. Did she have a girlfriend? And was she pretty? But not as pretty as Milena surely! Milena's discomfort in the oppressive, heavily furnished apartment grew as the questions intensified. It was only, she later told her daughter, when the diva tried to kiss her that she summoned the nerve to tear away.

There were also more customary fumblings in the world of love. The Minerva girls were allowed to go to dances arranged with a nearby boys' school, and the daily walk to school, as well as the afternoon promenades after class, presented plenty of opportunity for the girls to show off and the boys to admire. Milena, Jarmila and Staša knew they were objects of admiration; tall and spirited, they linked arms and sashayed along Na příkopě.

But her mother's illness was a shadow over these adolescent years. Milena Hejzlarová had never been strong, but as Milena entered her teens her mother's illness (variously described as pernicious anaemia and leukemia) worsened. Dr Jesenský believed it was good for Milena to share in the care of her mother. He would leave her to sit at the invalid's bedside when he went out for the evening. Milena inevitably felt torn, between concern for her beloved mother and frustration at being bound to this sick woman; she also felt rage at her father's neglect. Sometimes it was all too much, and she once threw her mother's meal tray on the floor. She had her father's temper.

At the close of 1912, when Milena was sixteen, her mother weakened even further. For several weeks Milena watched the final decline, until in January it was clear that her mother would not live much longer. Milena stood with her father and the doctor at the bedside. She later told her daughter that when her mother lost consciousness the doctor reached for another injection to try to revive her. Milena grabbed the syringe from him and smashed it on the ground. She could not bear her mother's pale, painful imitation of a life to be drawn out any further. Neither the doctor nor her father reproached her.

Milena responded to her mother's death with a mixture of pain and relief. She was free now, released from the sickroom. But she was also without one measure of her life, one necessary constraint, one fount of affection. Later she referred to her mother as a source of peace and love, telling Margarete Buber-Neumann, 'My mother never spanked me when I was little. She never even scolded me. Only my father did that.' Milena Hejzlarová's legacy to her daughter included both a sense of loss and a feeling of refuge, set against which most people in her later life, including her father, failed.

The following Christmas Dr Jesenský took Milena to Špičák. They arrived on Christmas Eve. 'We weren't alone, which drove out the memories of death from home. And so, high up in the cold and the isolation and the snow, during the long evenings, we celebrated a quiet Christmas more festively than those down in the town, full of the sweet magic of the intimacy of that miraculous land, locked away as one family, with Old Prokop at the head of the table.'

But back in Prague there was less intimacy with her father. Dr Jesenský in his own way too was a freer man, and he became even more absent. He expected his daughter to behave well, but by dint of his word not his example. Milena behaved accordingly. Rebellious and sentimental, she once took a room in a third-class hotel and stayed out all night. She hung about cemeteries, mournful and morbid. Artur Scheiner, a painter acquaintance of her father's, asked her to sit for him, to model for some illustrations for a fairy tale. Again she was drawn to an adult world where fairy tales were not so innocent, and Scheiner asked her to pose nude. This Milena did, curious but eventually disgusted by the atmosphere in the studio, by the painter and his friends, for whom she also modelled.

Her own friends became even more important, and attempts by Staša's father to keep her away from Milena did not work. They read sentimental novels together, including those written by two of Dr Jesenský's sisters, Marie and Růžena. Marie also translated foreign literature, while some of Růžena's novels were best-sellers, and her columns and features in *Národní listy* were popular. (She also took a great interest in her motherless niece.) But the girls preferred finer Czech literature, including the adult works of Božena Němcová, author of *Babička*. Němcová was a brave and unusual woman, an early feminist and socialist who fought to live and love how she chose. She left an early and unhappy marriage after bearing four children, championed the cause of the Czech Revival despite the problems this caused her with the authorities, and lived in poverty until her death at the age of forty-one. Her stories, based on rural life, and her beauty and emotional intensity ensured her reputation and she was one of Milena's heroines.

Milena and her friends read further afield – Dostoevsky, Knut Hamsun, Tolstoy, Ibsen, Oscar Wilde, Thomas Mann – tasting depths of experience which scorned the conventions of their family backgrounds. (Milena proudly told her history teacher Albína Honzáková that she had acquired more than 150 books.) They followed these writers in their search for an understanding of the godless individual for whom life is a solitary journey, a modern epic. Milena and Staša also became good friends with a young medical student, Jiří Foustka, whom they questioned for hours about literature and life.

The girls' philosophy demanded that they defy authority and explore the further reaches of life. They took to sneaking drugs from Dr Jesenský's medicine cabinet and experimented with the opiates, amphetamines and cocaine which they found. More healthily, Milena had a deep craving for flowers, rich, exuberant, scented flowers. The only way to satisfy this appetite was to take them from wherever she found them. She went on expeditions, sometimes at night, to the parks and cemeteries of Prague and plucked great bunches of white chrysanthemums, hydrangeas and camellias. More often than not she gave them away as gifts.

And then came war. When the First World War crept up on Prague, it hardly seemed the Czechs' battle. But it was the Empire's war and as such Bohemia had a part to play. When Gavrilo Princip, a young Bosnian Serb revolutionary, assassinated Archduke Franz Ferdinand, heir to the imperial throne, in Sarajevo on 28 June 1914, no one quite knew what would follow. Milena was at Špičák in the summer of 1914.

> We were sitting animatedly at the table after a delightful expedition, when Prokop came into the room and made straight for us, like a man who has something to say, something which won't bear delay. His news, that the heir to the throne had been killed, fell like a bomb among us. No one knew anything certain. No newspapers reached us. At Plzeň [Pilsen] railway station we at last got some details. And the stifling, stuffy air of the little railway carriages which rolled from the hills down to Prague was a taste of the tension which overcame everything before the beginning of the war.

Austria declared war on Serbia on 28 July, setting in train a much wider conflagration. Russia came to the defence of its Slav ally Serbia, France rallied to the cause of its ally Russia, and Britain stood by France. Germany of course backed the Austrian cause. Many Czechs were torn. The Empire, however greatly resented, was the guarantor of all they knew. But the Serbs were Slav brothers. Dr Jesenský's generation pondered what the war might mean for the future of the Czechs. When Vienna decreed a general mobilisation, young Czechs called up to fight made their feelings known, singing Slav songs as they set off. The general Czech population shared their mood. Vienna responded to such insubordination by imposing martial rule on Bohemia. Newspapers were subject to censorship and dissenters were arrested. Inevitably, the tension between Czechs and Germans in the city worsened.

The reaction of many young intellectuals was well caught by Max Brod, the young Jew and friend and champion of Kafka, who would become an important acquaintance of Milena:

> War to us was simply a crazy idea, of a piece with, say, the perpetual motion machine or the fountain of youth.... We were a spoilt generation, spoiled by nearly fifty years of peace that had made us lose sight of mankind's worst scourge.... And now, overnight, peace had suddenly collapsed. We were quite simply stupid ... not even pacifists, because pacifism at least presupposes a notion of there being such a thing as war, and of the need to fight against it.

The Minerva girls knitted socks, and talked about absent brothers fighting in this remote conflict. War for Milena was the sound of soldiers singing in train carriages, 'adding to the beat of the wheels and the monotonous song of the wagons the sound of male voices and the harmonica'. Her schoolgirl life remained remarkably unchanged. Milena could not guess that the war would herald a huge, unimagined transformation in the city, country and world in which she lived. In the summer of 1915 Milena graduated from Minerva. She and Jarmila lived up to their audacious image, appearing for the ceremony in lilac, flowing Grecian dresses. They knew nothing of the constricting wasp waists their mothers had worn. Milena had managed to fulfil the academic demands of the school, but Minerva, which had sometimes sighed at her excesses, had given her much more than exam results. She had already told Albína Honzáková, on whom she had developed an intense crush, that she wanted to grow up, so that she could go out into the world and achieve something with her life. Now she wrote: 'I want to thank you. Not only for my graduation. But for the whole eight years. For the fact that you never judged what I love, that you alone never laughed at what I read and what I liked. And that you never told me I am affected because I liked music, pictures, books.'

Here is the nineteen-year-old Milena's spirit: an appetite for the arts to feed her passion and imagination; a defiant belief in herself and her own way of doing things; a touch of sentiment, a touch of rhetoric; the appeal, tinged even with flattery, for someone else's sympathy; the vulnerable feeling that somehow she is strange and does not quite belong.

2

Freedom

Not long after Milena had escaped from her mother's sickroom she was driven back into the hushed world of the ill and weak. Her father, since he had no son to follow in his footsteps, enrolled her at medical school, a move which revealed respect for his daughter's intellectual capabilities but little insight into her nature. Milena hated the sight and smell of blood, and her active imagination hardly equipped her for clinical detachment. Not only did she have to contend with long lectures and gruesome practicals at medical school, but her father insisted that she help in his clinic. The war had brought him a new sort of patient, soldiers returning from the front with grim face wounds, torn cheeks and jaws blown away. Dr Jesenský welcomed the chance to develop new surgical techniques, but for Milena it was sickening to have to attend the operations and distressing to think what lay ahead for these young men. Her remonstrations eventually took effect, and when her father learnt that she had fainted at her first autopsy class, he gave in. Milena left medical school.

She had little idea what to do next. She considered studying music, but although she played the piano well and with love, she had neither the deep musical talent nor the discipline required to study at the Conservatory. She knew that there must be more to life than sitting in her father's house until she went to sit in a husband's house, but since her father could support her a career was not absolutely necessary just yet.

For now she drifted; but not into oblivion. Although she was young, she was in her own way a known figure in Prague. She was easily recognised – tall, elegant, with a flowing, rhythmic gait, swinging along but without any hint of provocativeness. She had large, expressive hands and long, wavy hair. Her clothes were always striking. Sometimes she wore flowing dresses inspired by the dancer

19

Isadora Duncan, in watery colours – blues, greys and purples melting into each other. Or she would adopt a more sophisticated style: while other girls pleaded with their mothers to be allowed to lengthen their skirts below the calf, arguing in vain over every half-inch, Milena, motherless, simply wore what she chose. The long narrow skirts suited her well.

When Milena joined Staša and Jarmila, also tall and striking, to stroll around Prague, they drew attention. Prague may have been a capital, but it was small enough for the people 'who mattered' to share the gossipy habits of a provincial town. As the trio joined the promenade on Ferdinand Street, they teased the Czech college boys, who in turn mocked them: 'Dívka z Minervy, nervi mi nervy' ('Girl from Minerva, don't get on my nerves').

The free spirits sought a different kind of audience, crossing the unwritten boundary onto Na příkopě where the German community preferred to walk, the boundary Milena's father had confronted. The writer Josef Kodiček later recalled:

> On Sunday morning Na příkopě was old-Austrian territory. The commanding figure of Count Thun, the six-foot, eight-inch governor of Prague, towers over the crowd. He's as thin as a stork and the best dressed man on the continent. He stands serenely, in celestial calm, with one foot tucked into the crook of his other knee, surveying the ebb and flow of the crowd through his black-rimmed monocle. Just then two young girls stroll by, arm in arm. They are both something to look at. The first Prague girls to give themselves a deliberately boyish look. Their style is perfect. Their hairdos are modelled on the English Pre-Raphaelites; they are as slender as willow withes, and there is nothing petit-bourgeois about their faces or figures. They are probably the first Czech girls of the pre-war generation to extend their world from the Czech promenade on Ferdinand Avenue to Na příkopě, thus making contact with the younger generation of German literati. They are genuine European women, a sensation! Count Thun swivels on one leg to look at them, and a wave of enthusiasm and curiosity passes through the crowd. . . . Milena and Miss Staša. Clearly it's Milena who sets the tone.

Tales of Milena's escapades spread. How she once flung herself, fully clothed, into the Vltava to swim across in order not to miss an appointment. How she was arrested in a park at five in the morning gathering flowers. How she sent huge bunches of flowers to her favourite actresses. But there was a more troubling side to her audacity. She had little respect for other people's property, least of all her father's. She would dress up her 'borrowing' in socialist ideas: after all, he had so much and her friends so little. Some of the stories are comic. How Dr Jesenský noticed a pair of his expensive, dandyish socks on the feet of one of his students. How he warned Milena that he knew exactly how many gold coins he had in his desk drawer, only to find that she exchanged the twenty-crown pieces for exactly the same number of smaller coinage. When prices rose, as Austria plundered fertile Bohemia for food for the war effort, Dr Jesenský still had a well-stocked larder, thanks to his grateful and often rich patients. Milena took bags of flour and bars of soap for her friends. When one of them unwittingly thanked Dr Jesenský for his gift there was yet another row.

Her 'borrowing' strayed further afield. She took things from her friends' rooms and from shops. Sometimes Dr Jesenský received the bills, sometimes she got away with it. There can be many causes of kleptomania; a craving for excitement and danger, a confused morality or perhaps a cry for help. Why not strike out at a world where she did not quite seem to fit; if life had uncertain value, why not gamble with it? The imperious Dr Jesenský could not cure his daughter. Why should she listen to his mean-spirited tirades? He gambled away enough of his money, why should she not appropriate a little more?

Much of the time, these shadows were kept at bay with the bright lights of all that Prague had to offer. Despite the war, the city was full of life. The conflict even gave new stimulation to cultural life as the Czechs began to stretch their wings against the collapsing cage of Austrian domination.

As the daughter of a cultivated professional who loved theatre and music, and the product of a high-minded school, Milena was quite at home among the cultural institutions of the city. There were concerts at the Rudolfinum, an airy concert hall by the river, and even here Milena would defy propriety, attend concerts with young men unchaperoned and take standing places in the gallery at the back of the hall.

Then there was the National Theatre, built in the late nineteenth century as a home for Czech rather than German theatre. As a child, Milena had listened to her father telling her how the theatre was built by popular subscription, and how, when fire razed the impressive building not long after its opening in 1881, the good Czech citizens rallied round again: 'People came and gave their last farthing.

That's why on the stage curtain is written "Národ sobě" [The Nation's Gift to Itself], and it doesn't matter if the phrase is a little trite.' The Czechs, like any small nation still in the throes of finding its place in the world, were busy myth-makers. Milena knew from her father and from her school that she was the child of a people on the rise, learning to look after themselves.

The war brought home this growing patriotism. One day Milena attended a performance of the musical *Strakonický dudák* (*The Piper of Strakonice*) by the celebrated mid-nineteenth century Czech playwright and patriot Josef Tyl, at the Vinohradské Theatre. The songs included 'Kde domov můj' ('Where is my home?), a hymn to the beauties of the Bohemian countryside, which would become the Czech national anthem. At this stage it was still only a much loved national song and Milena was moved to see how the audience, from children to usherettes, refused to sing the Austrian imperial anthem at the beginning of the performance but stood for the Czech song. Cultural life in Prague was a forum for citizenship as well as private aesthetics. For all Milena's uncertainty and resistance, her sense of not belonging, she enjoyed an underlying sense of place. Her Czechness was a thread which in the end would prove to hold remarkably fast through her life.

Another popular venue was the new Lucerna palace (designed by the grandfather of the post-Communist president and playwright Václav Havel), the first building in Prague to be built of steel and concrete. This art nouveau dance hall, with a series of galleries and salons, was a good place to meet friends, to dance and enjoy music. And in the rooms at the top of the building there were readings and lectures, about French symbolism, Rudolf Steiner and anthroposophy, Russian literature.

Milena and her friends embraced ideas from abroad, far from the preoccupations of the Czech promenaders on Ferdinand Avenue. They deepened their reading of Dostoevsky and Turgenev, Kierkegaard and Thomas Mann, and grappled with the ideas of Albert Einstein. Modernity beckoned.

Conversation about such things thrived in the cafés of Prague. Here, according to Max Brod, who lived at the heart of café life, one found an atmosphere 'free and open to ideas, crammed together in four or five rooms, smoky, stifling, thick with the fumes of mocha coffee'. One of the most popular cafés was the Holandská Kavárna, just off the Old Town Square, where Milena, young and watchful, moved among the different groups, each with their own table. The architects sat at one, at another were writers. Her father and other professionals sometimes joined a table favoured by artists, including Artur Scheiner, the painter who had enticed Milena to model for him.

Sometimes Milena sat with her father. But sometimes she joined another group, which included the famous Čapek brothers, writer Karel and illustrator Josef. Here, discussion often turned to the political situation, and Milena broadened her political education, away from the narrow bounds of her father's conservatism. War intensified the political tension between Prague and Vienna. Czech soldiers deserted or found their way to Czech units in Russia and then France. A number of Czech political leaders were imprisoned early in the war, accused of treason and impeding the war effort: 'The whole nation felt that it was on trial.' Others were in exile in Moscow, Paris and London.

One of these was the philosopher and politician Tomáš Garrigue Masaryk, who went into exile in 1914 because his dream of an independent union of the Slav Czechs and Slovaks in a new Czechoslovak state made him suspect to the Austrian authorities. As the war continued he established and led a Czechoslovak National Council abroad to campaign for the interests of the Czechs and Slovaks in any peace settlement. T. G. Masaryk and his supporters (including men like the Čapeks) believed that the only future for the Czechs lay in the defeat of the Central Powers and the dissolution of the Empire.

The Čapeks and their friends would leave the Holandská and stroll along the banks of the Vltava speculating on the outcome of the war and how it might affect the Czechs. All were touched by a sense of possibility. The young Milena was welcomed for the information she could pass on, gleaned from her father and his friends, some of whom were in close touch with politicians in Vienna.

Milena was infected by the excitement. But although she could recite Czech Revivalist poetry and sing Czech folk songs with the best of them, although she shared the developing pride of a people daring to contemplate independence, she would not be bound by any rigid nationalism. The war and political developments had unsettled relations between the country's coexistent peoples, especially between the Czechs and the German minority, but they could not destroy a world which Milena and her friends had joined not long before the war, a world where national boundaries seemed less important – challenges to be overcome rather than borders to be shunned. Although the Czech, German and Jewish parts of Prague largely kept to themselves, there were inevitably exceptions, places of intersection. With unerring instinct, Milena found them. She, Staša and Jarmila not only promenaded through the German sphere of Na příkopě, they penetrated the Jewish world too.

It was a particularly rich world and included a constellation in one city of some of the best of German Jewish writers. They were children of the new Jewish bourgeoisie and had been given a stern but rigorous education (in German). They were moving away from their parents' orthodoxy, but were at odds with the German culture to which their language ascribed them. They were a ghetto inside a ghetto in Czech Prague, a ghetto without walls since the ramshackle Jewish quarter had been razed, a culture needing to define itself anew. The younger generation struggled for answers. It included Max Brod, more than ten years older than Milena, a serious-minded young man who became involved in the Zionist cause. He had a curvature of the spine and a large head, which did not stop him being popular with women and optimistic about life. He was a writer himself but more importantly an inspired critic and champion of the work of others – Jaroslav Hašek's *The Good Soldier Schweik*, the operas of Janáček and, of course, the work of his great friend, Franz Kafka.

Then there was Franz Werfel, born in 1890, something of a literary prodigy as a child and a prolific poet and writer. He was a charming and extrovert man, a large figure with a large appetite for life and women. Willy Haas was another prominent figure in the cafés, an intelligent critic, a gentle man and a scrupulous editor, who became a good friend of Milena's and a lover of her friend Jarmila. And of course Franz Kafka, tall, bony, his seriousness lit by a smile.

These young men met in their homes, at the university, or at their offices, but their true theatre was the café. They avoided the smarter cafés of central Prague, where the Czech and German bourgeoisie congregated among the pot palms and chandeliers, and found more unassuming places. The Café Arco was a favourite. Only a ten-minute walk from the Old Town Square, it was another world. In the bustle and transience of a quarter near one of Prague's railway stations, the Arco served travellers, travelling salesmen, brokers from the nearby Corn Exchange, local residents and those seeking to escape their particular ghetto. The Jewish writers came here to sit at marble-topped tables under the high ceiling, to rifle through the café's spread of newspapers or meet their friends. Here too came the more bohemian young Czechs, and here, in search of sensation and difference, came Milena and her friends.

What did these Jewish men and Czech girls share? They carried the same map of tumbled streets and red-tiled roofs in their bones. From different quarters they knew theirs to be a proud city with a rich history. But even more perhaps, they shared intellectual curiosity about a broader Europe and imaginations which roamed among the questions facing a new age. For the Czech girls, the Jewish German writers represented a more cosmopolitan world within Prague. The Jews in their turn were interested in the Czechs, the authentic inhabitants of the city. Both groups shared a resentment of the Germans who, despite being a minority, had arrogated power. To the men these girls were freer than their Jewish sisters, who remained at home being groomed for marriage. To the Czech girls these men were utterly different from the less sophisticated Czech boys they knew.

Milena loved the atmosphere of the Café Arco and the welcome she found. She was ripe for the bustle and the debate and the laughter. She was also ripe for love. There had been tremors of her heart, including an intense crush on a singer and a slightly awkward relationship with the intelligent but overly respectable medical student Jiří Foustka. But nothing more. Now, in 1916, it was not Kafka who drew her attention. For one thing, he never stayed long in the café. 'He soon stood up, said farewell, bowed to everyone and with his long steps left. He smiled as he left, his smile seemed to come from endlessly far away.' Milena hardly noticed this tall, slightly remote figure. She was drawn to another German Jew who held court at the Café Arco, Ernst Pollak.

Pollak was not a writer, but he was a man of renowned critical faculties, at once a supporter, connoisseur and adjudicator of the writers around him. It was his taste and conversation, rather than his job as a translator for the Austrian National Bank, which earned him a place of honour in the Café Arco.

One account tells that he and Milena met at a concert. Milena was 'sitting on the steps of the centre aisle, immersed in the score. She was wearing a purple evening dress, as though at a royal reception. A man looked over her shoulder and read along with her. The man was Ernst Pollak.' But it seems more likely that they were at least aware of each other from the Café Arco, and that this incident marked a stage in their attraction for each other. Ernst was ten years older than

Milena, with rather soft features, which made him ugly to some; but he had arresting dark close-set eyes, a high brow and a smart demeanour. He was born in a small town and like many outsiders relished the ways of the city even more than its inhabitants. His authority and rakish charm captivated Milena. And Milena, turning twenty, was strong, vivacious, fresh inspiration for a man who had a way with women.

They discovered much in common: music, poetry, the search for a new literature for the new era. Soon Milena was visiting Ernst in his studio on the top floor of a neo-Gothic house on the embankment facing the castle, to listen to music and read scores together. They became lovers. Ernst was probably not Milena's first lover; there are suggestions that she had been seduced by one of the artists for whom she modelled, and she and Jiří Foustka may have been lovers. But Ernst was certainly her first lover of real importance or passion. She was swept away. She showered Ernst with her energy and enthusiasm, her strong will overwhelming his urban tastes. After one night together she dragged him up Petřín Hill to watch the sun rise. Ernst, a man more used to sunsets and the welcome arrival of night outside the windows of the Café Arco, grumbled the whole way up and taunted Milena about her Czech Revivalist sentiments about nature. But he was in love and followed her, and she was in love and ignored his indifference. She had at last found a focus, a target for her affections. Once, after Ernst had given her a key to his flat, Milena sneaked into his room and filled it with flowers which she had stripped from Stromovka Park on the other side of Prague. When she telephoned him later to see how he liked her gift, he claimed not to have noticed the flowers.

She was undeterred by the repercussions of this relationship. Ernst had other admirers. One of them learnt whole pages of Kierkegaard to impress him, only to be told mockingly by another of their circle, the Czech writer Johannes Urzidil, that this was not enough: she should take classes with a literary figure of the day, 'and then you will soon understand as much as Milena'. Urzidil himself enormously admired, even loved Milena. Milena gave him little. The cafés were rippling with the currents and undercurrents of desire fulfilled and unrequited. More seriously, Milena had swept upon Ernst when he was engaged in another relationship. For two years he had been involved with Amalie Kreidlová, a medical student, older than Milena, gentle and very clever. Milena and she knew each other at medical school, and the friendship may have helped bring Milena into acquaintance with Ernst. When Ernst and Milena took up together, Amalie was devastated. She buried herself in her studies, gave up concert-going, stopped having anything to do with Milena and 'never forgot'. Whatever the rights and wrongs of the affair, passions were strong. Milena was not one to hold back out of deference to another.

A potentially much more serious obstacle was her father. Dr Jesenský was appalled to find his daughter going out with a man much older than herself, of no clear profession, a German speaker and, worst of all, a Jew. Ernst's great friend in Vienna, Milan Dubrovic, described him as 'short, slight, with a stooped walk, like an intellectual Jew laden with problems ... Milena's father instinctively hated him.' But nothing Dr Jesenský could say deterred Milena, and so he resorted to more pragmatic methods of separating them.

In the summer of 1916, he encouraged Milena to join a group of her friends at the Hotel Prokop. Jarmila was there and they also made friends with another, German-speaking, guest, Wilma Löwenbach (known as Vilma Löwenbachová in Czech), a kind-hearted young woman who became a good friend to Milena. Wilma was involved in plans for an anthology of Czech poetry in German translation, an endeavour which grew out of the recognition by some young Germans in Prague that Czech poetry had matured from a folk tradition into a literary form, and out of their idealistic desire to challenge national boundaries, despite (or perhaps because of) the war.

Wilma had brought reams of Czech poetry with her and Milena had plenty of suggestions about what to pick. When other members of the editorial team arrived at the nearby German-run Hotel Ritz, it was natural that Milena should be involved too. Also inevitable perhaps that Ernst Pollak should turn up. Inevitable too that after the readings and discussions about the merits of rival poets the pair should find a way to be together. Wilma later reported to Margarete Buber-Neumann (a little floridly) how in the early hours of one morning Milena arrived in her bedroom, in a 'heliotrope-coloured dress and holding a bunch of flowers. Her bare feet were wet with the dew of the meadows. She jumped up on Wilma's bed, hugged her, and whispered, "Ernst spent the night with me." She was radiant, utterly exhausted, and entrancingly beautiful.' The hotel owner (no longer Old Prokop), who knew Milena well, discovered what was going on. He gave Milena a ticking off and told her he wasn't born yesterday. Such goings on were bad enough, but even worse with a gentleman from the German Hotel Ritz. But Milena's charms beguiled him, and he agreed not to tell Dr Jesenský.

Back in Prague, relations with her father remained sour. She would track him down in a café to ask for money. Slávka Vondráčková, Milena's friend from early childhood, remembered one such expedition with Milena when they found Dr Jesenský with Slávka's brother-in-law. There was a row, and later Slávka heard accounts of Dr Jesenský's rantings about his daughter: 'Always the same debts for someone to pay for this girl. And she's still going around with that Jew. . . . At home I have to hide ducats from her, gold for teeth, medicines and even new socks.' But Milena kept asking and in the end he always gave in. Dr Jesenský's friends and their wives tut-tutted about the doings of this father and daughter, raging away, living separate lives, utterly bound to each other.

Milena became a familiar figure at Ernst's boarding house. She slipped away from her father's home at all hours to be with him. From his little kitchen studio they could look over the trees to the river and the Castle. Ernst organised musical evenings for friends. They sang, played his piano, drank, danced. Milena wooed the landlady and her daughter, who lived on the second floor, with gifts of cream from her father's larder. Mrs Seidlová took her to her heart, and her daughter Mařenka was awed by Milena. She was too young to understand when her mother muttered about 'how Milena, from such a fine family, could behave so'. Nor did she quite understand what Milena wrote in her autograph book: 'If I wish anything for you, it is that you will stay a child for a long time even if you don't understand why. And when you do understand, you will no longer be a child. 19 August 1916. Your Milena Jesenská.'

Milena knew only too well that she herself was no longer a child. She was twenty, had grown up quickly, and been whisked by Ernst into a world of people much older than her. Her note to Mařenka suggests a nostalgia for a girlhood innocence which in fact she had hardly ever known. It was certainly too late now. That year, 1916, Milena became pregnant. She began to make enquiries about an abortion, a common enough but hardly respectable procedure. Some-how Dr Jesenský found out, and his rage at the relationship with Ernst transformed into fear and worry for his daughter. He looked after her himself, and after the operation he sat with her while a dose of morphine soothed her to sleep. Perhaps he was glad to have his wayward daughter restricted to her bedroom, under his care once again.

But the reconciliation did not last long. Milena was grateful for her father's attentions, but as soon as she was up and about again it was Ernst she wanted to see. That winter the war between father and daughter waged more bitterly than ever. Dr Jesenský felt himself to be the butt of bourgeois Prague for having a daughter who consorted with a Jew. There were more unpleasant incidents over unpaid bills, more arguments with Milena about her vanishings. There is a suggestion that she tried to commit suicide around this time. Whether or not the attempt was serious, the story suggests her volatility and vulnerability, her mood swings, her need for attention. For she had turned her back on her father for a man who could not always give her the love and understanding she craved.

The political atmosphere in Prague, meanwhile, was increasingly febrile. In January 1917, while Masaryk and others promoted Czech interests abroad, a few Prague politicians capitulated to Viennese pressure and made a declaration of loyalty to the Empire. Most Czechs were appalled by this pragmatic compromise. In April, a popular dramatist and poet, Jaroslav Kvapil, wrote an open letter to the Czech deputies in the Vienna Reichstag, signed by many other cultural figures: 'A democratic Europe, a Europe of free and independent peoples, is the Europe of tomorrow and the future. The nation demands of you, gentlemen, that, in this great moment of history, you bend all your energies, forgo all other considerations, and act as free men.' At the next Reichstag meeting the deputies took a stand and demanded federalisation. This heady talk of freedom and self-determination inspired Milena. She and friends like Slávka had had enough of Austria. 'We hated the black and gold colours, Tyrolese hats, white socks, capes and imperial symbols.'

By the summer of 1917, Dr Jesenský was at the end of his tether with Milena, her passion for Ernst and her escapades, which included further incidents of shop-lifting. What could be wrong with her? It was beyond reason. And so he had his daughter confined to a private psychiatric clinic on the outskirts of Prague. The register records that on 20 June 1917 Milena Jesenská (still interestingly registered as a medical student, a matter of form rather than reality) was received on the grounds of 'moral insanity' by a Dr Horníček. Milena was under twenty-one and therefore under her father's control. The head of the clinic was an acquaintance, and other colleagues and friends, including Staša's father Dr Procházka, all sympathised with Dr Jesenský, a Brabantio burdened with a daughter loving 'against all the rules of nature'.

The clinic at Veleslavín consisted of an elegant villa and two other houses in a park on the edge of Prague. Milena was confined, sometimes in solitary, in a room whose peephole made it seem like a prison cell. Locking his daughter up did not save Dr Jesenský from scandal. Milena got to know some of the other patients and the jewels of one old lady were too tempting for her. When the loss was discovered and eventually the culprit too, it was Dr Jesenský who again had to pay up to keep silence. On other occasions, Ernst paid her debts.

Milena was as defiant as ever, and as charming. In time she befriended a young nurse, Anka Schulhofová, who was susceptible to her romantic tales of thwarted love and perhaps realised that she was hardly mad. She lent Milena a key to the gate in the park's high wall and, with Staša's mediation, Milena was soon meeting Ernst again.

Ernst had not been lonely while Milena was away. There were other emancipated, cultured young women who enjoyed visits to his studio. But the bond with Milena was strong, and the affair restarted, as far as it could. Ernst and Milena both talked of wanting to leave Prague, and they decided to marry and go together to Vienna, a city Ernst knew well. Faced with this decisiveness, Dr Jesenský finally relented and agreed to Milena's release from Veleslavín and to the marriage. Milena's departure for Vienna might perhaps save him embarrassment, and he even gave the couple a dowry. In February 1918 Ernst wrote to his employers requesting leave for his wedding and on 7 March Milena emerged from Veleslavín. She had been confined for nearly nine months. She later wrote to Max Brod about the experience: 'Psychiatry is a terrible thing when it is abused; anything can be abnormal and every word is for the tormentor a new weapon.'

While Milena prepared hastily for the wedding, she caught up with her friends. Staša was planning to get married too, to Rudolf Jílovský, a journalist and publisher who was also fond of performing cabaret. (Jarmila would the following year marry a poet, Josef Reiner.) Milena also heard news of the wider world in turmoil: the winter's food riots in Prague; the fortunes of the war; strikes in Austria; and the 1917 Russian revolution, which had intensified the argument between those Czechs who wanted a revolutionary Czechoslovakia and those like Masaryk who wanted an alliance with the western democracies. Reports filtered through of his progress in persuading the Entente powers, who were now hopeful of victory, that the break-up of the Habsburg Empire was in their interests, as well as in the interests of the Empire's various nationalities.

The fractures in the Empire were not enough to deter Milena and Ernst from moving to the imperial capital. Milena's daughter suggests that there were some months between her mother's release from the clinic and her marriage, during which Dr Jesenský slowly relented and allowed an engagement on condition that Milena and Ernst met only at the home of her Aunt Mařena, a charming, forthright, artistic woman who lived above Petřín Hill. But official documents suggest otherwise, that in fact there were less than ten days between her release and the wedding, that all was negotiated during her stay in Veleslavín.

So on 16 March 1918, in a civil ceremony in Prague, Milena and Ernst were married. Milena, with more thoughts of her victorious battle with her father than of the implications of forsaking her homeland, left for Vienna.

3

Vienna

When I arrived in Vienna, I was a young girl, I couldn't speak a word of German and I had nobody to help me. Pollak left me at the station of the big city ... and went to his lover. ... At that time I had nobody in the world.

This account, written in the late 1930s, is perhaps overly bleak, a symptom of the emotional legacy of her time in Vienna. But as such, it contains the raw truth of what proved for Milena difficult years.

She was young, her German was stilted (although it improved rapidly in the German-speaking city), and while Ernst had many friends and contacts among the literary and Jewish communities of Vienna, she hardly knew anyone. Her triumph over her father, the adult freedom gained by marriage and the adventure of a new life away from Prague would not sustain her long.

Vienna in the spring of 1918 was not the most welcoming of cities. The Empire was in its death throes, its capital a faded beauty with rouge on its cheeks but skin and bone beneath. Its inhabitants were only just beginning to come to terms with the unimagined possibility of defeat. The more resilient prepared for a future without an Emperor; the Social Democrats, the Christian Social Party and the German Nationalists were wise enough to cooperate rather than to fight and destroy each other. Others saw the impending collapse of the Empire as a call to revolution, the inevitable spread of the victory of the masses from Russia to the West. Vienna was hectic with rumours, revolutionary fervour, mass meetings.

But the real division of power was being planned elsewhere, by the Allied Powers who now glimpsed victory. Was the break-up of the Empire really in Europe's best interests? Might it not bring even greater instability? Far from Vienna, T. G. Masaryk and his compatriots campaigned tirelessly to be free of the Austrian yoke. Their message was beginning to be heard: that the Empire did not deserve to survive, and that in an age of democracy and national determination it was inherently unstable. Peace would be better served by breaking it up. So while Milena's friends back home began to anticipate an independent Czechoslovakia, she found herself in a country facing defeat. There was little energy left to welcome strangers, least of all a Czech.

Milena and Ernst briefly took noisy lodgings in a modest house at Florianigasse 58, and then at Nussdorferstrasse 14 near the Franz Josefs Station. Both apartments were some way from the centre. After a few weeks they found more permanent accommodation, and in the middle of May they moved into a four-roomed apartment at Lerchen-felderstrasse 113, a little way up the hill from the city centre. It was a corner house, and their apartment looked out over a garden attached to the Alt-Lerchenfelder church. It was not a smart area; Ernst had been transferred to his bank's Vienna office, which contributed to the rent, but his salary was modest.

Ernst's acquaintances quickly began to draw them into the life of the city, in particular his friend Franz Werfel, the writer, who was also a friend of Max Brod and Kafka. Werfel had been conscripted but spent much of the war working for the Military Archive in Vienna. He lived at the grand Hotel Bristol on the Ringstrasse and was about this time embarking on the obsession which would lead to marriage with Alma Mahler-Gropius, widow of Gustav Mahler and a powerful Vienna personality and saloniste. Like many other German-speaking Prague Jews (including Ernst), Werfel regarded Vienna as a safer haven than Prague, which was beginning to reek of Czech nationalism and lust for revenge against the German oppressors and their Jewish sidekicks. Werfel introduced Ernst and Milena to the favourite cafés of these exiles. Milena had enjoyed Werfel's company in Prague and she admired his poetry. But she soon found herself ambivalent about his café swagger and his bond with her husband.

As well as working at the Austrian National Bank, Ernst soon took his place among the café circles of the Vienna intelligentsia. After a morning at the office he would head for the Café Central or the Herrenhof (his favourite) or the Griensteidl. The Herrenhof was art deco in style, with a clouded glass ceiling; the Central was more elaborate, with vaulted ceilings and marble walls. Milena would join Ernst and his friends at their table. Apart from Werfel they included Dr Otto Gross, an older psychiatrist, pupil of Freud's and cocaine user; the writer Hermann Broch; and Gina and Otto Kaus, she a writer and dramatist, a little older than Milena and at the heart of the social circle, he a writer and journalist. Ernst would discuss literature or his growing passion for philosophy, which was beyond Milena's education or interest. Although these people became friends, Milena did not find the same closeness she had known with Staša or Jarmila. Many of her new companions were older than her and more brittle. In Prague optimism and even sentimentality reigned. Here in Vienna attitudes were more fractured and cynical. The end of the familiar order raised enormous questions. The old certainties, the plush comforts of bourgeois Vienna, the luxuriant art nouveau curves which had dominated the city no longer seemed appropriate for harder times. These shifts had of course been happening for some time, expressed for example in Schiele's angular, angrily erotic paintings or Freud's research into the dark corners of the unconscious. The war exacerbated the intellectual uncertainty; if old meanings were empty the only meaning lay in the moment, a life lived for sensation and intellectual adventure. This was a hard, driven city, knowing and sophisticated. In theory this was what Milena craved. In reality it left her bereft.

The café culture rejected bourgeois conventions, in particular sexual puritanism and propriety. Ernst had made clear to Milena that marriage for him did not mean monogamy. She knew that his life in Prague had included many liaisons and her own creed required her to be free-minded. But she was not prepared for the cult of promiscuity prevalent at the Café Herrenhof, and certainly not for the way it took Ernst away from her. She became the object of other people's more or less casual appetites. Even Werfel (despite his interest in Alma Mahler-Gropius) seems to have paid her cloying attention. She was at sea in a culture with its own code, unsure what to take seriously, what to dismiss. In time she learnt, hardened, and sought her own consolations. For now, she did not feel at home.

For all her charms Milena was not coquettish, and with her firm chin and intelligent blue eyes she appeared more self-assured than she felt. Other women, more sophisticated and flirtatious, flocked around Ernst and he took lovers. (In the post-war years they included Mitzi Behr, a fashionable and pleasing companion, and Mia Weiss, the wife of one of his colleagues.) Ernst and Werfel were a charismatic pair, clever, ebullient, dissolute. Ernst brought friends, including women friends, back to Lerchenfelderstrasse. When Milena awoke in the morning, there would often be a guest asleep on the sofa. There were easier times too, when they recreated the Prague musical evenings, but she frequently felt excluded from Ernst's life.

By day, while he was at work, Milena explored the city and looked for provisions. Food was hard to find in the shops and it was expensive on the black market. They were both careless with money; Milena's dowry soon went and in time her trousseau was pawned. She walked for miles and came to know the city's different layers, the still elegant centre, the drabber suburbs, the black marketeers, the beggars, the rich inhabitants of the grandest cafés.

Through the late summer and autumn it became clearer that the Central Powers were losing the war, and that if there was to be any chance of survival Austria must sue for peace. Through October, the Empire began its final disintegration as the South Slavs (Yugoslavs), Poles, German Austrians and the Czechs declared their intention to break away from the Empire. In Prague on 28 October an independent Czechoslovak Republic was declared. Within a few weeks, T. G. Masaryk was elected president and returned from exile to be greeted by jubilant crowds in Prague's Old Town Square.

Vienna by contrast was a humiliated city. On 3 November Austria surrendered. On 11 November the Emperor left Vienna and on the next day the Republic was declared. Gina Kaus described how: 'Our entire group was sitting in the Herrenhof Café when we saw a crowd of people gathering opposite the parliament building. Milena, Werfel and I went out. The Social Democrat Karl Leuthner was speaking from the balcony. The crowd was yelling all sorts of things. Werfel tore off his hat and shouted "Down with the Habsburgs! Long live the Republic!" Thousands of weary, starving labourers came marching in from Florisdorf and we marched along with them for a while.'

The Social Democrats had the strongest base in the new country. With an efficient party organisation and a direct appeal to workers, they absorbed support which might otherwise have gone to more revolutionary, disruptive forces. In cooperation with the Christian Social Party and the German Nationalists they took up the harness of state; all were determined to prevent civil war between left and right.

There was much to be done, from choosing a national anthem and flag for the new country to preparing fresh elections. But the most pressing problem was food. With the loss of the Empire, Austria's population shrank from fifty million to six and a half million. The fertile lands of Hungary and Bohemia and the coal fields of the northern reaches of the Empire had gone. Food had to be requisitioned from the agricultural hinterland around Vienna to feed the urban masses. Prices rose and goods vanished from the shops. Milena, the outsider, observed these developments closely. She was shocked by the suffering of the poor and stirred by the politics of the Social Democrats; they were indeed a radical break from the decadent Empire.

As the autumn passed, Milena began to find friendship and threw herself into it with the same generosity and intensity as in Prague. She renewed acquaintance with Alice Gerstlová, a friend from Prague, who came to Vienna to attend Freud's lectures. She and her future husband, Otto Rühle, in time introduced Milena to Vienna socialists.

Another friend was Willy Haas, also an acquaintance from Prague who moved between the two cities and who was close to Milena's friend Jarmila. He described how giving but also demanding Milena could be. Once he wanted a room to take a new girlfriend to. Milena arranged for an acquaintance to lend a room, and borrowed money from another to fill it with flowers. The problem was that she expected friends to match this sort of generosity. Willy Haas recalled failing to live up to her standards. He had kept his soldier's pay vouchers which many others, convinced they were worthless, had thrown away at the end of the war. In fact they were redeemable and Haas proudly showed them to Milena. She declared that she was in need of money; could she have some? When Haas prevaricated she simply reached out and took a bunch of notes. He was outraged at first, and then ashamed. 'Milena had taught him a lesson.'

Haas left a powerful description of Milena at this time.

> She sometimes gave the impression of a noblewoman of the sixteenth or seventeenth century ... passionate, bold, cold, and intelligent in her decisions, but reckless in her choice of means when her passion was involved – and in her younger days this was almost always the case. As a friend, she was inexhaustible, inexhaustible in kindness, inexhaustible in resources, the source of which often remained a mystery, but also inexhaustible in the demands she made on her friends, demands which she as well as her friends took for granted.....
> Out of place amid the erotic and intellectual promiscuity of Viennese café society during the wild years after 1918, she was very unhappy.

Perhaps to assuage her unhappiness, Milena followed Ernst's example and took a lover, the writer Hermann Broch. He was, like Ernst, a Jewish intellectual ten years older than her, tall, with piercing eyes, an aquiline nose and a kind smile. Although he was involved in his father's textile business his real interests were philosophy and literature, and he was an entertaining conversationalist with an appealing, self-deprecating sense of humour. Under the pretext of taking Czech lessons with Milena, Broch allowed an affair to develop and Milena responded passionately. But during 1918 Broch also became involved with an older woman who would be his mistress for ten years, Ea von Allesch, an elegant fashion writer and sophisticated grande dame of the Café Central who, no doubt, both inspired and intimidated Milena. Broch's interest in Milena was a dalliance in comparison; this at least is what Ernst understood and he therefore asked Broch to break off the relationship. Whether Ernst really felt protective towards Milena as she made forays into his world of free love, or was in fact jealous, is not clear. Milena's confusion can only have increased. To his friends, Ernst was a kind-hearted, companionable man. His affection for Milena was not in doubt but, having brought her to Vienna, he was unable fully to acknowledge or satisfy the complicated needs of his young, homesick wife. Milena still looked up to him, but emotionally he seems to have left her behind and wandered out into the Vienna night.

Occasionally she found respite in a visit to Prague, now the capital of independent Czechoslovakia. It was a confident, optimistic place, governed by the largely liberal hand of President Masaryk. Milena could not but feel the contrast with Vienna. Her friends also came to visit her. It was only a few hours by train or car, or a short flight from Prague to Vienna. Once when Milena and Ernst had visited Prague, Jarmila went to the airport to see them off. Milena suddenly suggested that Jarmila return with them. And she did, with just her coat and bag. In Vienna, Milena showed guests around the old town or took them to the Prater, Vienna's huge funfair.

Milena found other, more unlikely companionship with the concierge at Lerchenfelderstrasse, Paní Kohler, a warm-hearted, bustling middle-aged Hungarian woman. (Paní means 'Mrs' but she was always known as Paní Kohler as if it was her real name.) Milena described her face: 'round like the moon, with a little blunt nose right in the centre, and underneath yawns a broad, full, toothy mouth.' Paní Kohler served as housekeeper as well as concierge. Times might be hard but it was unimaginable for Milena, a daughter of the bourgeoisie, to be without help in the house. Paní Kohler cleaned, cooked and even woke Milena each morning. 'I can't get up in the morning if she doesn't stand by my bed with her broom and tattered apron.' The two became friends of sorts. Milena was touched by Paní Kohler's care and impressed by her energy as she scoured the town driving hard bargains to feed the Lerchenfelderstrasse brood. Paní Kohler was popular with Ernst and his friends; she would mend their socks, clean their shoes, feed them, clean up after them. But Milena felt her to be her particular ally. She never quite managed to stop thinking of Paní Kohler as a character in some folk tale, or of herself as her mistress, counting the sugar lumps in the bowl to see how many Paní Kohler might have 'borrowed'. But her fondness and reliance were real. They shared a sense of exile, Milena from Prague, Paní Kohler from Hungary. In Paní Kohler, Milena found a maternal ear for her woes.

She found it harder and harder to keep her spirits up. Franz Blei, a writer, editor and admirer of Kafka's, observed her at the neighbouring table in the Café Central (which he regarded as 'not a café like other cafés, rather a whole philosophy of life'): 'What's up with Milena? She looks as careworn as six volumes of Dostoevsky.' Around this time Milena resorted to drugs. She and her girlfriends had experimented in Prague, but this was different, a craving not for adventure but for oblivion. A friend of Ernst's supplied her with cocaine to ease her headaches, and she came to know the inevitable highs but also the concomitant lows, as well as the intensified money worries. It was a dark, dark winter. At some point Milena tried to leave Ernst; exactly when or where she went is not clear, and in time she returned. But it was a sign of her desperation.

Outside the 'lair', as she dubbed their apartment, Vienna was on edge. Elections in early 1919 brought the Social Democrats firmly to power and the government was involved in lengthy negotiations at the Paris Peace Conference. The economy was a wreck. Ernst could not give Milena much money and the dowry had gone. Milena resorted to her old tricks and stole jewels from her rich and sophisticated acquaintance, Gina Kaus. There was embarrassment but the police were not involved. She was not to be so lucky on a later occasion.

Milena observed and wondered. What was the future of this city, and what was her own future here? Her husband gave her neither adequate emotional nor financial support. But what could she do? She was not trained for any employment and in any case Vienna was suffering from high unemployment and there was little room for an unqualified Czech. But Milena proved resourceful. She started to teach Czech to classes of between 50 and 200 schoolchildren, and gave private Czech lessons to factory owners whose property was now in Czechoslovakia.

There are also several accounts that Milena took work as a porter at the Westbahnhof railway station, carrying suitcases to hotels. While this may seem surprising, such heavy work was permitted to women and Milena's later journalism certainly reveals her familiarity with the bustling pageant of the station.

> Every morning a train leaves for Amsterdam and the Hague. . . . In the restaurant car, at the big windows, sit beautiful men and women drinking hot chocolate from silver cups . . . nowhere in the surrounding streets is there such blazing elegance as here, the moment before the train leaves. But hardly has the train been swallowed up by the open sky beyond the platform than a crowd of gaunt, frozen figures in rags emerges onto the platform, women with terrible coughs, irascible, bitter, unshaven men carrying satchels, sacks, milk-cans from dawn to dusk. Hundreds of people come to pick up what they can: a little milk, bread, eggs, potatoes, wood. The Austrian farmers do famously by it. . . . They have more food than they need and they exchange the surplus for things which the hungry townfolk bring them: linen, shoes, clothes, even furniture and quilts. Once a farmer's wife, who had been brought everything she might wish, demanded – opera glasses! And in return she handed over a few kilograms of potatoes.

All life was here. Milena observed her alien surroundings carefully, always sensitive to those in difficulty and shocked by the contrasts she noticed between rich and poor. These contrasts were present in her own life. She had little money of her own yet wanted desperately to keep up the glamorous appearance of which Ernst approved. She succumbed to theft, again from an acquaintance. This time she was accosted and on the day after her twenty-third birthday, 11 August 1919, she appeared before a local court. Her friends hired a good lawyer, who got her off on grounds of 'incapacity'. When asked why she had stolen, Milena said it was because of an 'erotic crisis'. It seems that she had been driven to despair by Ernst's apparent preference for more sophisticated women in the Café Herrenhof. She had decided to challenge him. With the money from the pawned stolen jewels she bought a new dress and hat and make-up. Late in the evening she swept into the café and presented herself before Ernst. But the welcome and admiration which her restored glamour aroused was not, after all, what she really wanted. She wanted Ernst to notice her even without new finery. Ernst received a slap and Milena a humiliating court appearance.

So in the autumn of 1919, more than a year after her arrival in Vienna, Milena was still searching for greater purpose to her life. She was made for more than carrying luggage, more than playing house-wife to a promiscuous literary figure. She was still an outsider in Vienna. But perhaps here lay her chance, if she could turn her status as an observer to advantage. She wrote to the mother of a friend in Prague, who worked for the newspaper *Národní politika*, offering fashion articles. The response was disappointing but Milena persev-ered. She wrote a handful of pieces about life in Vienna and sent them to Staša, who had connections at *Tribuna*, a progressive liberal paper. The editor, Arnošt Lustig, was impressed and asked for more. And when the paper's fashion correspondent, Zdenka Wattersonová, left for the United States, Milena also began to contribute fashion columns. She soon had regular space, especially in the Sunday editions of the paper; her journalistic career was launched. With pride she sent a copy of the first edition in which she appeared to her father (it was not a paper he read regularly). He apparently did not respond.

Milena's daughter Jana later wrote how journalism was absolutely the right choice of profession. 'Milena needed immediate contact with the reader and she needed to involve herself actively with events around her. Besides, she never had the stamina for long prose. She expressed herself best on a small canvas.' She would in time write hundreds of articles, under various names: Milena Pollak, Milena Krejcar, Milena Jesenská (most commonly), A. X. Nessy (Jesenská backwards), MP, MJ or simply Milena. From now on, Milena's own words help paint the story of her life.

Christmas 1919 found her very low. But at least now, in one of her very first articles, she could make something out of her experiences in Vienna.

> Best to get under the quilt, cover yourself up to your ears and stay there right through the holiday. That's how I decided to celebrate Christmas! . . .
>
> There is no fuel, no coal, no wood, no coke. No trains are running in the whole country, the factories fall suddenly silent, the shops shut at five o'clock and from eight o'clock the restaurants and cafés are lit only with flickering acetylene lamps. They're threatening to cut off electricity for domestic use so that we'll have to use candles, which are

impossible to buy! There's nothing to heat with, nothing to cook with. Every day thousands of people go to the Vienna woods to collect wood and they return with damp bits of tree which bake in the stove but give off no heat. At the terminus stations on the edge of Vienna crowds of people wait patiently with sacks and satchels full of wood; women, old people, children, with huge loads. In the darkness the whole caravan looks grotesquely horrible, as if the forest was secretly on the move....

The other half of the population sells wood. For two crowns a kilo. At the stations boys stand with sacks and little carts. Wagons laden with wood roll through the streets. If you want fuel, go through the streets and look for a man with wood, stop the cart and pay, haggle, pay and pay again. The wood, however, is neither chopped nor trimmed. For chopping you pay again. For transport you pay again. Of course by the time you get the wood to your apartment half of it has gone. Then take the good man by the hand, thank him, and give him a big tip and a glass of wine. And be glad that you have anything at all.

It's the same with food. What you get weekly is enough for only the most modest needs – quantitatively and qualitatively – a wretched dinner once a week. A loaf of bread per person – and despite two winters' schooling in Viennese poverty, I have not managed to succeed in swallowing this yellow, hard, mouldy old 'gift of God'. There's no other choice but to provide for yourself on the black market, which flourishes here perhaps more than anywhere else.

At the same time Milena noticed the busy stock exchange, the full restaurants, cabarets and theatres, observed people for whom nothing was expensive enough.

Vienna is mad – or is the world mad? – Vienna is in the last stage of its fame. The only thing that can save it is its old tradition as a metropolis, the fact that after all these years everything still works, that public buildings, hotels, restaurants, bars, theatres are being built, that the whole mechanism still runs even where there is a vacuum. But it's worst of all for us Czechs. In Czechoslovakia we are at home but here we are forced to carry the burden of others, without our own people being able to help us at all! Would it not be possible for representatives of the Czech Republic to open the borders or allow post and travel? Could we not at least have a piece of Christmas cake from our families or a little flour for Christmas?

As I said – there's nothing for it but to sleep out Christmas under my quilt like a marmot.

Kafka, Love and Courage

In the informal style which she adopted from the start, Milena gave her readers in Prague a vivid picture of life in post-war Vienna. But she was not just a reporter. This was her life too. She also had to hunt for food and resort to the communal kitchens. 'There are all sorts: for journalists, artists, ordinary people, academics, clerks ... they are all the same, like peas in a pod ... they all have the same unbearable smell of cabbage and rancid butter.' After a couple of weeks of trying to eat the watery soup and solid plum cake she gave up. 'After two weeks it's simply impossible to go to these places without throwing up just from the smell. And yet what else is there? For six crowns no one could cook much more than carrots at home, or perhaps cabbage, that terrible, sickening cabbage, which the whole of Vienna smells of, from top to bottom of every house ... nose, mouth, stomach, all are full of cabbage.'

But she also described life in the best restaurants, like the Opera or the Imperial.

The waiter will lean over and quietly whisper: 'Do you like Hungarian cabbage?' Cabbage! You take fright and ask, 'What is it?' 'Ah, something delicious,' he replies condescendingly. If you have to ask what it is you are not 'au fait', my dear; if you were, you would know. 'So, bring me the cabbage,' you declare. In a moment he weaves towards you with a plate of food which looks indeed like a pile of cabbage. But underneath there really is 'something delicious', roast pork for example! Or veal! A cutlet! A joint of chicken! Goose! A leg of venison! Ah, miracles!

It's the same with dessert. On the menu is macaroni, plum strudel, semolina pudding. But if you can enter intelligently into discussion with the waiter, he will investigate the corner of the cupboard and find cakes with whipped cream, butter biscuits, the best crumbly little jam-filled cakes which you can eat twenty of at one sitting, slices of sugared gateau ... From time to time one of these restaurants is closed by the police for a few days. But this does no harm. On the contrary, it's like an advertisement – it's true! Everyone knows why it was closed – because the food there is as good as in peacetime!

She was more familiar, however, with the city's varied cafés.

It would be hard to think of a town with as many cafés as Vienna. There is hardly a street without at least one, more probably three or four, and they are always completely full ... even here it's possible to eat, and what's more it's possible to eat on credit. The waiter Anton or Franz is always around and he knows his poets and critics, and knows at once how much he can expect from them.... However, it's all incredibly expensive. But to eat expensively on credit is sometimes cheaper than to eat cheaply and pay – a secret not everyone understands.

At less salubrious cafés she watched the black marketeers at work under the attentive eye of the head waiter.

It's enough to go to him, press a note into his hands – in this way he earns thousands a day – and say, 'Sir! I have so many wagons of coal, flour, candles, condensed milk, oranges, whatever – who can I sell it to?' He replies, 'That man at the third table on the left would perhaps buy, but not the whole wagon.' Or, 'Ah, sir, the man you need was just here. But come tomorrow at half past three and he'll be here.' Or, 'No, coal you won't sell today, but do you have medicine? Well sir, there in the corner at the table on the right you will sell.'

Through these hands pass medicines which cannot be bought in the whole of Vienna, and which go immediately to a country with a stronger currency. Meanwhile, people in hospitals and sanatoriums are in agony and will perhaps even die.... How much madness lies in the machine which we call a Metropolis!

But Vienna had its delights too. Milena wrote articles about the fashion world, the rich women who could afford hàute couture, the slow resuscitation of the fashion houses. And she went often to the cinema. She loved films and the cinema was a welcome refuge while Ernst was at work or out on the town. She wrote a delightfully wry article celebrating its charms.

I know people who can go to the cinema day after day. It's not that they don't want to work, or that they don't know what to do. But the soul is so comfortable sitting in the cinema.

Everything on the screen is apparently the same as in life. And yet how vast, how comforting the difference. Whether it's about love and hatred, good and evil, fortune and poverty, or whether it's an intrigue to make your eyes roll and your fists clench, you know with all certainty that in the end it will all fall out right.... Nothing can happen which would not be right and fitting, else it would not be passed by the censor. Here are wicked women who smoke and lie about half-dressed on the ottoman, and good women who sew linen, read books, play the piano or love curly-haired little children. You know for certain that they are good, and that it is absolutely impossible for them to have anything bad in their hearts, and you know that the wicked ones are evil, and that they deserve your merciless scorn. You do not have to fear that you are doing them wrong, and you can be satisfied that they will be punished before you leave, and justly punished. Here the heroes, honest men, risk their lives for their beloved, staking their honour, reputation and very existence. And others, who just want a woman, approach her from behind and with a devilish expression take her by the shoulders. If they are refused they elegantly incline their head; if they are not, they sit 'afterwards' on the sofa. In either case they smoke a cigarette out of the corner of their mouth and look very cynical, they wear pyjamas and have black hair, you can recognise them immediately and scorn them with proper hatred.

In truth, how wonderful the world would be if it was like this.... In our world people are good and bad at the same time, trustworthy and untrustworthy, ignominious and heroic. Every heart is complex, every life hard and unfathomable ... We do not know how to vanish at the last minute through the window of a high prison on a rope fashioned out of our own shirt; we do not know how to jump, accurately if we are good, inaccurately if we are wicked, from the roofs of moving trains, and from bridges into the water.... The brides we meet are neither demonic women nor women of tragic fates who pierce our hearts with desperate laughter; our men deceive us without being expelled from human society; and our loves are quite ordinary clerks, shopkeepers, ministers, actors, not seducers and irresistible devils...

How sweet it is to let the brain contemplate these people on the screen, to rest from the problems of our lives....The cinema is something which makes it easier to bear life.

It is hard not to read into this article her own sense of disappointment, the compromises and moral confusion of her married life with Ernst. On top of his work and social life he had started to study philosophy and attended demanding seminars run by a group of professors exploring logical positivism, a scientific approach to philosophy which tended to regard moral concerns as metaphysical, unverifiable and therefore meaningless. Milena was left very much alone to try to find her own meanings in life.

One treat came in February 1920, with the carnival which transformed Vienna. 'Carnival is something which the good Lord invented especially and above all for Viennese blood.... For heaven's sake, everyone should paint the town red at least once a year.... And Vienna forgets the hard times and opens its pockets.' She loved the colour in the streets, the streamers on the pillars and horse carriages, the posters everywhere advertising concerts and shows, the bands in the cafés. She walked the streets in the evening and soaked up the scent of life, of pleasure, of the figure passing by in a harlequin costume. 'You forget for a moment that before you lies a town where hunger kills and you ask – peace?'

Her articles belonged to the tradition of the 'feuilleton', personal observations and musings rather than news reports. The stern moralistic Vienna writer and critic Karl Kraus criticised feuilletons for drowning important matters in a tide of personal superficialities. In his 1921 operetta *Literatur oder Man wird doch de sehn* he satirised the literary café society world of the likes of Pollak and Werfel. He was particularly scathing of how the press dictated fashion and thought: 'In the beginning was the press and then appeared the world.' But for others the feuilleton was an exciting form, allowing writers to bring their own sensibility to bear on what they observed. The writer of course always faced the danger of 'falling in love with his own spirit and thus of losing any standard of judging himself or others'. Milena did not always resist this danger. But at her best her articles are vivid, a mix of the concrete and the reflective. Their voice is fresh today. They are like letters home to a good friend, a repository for what she saw and thought; indeed some were printed under the rubric 'Letter from Vienna'. But a newspaper audience is no substitute for a real friend, who will, for one thing, write back. Milena lacked a true kindred spirit in Vienna itself. In early 1920, from a surprising quarter, she found her own personal, all-consuming correspondent.

4

Kafka

Franz Kafka was a little-known writer, a Jew living in Prague and writing in German. His friend Max Brod already regarded him as a genius but as yet he enjoyed little fame among the German community and even less among the Czech. Although he had written some of his greatest stories and begun work on *The Trial* by the early 1920s, only a few stories had been published (including *Metamorphosis*). After a day at his office in the Workers' Accident Insurance Institute he would sit for a while in one of the cafés, a lean, angular figure, engaged in philosophical discussion or literary gossip with his few close friends. He was elusive. He liked best to write in the small hours of the night.

Milena knew his face from Prague, but little else about him. In Vienna, where she was even more closely entwined with the German Jewish world than in Prague, she was introduced to his stories and was immediately taken by them. (Ernst was one of those who encouraged her to translate Kafka). Around October 1919, on a visit to Prague, she talked briefly to Kafka in a café (probably the Arco), and soon after she wrote to him, praising his work and asking for permission to translate some of his stories. He was flattered, found her interest 'somehow moving and embarrassing' and asked his publisher Kurt Wolff to send her some texts. In a series of letters in April 1920 he charted the beginning of their acquaintance. He recalled meeting her husband in Prague: 'I remember a Sunday afternoon years ago, I was creeping along the embankment close to the walls of the houses and ran into your husband who was coming towards me in a not much more brilliant condition, two headache experts, though each in his utterly different way. I no longer remember whether we then walked on together or passed each other, the difference between these two possibilities wouldn't have been very great.'

In another letter he enquired after her work and well-being. He was writing from the spa resort of Merano in the Italian Dolomites (formerly part of the Empire) where he hoped to heal the tuberculosis which had been troubling him for several winters. In a postscript he wrote of their autumn meeting: 'It occurs to me that I can't remember your face in any precise detail. Only how you finally walked away between the tables of the coffee-house, your figure, your dress, these I can still see.' Kafka had evoked the ghosts of Milena, her husband and himself. The players in the triangle were laid out.

Milena wrote back, telling Kafka about her life in Vienna, with something of its pains and claustrophobia. He replied, as a way of 'celebrating' the end of a rainstorm, and explained how he enjoyed his position as a 'foreigner' in the mountains. 'You too, if my impression was correct (a short, isolated, semi-silent meeting can evidently not be exhausted in one's memory), enjoyed being a foreigner in Vienna, although later on it may have been dimmed by the general conditions, but do you also enjoy being a foreigner as such?' He described the garden outside his room, the lizards and birds that occupied it. 'I so much wish you could be in Merano, recently you wrote about not being able to breathe, in this word image and meaning are very close and in Merano both might become a little easier.'

Here was somebody who understood her and her sorrows even without her having to spell them out, someone who showed her concern. And when her first translation of one of his stories, 'The Stoker', was published in the literary weekly magazine *Kmen* (*Tree-trunk*) on 22 April 1920, 'translated with the permission of the author by Milena Jesenská', Kafka was likewise convinced that here was someone who understood him. The story was the precursor of his novel *Amerika*, a fragment about a young man who is moved by the thwarted struggle of a ship's stoker against his unjust superiors. Its few pages conveyed with force some of Kafka's insight into exile, injustice, and the currents between people. *Kmen* was edited by Stanislav K. Neumann, an energetic socialist of broad tastes, and Milena cannily sold the fragment to him on the strength of its credentials as a story about the oppression of a worker. An editorial note in *Kmen* explained that the story was printed in full, rather than in instalments, since it 'belongs to the best modern German writing'.

Kafka wrote to Milena with one or two detailed comments on the translations and added, 'I'm deeply moved by the faithfulness with which you've done it, sentence for sentence, a faithfulness I wouldn't have thought possible in the Czech language, as little as I would have suspected your beautiful natural qualification for it.' The professional connection was fast becoming a deeper admiration.

What was it that drew these two together? Milena was 23, Kafka was 37. At first glance the spirited, full-blooded, broad-cheeked Czech adventuress and the pale, gaunt ascetic Jew were ill-matched. But if the clichés are discarded it becomes easier to discern the bonds. The ghostly posthumous portrait of Kafka is belied by the testament of his friends. They recall him swimming energetically in the Vltava, as Milena had. His smile, his sympathy, his enthusiasm charmed them all, as Milena charmed her friends. Life may have treated Kafka harshly but he did not scorn it, sought rather to understand it, grappled with it body and soul. He did not despise what in the end Milena wanted and what he could not have – love, family, the stuff of life. Indeed his tragedy was that, like a street urchin standing by a brightly lit shop window, he pined for what he could not share. Milena was more likely than Kafka to reach out and take what dazzled her, but she also knew what it was to be fearful.

There was also the attraction of difference, a mutual curiosity about another world. Kafka's parents were rural Jews whose first language was Czech: Kafka is a corruption of Kavka, or Jackdaw. When they moved to Prague and prospered, they began to inhabit a German-speaking world and Kafka's schooling was in German. But he took voluntary Czech classes at school and was interested in Czech politics and literature. He implored Milena to write to him in Czech. 'I'm not suggesting that you don't master German. Most of the time you master it surprisingly well and if once in a while you don't it bows before you of its own accord, and this is particularly pleasing. ... But I wanted to read you in Czech because it is part of you, because only there is the whole Milena.' When she did he was delighted: 'German is my mother-tongue and therefore natural to me, but Czech feels to me far more intimate, which is why your letter dispels many an uncertainty. I see you clearer, the movements of your body, your hands, so quick, so determined, it's almost a meeting, although when I try to raise my eyes to your face, then in the flow of the letter – what a story! – fire breaks out and I see nothing but fire.'

Milena had already strayed across national boundaries in her relationship with Ernst; Kafka took her deeper. Her relationships with Jews horrified not only her father but other members of her family, and arguments about Jewishness and Zionism at times brought conflict with Kafka.

Despite their very different backgrounds, they shared one family trait. Both were engaged in lifelong struggles with their fathers. They found relief discussing these bonds of love and hate. Milena's relationship with her father had erupted into more open conflict than had Kafka's with his father, a patriarchal businessman, but they recognised each other's hurt. They shared, too, the egotist's interest in the inner workings of the self, and the altruist's desire to help and heal others. Above all they were intellectual equals, and in this way, Milena stands out from the other women Kafka had been seriously involved with (all Jewish). The first woman he was engaged to, before the war, was a practical, outgoing young businesswoman, Felice Bauer. She signally failed to appreciate his writing. Her friend Grete Bloch, to whom Kafka was also drawn, was an intelligent woman but their correspondence was preoccupied with emotional matters. Finally there was his current girlfriend, the shy dressmaker Julie Wohryzek.

Kafka projected his dreams of family and of understanding onto these women, but the relationships became battlegrounds about marriage, his writing, living arrangements, furniture. Milena's appreciation of Kafka's work took this relationship into different territory. Kafka later wrote, 'No one has ever taken my side as knowingly and willingly as you, in spite of everything, in spite of everything'. They discussed books, especially Dostoevsky whom they both deeply admired, as well as intellectual currents of the time like psychoanalysis and Marxism. They were both interested in the unconscious but sceptical about the therapeutic value of psychoanalysis. They were both interested in socialist and radical politics, although Kafka was warier than Milena.

While much of his correspondence with Felice seems obsessive, complaining, inappropriate, his letters to Milena met their match. Sadly, Milena's letters to Kafka have not survived. But sometimes Kafka quotes Milena back to herself, and from later letters which she wrote to others it is possible to imagine her letters to Kafka – frank, sometimes funny, sometimes mournful, sometimes overwhelming, always questioning. And from Kafka's letters it is clear that the two were soon engaged in an intense, almost daily, correspondence. Milena asked Kafka to write to her at a poste restante address. Although it seems that Ernst knew of the letters, and even read some of them, collecting the letters from the Bennogasse post office near her home soon became a ritual part of Milena's life. The correspondence gives a remarkably dense picture of this period of her life. It reveals shifts of mood which feel as if they took place over months but in fact occurred over weeks or days.

At the time they met, both were damaged creatures. Kafka had recently broken off his engagement to Julie in despair (although they still saw each other) and his health was failing. He wrote from Merano that despite the rest and the mountain air he was not making good progress. Milena was at a wretched point in her life. She wrote a letter in which she exposed without self-pity the raw misery of her life in Vienna; her unhappy marriage and the pain caused by the fact that she still loved Ernst, the friends left behind in Prague, the loneliness, the financial straits, 'not a heller – tea and apples'. There was also a recurrent illness which left her coughing and weak. He replied with tenderness. 'So it's the lung. . . . Let's hope – your hints seem to suggest this – it is showing itself gently in your case . . . (half of Western Europe has more or less faulty lungs). . . . And what are you going to do now? It's probably only a trifle if you're given a little care. But that you need a little care, anyone who is fond of you must realise; for this everything else must take second place. . . . One more thing today: if you miss so much as one minute of your sleep by translating, it will amount to putting a curse on me. For when the Day of Judgment comes it will not be a question of closer investigation but simply of establishing: He has deprived her of sleep.'

And, in another letter, 'now and again there should be a deck-chair ready for you somewhere in the garden, half in the shade, and some ten glasses of milk within reach of your hands. It could also be in Vienna, especially now in summer, but without hunger and restlessness. Isn't this possible?'

For now it was not. This sort of tender care was exactly what Ernst did not give Milena. Their fraught life continued, and so did her work. Against this background, the correspondence with Kafka became a vital source of love and support. But she needed to know her ground. She demanded information about his past relationships. He replied, 'You ask about my engagement. I've been engaged twice (three times if you wish, that's to say twice to the same girl), so I've been separated three times from marriage by only a few days. The first one is completely over . . . the second is still alive but without any prospect of marriage.'

Kafka

He responded to her descriptions of her emotional difficulties with sympathy and tact, accepting her law that she was responsible for herself, it was she who must pay. 'That you don't want to be pitied . . . is quite natural. . . . But independent of all this it's terrible for a limited human intelligence to see you in the overheated oven in which you live.' His letter gives a clue to hers, in turn wretched and defiant, trying to protect herself a little. 'A small effort does show itself in your letters. Frequently I read of calm and fortitude, although recently often of other things, too, and in the end even of: "réalná hrůza" – "real horror".'

A letter from Kafka came most days, and Milena replied almost as often, writing letters and cards and telegrams in her apartment or a café. She was working too, but with uncertain confidence. She refused to send her articles to Kafka and wrote to him of her 'poor brain, unable to think'. He replied that he wished she could be with him, except that, in the way of lovers, she already was: 'It would be a lie for me to say that I miss you, it's the most complete, most painful magic, you are here, as much as I and more intensely; wherever I am you're there as much as I am, and indeed more so.' Reality and fantasy were already merging for Kafka, as he sat in a deck-chair in Merano and wrote to Milena of the beetle he had just watched writhing desperately on its back.

They were locked in their separate worlds, and trust did not come easily, especially for Milena. When Kafka was kind, she charged that he was not sincere. She appealed for his sympathy, yet tantalised him with accounts of her life in Vienna. 'How does it happen,' he retorted, 'that you're not fed up with the absurd people whom you describe (you describe them with love and therefore enchantingly). . . . I'm under the impression that you condone the absurdities as such, understand, love and ennoble them by your love. These absurdities are nothing but the running zig-zag of dogs, whereas the master walks straight ahead, not right through the middle but precisely where the road leads.' She, not surprisingly, was hurt: 'This has offended me.' In a later letter he said she had misunderstood him, that 'my "absurd" people are precisely yours'. Jealousy, and the frisson of a lover's tiff, of conflict and reconciliation, was possible even in letters.

It was as if Kafka wished Milena had no other life, certainly no husband. After only a few weeks, the intensity of the correspondence, both in number and content, was at fever pitch. In a letter to Max Brod at the beginning of May, Kafka wrote: 'I would be doing well, as far as my health goes, if I could sleep. . . . There may be various reasons for it, of which one perhaps is my correspondence with Vienna. She is a living fire, of a kind I have never seen before, a fire moreover that in spite of everything burns for him [Ernst]. Yet at the same time she is extremely tender, courageous, bright and commits everything she has to her sacrifice, or to put it another way perhaps, has gained everything she has by her sacrifice. Yet what kind of man must he be, who could evoke that?'

These first few weeks of Kafka's letters and his interest in her work were doing Milena good. She sent him a cheerful letter to which he replied, 'Where does this liveliness, the good humour, the carefreeness in your last letter come from?' And she now agreed to send him some of her articles, although she demanded he return them soon. He was enchanted. They may well have included the articles about the hardships of post-war Vienna, but she also wrote of the city's pleasures. In May she sent *Tribuna* a piece about the Prater fair under the viaduct in Vienna, a hectic jumble of thrills and delights. She described the hall of mirrors, the panoptikon with its ghastly wax figures, as frightening to her now as when a child. 'What is it in human nature which thought up this devilish scheme, where for a crown entrance fee all the bloody and painful scenes from human life imaginable are depicted for your pleasure?' More cheerful were the fire-eaters and the merry-go-rounds, above all the roller-coaster. 'Ten great hills, ten valleys, the carriage flies like the wind up, down, up, down, your hat flies away, your hair flies behind you. . . . It is beautiful, magnificent.' But rising high above the streets of Vienna brought home her disillusionment with the city. 'The town below is a boring, extended spider with endless legs. Perhaps there is no other town so faceless, so characterless as Vienna. . . . Suddenly you realise what is so oppressive down in the streets: it's never possible to get above the town, it's all on the level and you can never, never rise above the roofs.' How she missed the views down on Prague's spires and red-tiled houses from the Castle or Petřín Hill. Her visit to the Prater ended with her singing Czech folksongs with an old Czech busker. She was as sentimental and homesick as ever.

There was plenty of material here for Kafka, who scoured Milena's articles for clues to her person. But he also enjoyed them in themselves. 'That's no ordinary writer who wrote this. Having read it I have almost as much confidence in your writing as I have in you as a person. I know in Czech (with my limited knowledge) only one music of language, that of Božena Němcová, here is another music, but related to the former in determination, passion, loveliness and above all a clairvoyant intelligence.... Did you always write? Of course you'll say I'm ridiculously prejudiced and actually you're right, of course I'm prejudiced, but prejudiced not by what I discovered in the articles (which by the way are uneven, occasionally show the harmful influence of journalism), but by what I rediscovered in them.' Such praise!

Milena wrote to Kafka in more detail about Ernst, about his affairs and his reproaches. Kafka was surprised. 'Of your husband I had made myself another picture. In the coffee-house circle he appeared to me as the most reliable, most understanding, the calmest person, almost exaggeratedly paternal, though also inscrutable, yet not to a point that would cancel what I've just said. I always had respect for him, for further insight I had neither opportunity nor ability, but friends, especially Max Brod, had a high opinion of him, and of this I was always conscious when I thought of him. At one time I particularly liked his peculiarity of being called to the telephone in each coffee-house several times during the evening. Presumably there must have been someone who, instead of sleeping, sat by the telephone dozing, his head on the back of his chair, and who started up from time to time to telephone him.'

As their letters criss-crossed the new border between Austria and Czechoslovakia, Milena and Kafka described daily events and told amusing stories, but the burden of their correspondence was darker. Kafka wrote of his illness, his sleeplessness, his self-doubt. Milena tried to rouse him. He was not convinced: 'I don't believe what you say, Milena, and there's no way in which it could be proved to me.'

His resistance unsettled Milena. Indeed the whole correspondence unsettled her. A few days without a letter (even if several then arrived at once) left her anxious; perhaps Kafka was angry with her or did not like her articles. Sometimes his letters were unsatisfying, sometimes he seemed casual. She wrote him a letter full of anxiety and reproach. He replied with a long letter which is enormously revealing about the innate contradictions in their relationship.

She had written that she was frightened about the relationship 'which has fallen into my lap', and Kafka compared it to the fear of a prophet who hears a voice calling and is afraid to obey. 'One peculiarity I think we have in common, Milena: We are so shy and anxious, almost each letter is different, almost each one is frightened by the preceding letter and even more so by the reply. You aren't like this by nature, that's easy to see, and I, perhaps even I, am not like this by nature, but it has almost become my second nature already, it disappears only in despair and sometimes in anger and, needless to say: in fear.

'Sometimes I have the feeling that we're in one room with two opposite doors and each of us holds the handle of one door, one of us flicks an eyelash and the other is already behind his door, and now the first one has but to utter a word and immediately the second one has closed his door behind him and can no longer be seen.... Agonising misunderstandings come out of this. Milena, about some letters you complain that you turn them in all directions and nothing falls out of them, and yet they are, if I'm not mistaken, just those in which I feel so close to you, so tamed in my blood and taming yours, so deep in the forest, so restful in rest, that one doesn't really want to say anything but that up there through the trees the sky is visible.

'And don't demand any sincerity from me, Milena. No one can demand it from me more than I myself ... encouragement on this hunt does not encourage me, on the contrary, I can then no longer take one step, suddenly everything becomes a lie.... I can't listen simultaneously to the terrible voice from within and to you, but I can listen to the former and entrust it to you, to you as to no one else in the world.'

It was a very direct letter, a contrast to the 'eyelash flicking'. Kafka wanted an audience, not a partner, certainly not another preacher or performer. Kafka's search for understanding cut him off from real contact, the muddle of life; he was caught between those old antagonists, art and life, work and love. 'The terrible voice within' was stronger than Milena's voice. Yet he trusted her to listen. And he knew he hurt her. He later dreamt: 'We were sitting side-by-side.... I was very unhappy. Not about the warding off, but about myself who was treating you like any other silent woman and failed to hear the voice which spoke out of you and spoke expressly to me. Or perhaps it wasn't that I had failed to hear it but that I couldn't have answered it.'

The correspondence spiralled into hurt. Milena replied furiously (letters to others show that she was good at indignation, hurt, chagrin), and accused him of taking sides with her husband. He told her she had misunderstood. 'Who am I to condemn, I who in any real respect – marriage, work, courage, sacrifice, purity, freedom, self-sufficiency, truthfulness – stand so far below you both that it sickens me even to talk about it.' She stormed and the storm passed, she had her reassurance and could respond in kind. A breakdown of communication was unthinkable. She sent him a 'sweet' telegram which he found 'a comfort against the night'.

Milena was drained by her life in Vienna, and susceptible to nervous tension and mood swings. One day she would write to Kafka a letter in which he found her 'so strong that I watched you as I would watch mountain-climbers from my deck-chair', the next an outpouring of depression: 'I've read the Sunday letter once again, it's even more terrible than I thought after the first reading.'

He made a proposal: 'You leave your husband for a while, that's nothing new, after all it's happened before. The reasons are: your illness, his nervousness (he would also benefit from it), and finally conditions in Vienna. Where you'd like to go I don't know, the best for you might be some peaceful part of Bohemia. It will also be best if I neither personally interfere nor show myself. The money required for this you take for the moment (we'll come to an agreement about the conditions of repayment) from me.' (On another occasion he does not seem to have sent her money.)

She could not accept, but he was right that she needed a holiday. He suggested she go away with Staša (now Jílovská), whom he knew from Prague, reassuring her that Ernst need have no fear. 'I won't see you at all, not now, not later. You'll be living in the kind of country you love. (In this we are alike: rolling country, not yet quite mountainous, with woods and lakes, is what I like best.)' But Milena began to suggest instead that he come to Vienna.

The question of a meeting was laden with problems: Milena's guilt about her husband, Kafka's resistance to any disruption of his routine, and his fear of confronting his fantasies with reality. He dreamt about an encounter: 'I was in Vienna, of which I remember nothing, but then I came to Prague and had forgotten your address. . . . So you were completely lost to me. In my despair I made several very cunning attempts which, however, I don't know why, were not carried through and of which I remember only one. I wrote on an envelope: "Milena", and under it, "I beg that this letter be delivered, otherwise the Ministry of Finance will suffer an enormous loss".'

But Ernst remained a constant presence. 'Perhaps I do him an injustice – I can't think about this – terrible injustice,' Kafka wrote, 'but almost equally strong is the feeling that I'm now bound up with him and more and more closely, I almost said: in Life and Death. If only I could talk to him! But I'm afraid of him, he's very superior to me. You know, Milena, when you went to him you took a large step down from your level, but if you come to me you'll leap into the abyss.'

Their arguments about Ernst were reflected in a battle about Ernst's great friend Franz Werfel. The two men were extremely close, with Ernst acting as trusted literary adviser to Werfel and both of them sharing their explorations of philosophy and the company of women. Milena had come to resent Werfel's appropriation of her husband's time and energy and their partnership in promiscuity. When Milena wrote to Kafka complaining of his lack of understanding about human nature, he countered, 'How about your knowledge of human nature, Milena? I've doubted it several times already, when you wrote about Werfel for instance.' She had expressed her visceral dislike of Werfel by criticising his swelling figure. Kafka, who hated his own skinniness, was outraged: 'If one leaves out all that Werfel really is and harps only on the reproach of fatness . . . don't you know that only fat people are trustworthy? . . . only these capitalists of the airspace are, as far as it is possible for human beings, protected against worry and madness and are able to go calmly about their business.' Kafka's sense of humour flashes like glittering veins in the rock of his seriousness; Milena's writing reveals the same capacity for irony and self-critique. But she was more literal than he, and his jokes sometimes made it hard for her to trust him.

And so their letters went back and forth day by day, sometimes full of sympathy, sometimes of friction. Kafka teased her. 'That's just the beauty of your translation, that it is faithful (scold me by all means for the "faithful", you can do everything, but what you can do best perhaps is scold, I'd like to be your pupil and make mistakes all the time, just in order to be scolded by you all the time).' The fantasy recurs, of her teaching in her Vienna schools. 'I'd love to have a window-seat in that last row for an hour.'

They wrestled with each other. Milena repeated her desire for Kafka to come to Vienna. 'I don't want to,' he wrote 'because I couldn't stand the mental strain.' He described the tension of the past years with engagements broken, patched, broken again. He was still in contact with Julie, and he explained to Milena that with his vacation soon ending at the end of June, instead of returning from Merano to Prague via Vienna, he might visit Julie in Karlsbad

(Karlovy Vary in Czech). Would she understand his constitutional incapacity to go to Vienna, 'his whole frame of mind'?

No, she did not understand. She wrote him an angry, hurt letter and suggested they stop writing. He replied in similar vein: how could she pretend to be 'fond' of him yet deprive him of letters; then again, 'perhaps you'd be right not to write to me any more, several passages in your letter suggest this necessity. I can't plead anything against them.' In another letter he characterised her letters as of two kinds: gentle, cheerful, 'peaceful' letters, which were 'rain on the burning head'. Others were shattering: 'Letters which begin with exclamations (and I am after all so far away) and end with I know not what terror, then Milena I actually begin to tremble as under an alarm-bell, I can't read them and yet read them I must ... trembling and almost unconscious I pray in the corner that you may fly out of the window as you have rushed in in your letter, I can't after all keep a storm in my room.'

She could not in the end bring herself to break off the correspondence. Threats had not brought Kafka to Vienna, so she turned to entreaties. He continued to resist and tried again to explain. He recalled a happy time in a village two years ago, after his final break with Felice, 'in the shelter' of his illness: 'All right, and now Milena calls you with a voice which penetrates your reason and your heart with equal intensity. Of course Milena doesn't know you, a few stories and letters have dazzled her; she is like the sea, strong as the sea with its vast volume of water, and yet, mistaken, tumbling down with all its strength when the dead and above all distant moon desires it.... Milena thinks only of the opening of the door. It will indeed open, but then? Then a long thin creature will stand there, with a friendly smile ... he's unlikely to talk much, lacking the vitality ... You see, Milena, I'm speaking frankly.' He prolonged his stay in Merano.

Milena was uncertain how to proceed, what effect their correspondence was having on Kafka. In a letter to Max Brod responding to a query about a mutual acquaintance, she also appealed to him as Kafka's best friend to tell her what she knew Kafka himself would not reveal: 'I beg you, really beg, beg you, if you see, if you feel that thanks to me his health suffers, please write to me at once, I won't tell him I know from you, and I will be calmer if you promise. How I can help him I don't know, but *that* I can help him I know quite certainly.'

Kafka, Love and Courage

Kafka too was troubled. 'This criss-crossing of letters must stop, Milena, they're driving us mad, one doesn't know what one has written, nor what one has answered, and trembles all the time however it is.' The crisis drove them to face the implications of the strength of feeling between them. 'How shall we continue to live?' wrote Kafka. 'If you say "Yes" to my letters, then you must not continue to live in Vienna, that's impossible.' But at once he retracted the implicit offer: 'Milena, for me you are not a woman, you are a girl, as girl a one as I ever saw, I don't think I'll dare to offer you my hand, girl, this dirty, twitching, clawlike, unsteady, uncertain, hot-cold hand.'

But the suggestion was gaining a life of its own. They were drawing closer. As Kafka finally began his return journey from Merano to Prague towards the end of June 1920, he wrote to her, answering her uncertainty about what he was proposing. 'Your interpretation of my "You must get out of Vienna" isn't quite correct. I didn't write it thoughtlessly and I'm not afraid of the material burden (I don't earn much, but I think it would be enough for us both, provided of course no illness interferes), I'm also sincere according to my power of thought and expression. . . . What I'm afraid of, afraid of with wide-open eyes, helplessly drowned in fear . . . is only this inner conspiracy against myself . . . That is why the suggestion which I made to you has a far greater significance for me than for you. For it is, at the moment, the only thing that is unquestionable, free of morbidity and making me completely happy.' He reserved the option to come to Vienna. 'Today for instance I would say that I shall certainly come to Vienna, but since today is today and tomorrow tomorrow I shall leave myself some freedom. . . . I would arrive at the South Station. . . . Today I saw a map of Vienna, for an instant it seemed incomprehensible to me that they built such a big city when you need only one room.'

The following day another letter arrived. In fact he would arrive, if he came, at the West station. He would not surprise her, but if she heard nothing by the following Thursday she should assume he had gone straight to Prague. A trip to Vienna 'after all, is no trifling matter, nothing to joke about'.

Circling, circling. The next day he was more committed. 'If nothing unexpected happens, outwardly or inwardly, I'll be in Vienna on Tuesday.'

So, at the very end of June 1920, little more than two months since

their correspondence began in earnest, Milena received a note from
Kafka, written at a coffee-house near the South Station in Vienna.
'What kind of cocoa is this, what kind of pastry? Is this what you live
on? ... I am nevertheless not yet completely here, haven't slept for
two nights ... I expect you Wednesday morning at 10 in front of the
hotel. Please, Milena, don't surprise me by approaching me from the
side or from the rear, I promise not to do it, either.'

They kept the appointment, and spent four full days together. It
was a concentrated, happy time, and some of what it meant for them
can be pieced together from later accounts. Kafka saw the house
where she lived and met Paní Kohler. Milena and Kafka explored
Vienna, walked in the Volksgarten with the chestnut trees in bloom,
went to a stationer's shop. They drove through the suburbs and spent
whole days in the woods. They lay on a 'wretched bed', perhaps in
Kafka's station hotel. They talked, of their lives, their dreams, their
families, their fathers, and Milena told Kafka about her little brother
who had died. He found her beautiful and stylish, especially on the
Saturday, their last day, 'really quite fabulously beautiful'. It was just
as they had both imagined. Kafka later characterised the days: 'The
first was unsure, the second was oversure, the third remorseful, the
fourth was the good one.'

For Milena the visit brought real intimacy and energy, and she
tried to give Kafka the sort of support and confidence in himself and
the world which she felt he needed. She also tried to help him
overcome his 'fear', his fastidious distaste for the physical, ripe,
material nature of the world. The word fear, often capitalised, tolls
through Kafka's letters to Milena and, one can assume, through hers
to him, as they tried to understand and assuage their mutual anxieties.
Milena regarded Kafka's nervousness as the foundation of his ill
health; by calming his fears she could bring him physical strength.
She later wrote to Max Brod: 'For the four days that Frank was with
me, he lost his anxiety. We laughed at it. ...This anxiety does not
refer only to me, but to everything which lives without shame, to the
flesh for example. Flesh is too bare, Frank cannot tolerate looking at
it. That was what I managed to lay aside at the time. Whenever he
felt that fear, he looked into my eyes, we waited a while, as if we
could not draw breath or as if our feet hurt, and in a moment it
passed. Not the slightest effort was necessary, everything was simple
and clear, I ploughed ahead of him through the hills behind Vienna,
I ran in front, because he went slowly, he tramped behind me, and if

I close my eyes, I see his white shirt and tanned throat, and how he exerted himself. The whole day he ran up and down, walked in the sun, without coughing once, he ate a great deal and slept like a log, he was simply healthy and his illness seemed to us during those days like a little chill.'

They were exhilarated and entranced by each other. They were certainly physically affectionate, but the relationship remained unconsummated. Kafka had slept with women, including prostitutes, but the closer he was to a woman emotionally, the harder it seems to have been for him to be sexually involved. Physical closeness was certainly part of his fantasy about Milena: he envisioned resting his head in her lap, or lying in a bed with his mouth close to her ear. But they did not cross his carefully defended threshold. In a later letter to Milena he referred back to their time in Vienna. 'You once asked me how I could have called that Saturday "good" with that fear in my heart, it's not difficult to explain. Since I love you (and I do love you, you stupid one, as the sea loves a pebble in its depths, this is just how my love engulfs you – and may I in turn be the pebble with you, if Heaven permits), I love the whole world and this includes your left shoulder, no, it was first the right one, so I kiss it if I feel like it (and if you are nice enough to pull the blouse away from it) . . .

'But just between this day-world and that "half-hour in bed" of which you once spoke contemptuously as "men's business", there lies for me an abyss which I cannot bridge, probably because I don't want to.'

Milena was no doubt puzzled and even frustrated but she showed great tact. Kafka was enormously grateful to her for not pushing the question of sex, for reassuring him that they were 'already one'. 'It is therefore "samozřejmé" (natural) that by your side I'm most quiet and most unquiet, most inhibited and most free.' If the four days in Vienna were not sexually consummated, they were a consummation of the correspondence.

5

Love Letters

Having brought their relationship into the real world, Kafka and Milena found it hard to push it back onto the page. Kafka left on Sunday, when Milena was most compelling and beautiful to his eyes, with a 'dear sad station-face'. The visit to Vienna had convinced him of one thing, that Milena and he must be together; she would join him in Prague and he must therefore break once and for all with Julie. He met his seamstress in one of Prague's squares and, as he reported to Milena, 'I could only say that compared with you everything else, however unchanged it may remain, disappears and turns into nothing.' Julie fought back, pointed out that Milena was married, was meeting Kafka secretly, and was infamous. She wanted to see Milena's letters to him. He refused, but gave her permission to write to Milena.

Kafka seemed in the first days after Vienna to be trying to clarify things. He explained his feelings about Milena to Max Brod; he sent Milena, in a gesture of great confidence, a copy of his extraordinary 'Letter to His Father' (a bitter, lacerating account of the pained relationship between Kafka and his father which he wrote in 1919 and in the end showed instead to his mother); and he poured out his excitement about the encounter in a letter to Milena: 'Now in the evening as a Goodnight receive the flow of everything I am and have and everything that is blissfully happy to rest in you.'

But for Milena the aftermath of the visit was different. The meeting had confirmed that she loved Kafka, but it had also shown her the obstacles in the way of a lifelong partnership. She also faced the fact that she felt bound to Ernst. In response to Kafka's exhilaration she wrote to him of her worries, and wondered whether she should say anything to Ernst. The letter, with its tale of a commonplace, even sordid, ménage à trois, 'frightened' Kafka out of the 'comparative calm which still remained from our being together'. He replied at once and claimed of the 'special mutual relationship of us three' that since Ernst Pollak was not his friend, he had not betrayed a friendship. 'You on the other hand have not betrayed him, for you love him, whatever you may say.'

Milena made clear that she did not want Kafka to come to Vienna again, but she followed the letter with a more conciliatory telegram. Kafka proposed coming to take her away, or perhaps recruiting Staša to bring her back. 'The only thing to fear at the moment is, I think, your love for your husband.' Their love had become a murky world of secrets, intrigue, jealousies. Kafka was jealous that Milena seemed to want Staša's presence in Vienna more than his. He knew Staša and Jarmila from Prague. (Jarmila and Willy Haas's acquaintance had developed into an affair, which, tragically, was followed by the suicide of her husband Josef Reiner. Milena wondered if Kafka regarded this tragedy as a warning; reluctantly he conceded that he did. Jarmila and Willy later married and moved to Berlin.) But Kafka sometimes resented Milena's closeness to her girlfriends, creatures of the 'underworld', and especially 'the incredible accord' he sensed between Milena and Staša, who he regarded as a chilling 'fallen angel'. He was anxious: 'How dark Vienna has become and it had been so bright for four days.' He was worried when Milena, his 'life-giving power', his 'Mother Milena', did not reply and he even sent concerned telegrams to Paní Kohler.

While Milena was being bombarded by Kafka's daily missives she tried to think what to do, what she really wanted. Could she be confident that Kafka would not rush straight back to see her in Vienna, or write to her husband? She wrote several letters to Prague, one reproaching Kafka for acting without consulting her and writing to Paní Kohler, another reproaching herself, in which she told Kafka she had not been kind enough to him. She summed up the dilemma she faced between Kafka and Ernst in a sentence: 'Yes, you're right, I love him. But Franz, I love you too.'

She was fighting a 'terrible battle' in her ambivalence. She decided to talk to Ernst. He seems not to have been too concerned about his position, but he nonetheless made some effort to keep Milena for himself. Kafka respected her decision to talk and tried to keep silent, 'but it's impossible, it's part of it, it is after all *my* battle.' She tried to lessen the intensity of their correspondence, saying that 'what's at stake here is not of ultimate value'. Neither believed this. Kafka's anxieties grew, and with them his sleeplessness.

Milena, despite her own 'sufferings', turned her attention to his. She wrote fretting about his illness, asked if he needed money, and above all whether she was somehow contributing to his unease. He replied, reassuring her on all three points, but agreed that it would be unwise for her to visit. He acknowledged the potency of their triangle: 'Even by the Vienna days you should not be misled. Didn't we perhaps even there owe many things to your unconscious hope of seeing him again in the evening?'

It was true that in many ways Ernst was still the measure of Milena's life in Vienna. He was her first real love, in many ways her mentor and protector, and an ally against her father. She still admired him for his charm and brilliance and wanted his admiration. The crisis made him pay her more attention and they drew closer to each other – Ernst was the sort of man to feel challenged by a rival and to want to reclaim his ground. He was unsatisfied with his job at the bank in Vienna, and they discussed moving to Paris, Heidelberg, even Canada.

It was Kafka who expressed the truth: 'We are now both married, you in Vienna, I to my fear in Prague. . . . For, look, Milena, if in Vienna you had been completely convinced by me (agreeing even with that step the wisdom of which you doubted), you would no longer be in Vienna in spite of everything, or rather there would be no "in spite of everything", you would simply be in Prague.'

Milena gave an explanation of her position in a letter at the end of July 1920 to Max Brod, who had written to her about Kafka's poor health. 'The history of my marriage and my love for my husband is too complicated to tell you about here. But such it is that I cannot leave now, perhaps I won't be able to at all, I – no, words are only stupid. But I am looking for an escape for myself, I am always looking for a solution, I am always looking for what is right and good. Please, Max, be assured that I will not let Frank suffer, please believe me that he is more important to me than anything else in the world.' She said she had not realised he was so ill; he had seemed so well in Vienna. And she begged Max to encourage him to take a holiday.

Meanwhile Milena received a letter from Julie, which made clear that she was still in touch with Kafka. Milena wrote angrily and jealously to Kafka. She might not be able to leave Ernst, but she still entertained the idea of a future with Kafka. He seems to have been almost amused by her jealousy but he admitted that he had been wrong to allow Julie to write to her or to ask her to reply to 'the girl'. She told him he was 'really a person who has no idea' about certain complexities of life, especially sexual ones. He could only agree.

Milena tried to break out of these endless circles. She looked back on what had so far been a stormy year and wrote to Kafka that she wanted to tell him all that it had involved. He already knew of her lung trouble the previous winter, the unhappiness at home, even the cocaine, and of her 'terrible battle', the 'real horror'.

But there was something else which he may not have known about. During this period Milena had got to know an Austrian aristocrat with an unusual history, Count Franz Xaver Schaffgotsch. He had been an officer in the Austrian Army and was in Russia during the Revolution, where he converted to the Communist cause. He returned to Vienna in the autumn of 1919, and moved in left-wing circles. He was a regular at the Café Herrenhof. Although he was married with two children, he and Gina Kaus became lovers. For a while Gina maintained the affair and Schaffgotsch even lived with her and Otto. But at some point Otto's tolerance broke and the marriage was threatened. Gina asked Milena to befriend her unhappy lover while she consoled her husband. Ernst disliked Schaffgotsch and regarded his views as totalitarian, but Milena and Count Schaffgotsch, who was four years younger than her, found common ground in their indignation at social injustice. He talked to Milena for long hours about the Soviet Union and Communism, and about what more the Social Democrats in Vienna should be doing to usher in a new world. He introduced her to the writings of Rosa Luxemburg, the Polish-born socialist who was one of the founders of the radical Spartacus League in Germany and co-founder of the German Communist Party. Rosa Luxemburg argued against Lenin's more totalitarian methods and in defence of democracy within the party, but her revolutionary writings and her role in the Spartacist revolt against the German government in January 1919 led to her assassination in Berlin by German troops (together with her friend and colleague Karl Liebknecht). Milena was drawn to this woman and to the Communist creed.

She was also drawn to Schaffgotsch. He was tall, with a high forehead, a full mouth and thoughtful eyes, dashing and extremely charming; an aristocrat with politically acceptable credentials. In time they became lovers. Whether this happened before or after her meeting with Kafka in Vienna is unclear, but the close friendship with Schaffgotsch would have been enough to complicate Milena's sense of the tormented year which she yearned to unburden to Kafka. Often it seemed, she wrote to Kafka, that 'what I would like best is to take a third way out, which leads neither to you nor with him [Ernst], but somewhere into solitude.'

It was a vision of independence, a woman standing alone. But perhaps too, in her darkest moments, she may have meant a different kind of way out. Milena certainly made one attempt at suicide in Vienna before the end of 1920, and this period, when the promise offered by her relationship with Kafka was offset by the almost unbearable pressure it put on her already strained life in Vienna, may have been the occasion. She later described how she had acted on the 'stupid idea' of poisoning herself: 'When I lay for a week in the empty flat, not knowing a living soul, half unconscious, I woke each noon with the violent shaking with which Paní Kohler brought me back to life.'

As Milena sought to understand her Vienna life, Kafka wrote that he felt like 'the mouse in the "great household" who is allowed at best once a year to run freely across the carpet.' But as before, letters that confronted the truth were hastily followed by reconciliation. Neither could face the implication that they should break off their connection. Milena wrote that she was planning to come to Prague in August or September, when they could talk. She sent consoling telegrams, messages via Staša, and a photograph, which Kafka found beautiful but worrying because of the dark rings under Milena's eyes.

He wrote to her that he had done as she had asked and gone to seek her little brother's grave in the cemetery in Prague. The first grave he described was the wrong one; he later found the right one.

Milena replied with tales from Vienna – of carrying luggage at the station, of food shortages, of hunger, of sadness, of pleasure in her work, of summer trips into the countryside – and sent him more of her articles. She and Kafka played with the idea of his return to Vienna, but Kafka rejected it, preferring to live off her letters. He was even nervous of her planned autumn trip to Prague, but when she wrote that she would not after all be coming but needed to see him, he was overwhelmed. He almost succumbed to the impulse to go straight to Vienna. But, he wrote, he would not be able to get leave without telling a lie, and that he would not do. Milena was exasperated; lying came easily to her if the end seemed to justify it. She would not let him be and in time Kafka began to propose another meeting, if not in Vienna then at Gmünd on the Czech-Austrian border. He could fit this into a weekend.

Now Milena was not sure. The Vienna visit had brought pain as well as pleasure. And another thing, she was coughing blood. Tubercular and bronchial illness was common enough in an age before antibiotics; and blood on the lung had acquired almost mythical proportions as the shadow of a disease which could strike at young people, and was still thought by some to cause 'spes phthisica', a burst of creative energy in the last stages of tuberculosis. For Kafka, blood was almost a familiar, but the word beat through his letters in reply to Milena's news. 'One should not exaggerate it, perhaps it's nothing at all, blood comes for many reasons, but it's still blood and one can't forget it. And you of course live your heroically gay life recklessly toward it, you live as though you were persuading the blood: "Well, come on then, come at last!" And then of course it comes.'

He tried to reassure her of how much she meant to him. He wrote that her letters and all they brought were 'the most beautiful thing that ever happened to me in my life' and he tried to explain the complications between them, what he would later call the 'fear-desire' that overwhelmed him.

She replied with a 'beautiful' letter of consolation – at once understanding his fears, but trying to draw him away from them. But in an equally 'beautiful' letter he defended his fearfulness: 'It is part of me and perhaps the best part. And as it is my best, it is also perhaps this alone that you love.'

These intense, revelatory letters from Kafka found Milena once again in turmoil. Her discussions with Ernst had brought about a temporary truce (he even proposed writing to Kafka), but they had not really resolved anything. Plans to go abroad had come to nothing and Ernst's mistress, Mitzi Behr, was a constant presence in his life. Milena was overwhelmed with the desire to see Kafka. She wrote to Kakfa of the 'little animals' haunting her and her renewed hopes of a future with him. As before he tried to put her off, reminding her of his fearfulness and his Jewishness. He did not often raise this last point, but at times it was a cause of misunderstanding between them. Milena sometimes felt excluded and Kafka sometimes felt that she did not understand the suffering of Jews. His friend Max Brod was a fervent Zionist, and although Kafka was more cautious, he believed that as a western Jew 'not one calm second is granted me, nothing is granted me, everything has to be earned'. Later that summer Milena argued with Max's Zionism. Kafka pointed out to her, 'You have your homeland and can also renounce it and that's perhaps the best one can do with one's homeland. . . . But he has no homeland, and therefore nothing to renounce and has to think all the time of seeking or building it.' Milena complained that Max did not like his friend consorting with a non-Jewish woman and was trying to come between them. Kafka said nothing could.

Throughout these weeks of emotional turmoil, Milena worked. Encouraged by Schaffgotsch she began translating some of Rosa Luxemburg's *Letters from Prison* to Sonia Liebknecht, the wife of Karl Liebknecht with whom she had founded the German Communist Party. Milena sent one to *Tribuna* at the end of August, describing the sights and sounds Rosa could see and hear from her cell which brought her joy. Milena was also busy with fashion pieces. She now 'allowed' Kafka to read her fashion articles (in fact he already had). He wrote gently to her: 'You, poor dear, how much work you burden yourself with from a sense of guilt, I see you bent over your work, your neck is bare, I stand behind you, you aren't aware of it – please don't be frightened if you feel my lips on the back of your neck, I didn't mean to kiss, it's only helpless love.' He said he enjoyed her articles and told her not to underrate them. Despite the war, despite shortages, fashion thrived in Vienna. There were always a few who could afford haute couture, and others who strove to follow the latest trends and the influence of Paris and London. But Milena rarely wrote about hemlines alone – her best fashion pieces are part of her overall theme, the search for the appropriate way to live. For Milena, women should not be fashion's victims; fashion should be an expression of a woman's being and, if chosen with care for comfort and style, an expression of a modern way of living. Clothes, even in hard times, were a means to maintain the dignity of woman, and encourage her freedom. An article called 'Travelling' was about clothes, but also became a celebration of travelling itself.

'What a delight it is to prepare for a journey! Today, after so many years when we were locked in, we can once more escape to foreign lands in express trains, to unfamiliar hotels and cities, to new seas, to foreign mountains and spas.' Milena herself might not yet have been far afield, but she had travelled enough to know how it should be done. She gently chided her Czech readers. 'We as a nation are rather neglectful when it comes to travel.' As an independent nation which needed to make its mark on the world, this must change, and so must her compatriots' vulgar travelling habits. 'Since they say "clothes make the person" let's start with the question: What to wear?'

She recommended an inconspicuous, hard-wearing suit, 'not slavish to fashion, with a comfortable skirt' and a jacket with pockets, a raincoat and leather gloves. 'Do you not look tasteful, "cosmopolitan", elegant, is it not practical and are you not a picture? Leave your straw hat with feathers quietly at home, along with your fine shoes and lace blouse – and above all, above all, your jewels.'

It was good advice, a little snobbish but based on her instinctive eye. She also recommended a good suitcase. 'Ten boxes, a cage with a canary and a basket of cakes and cooked goose – that's a mark of a Czech. Just look at English luggage: such harmony, it drops into your hands and you can laugh in the porters' faces. And if you open it, what miracles.' Toiletries in one corner, a little bottle of cognac in the other, a penknife, some visiting cards; and underneath one change of suit, shirts, lots of handkerchiefs and a layer of books. 'An Englishman can take his whole life with him in his suitcase. . . . The more self-sufficient you are, the more independent.'

How greatly Milena wanted to be self-sufficient and how little she was. Travel was the last thing she could enjoy just now. She lay in bed with fierce headaches and wrote to Kafka that she felt more ill than for a long time. She sent him another photograph, 'a sad picture', and asked him for books. A doctor reassured her that the blood she had been coughing meant nothing serious, but that she should rest in the country. Davos was mentioned, but she felt unable to leave the city.

In her present crisis, Milena wrote to her father and told him something of her illness and distress and how she was considering leaving Vienna. Perhaps she mentioned Kafka. Shortly before her twenty-fourth birthday on 10 August 1920, for the first time in two years she received a letter in return. Dr Jesenský was as firm as ever, even (as she characterised it to Kafka) 'tyrannical'. Dr Jesenský had already given her financial help in Vienna; now, partly through the mediation of Kafka, who made contact with Dr Jesenský's assistant Vlasta and kept her informed about Milena's situation, he proposed an 'arrangement', probably including a stay in a sanatorium. The form his love took was still imperious, concentrating on practical solutions. Milena was very upset by the letter, and Kafka explained that he believed she was longing for her father to accept her way of life and 'speak to her as one human being to another, on equal terms'.

She suggested to Kafka again that he come to Vienna. He repeated his objections – that he could not, would not lie. If he could not come to Vienna, he nonetheless encouraged Milena to leave Ernst. He pointed out that she had nearly left him during the previous winter and 'that under the much greater pressure of the present you could leave him all the easier'. It provoked her to respond more clearly than ever, that she would not leave. He replied, 'I've known all along what would be in the letter, it has been in the background of almost all your letters. . . . And I see how you torment yourself and wriggle and cannot get free and – let's throw fire into the powder-keg – never will get free.' She wrote that despite everything, she loved Ernst too much to leave him and they still shared something of a life together; and that even if she could, he needed her too much 'inwardly' and couldn't live without her. And Kafka acknowledged, yet again, the strange disability of his fear of intimacy, describing with extraordinary openness his first sexual encounters and the 'obscenity' that was for him inseparable from sex.

Nonetheless, Milena finally agreed to meet Kafka in Gmünd, despite feeling ill and suffering fainting spells (she did not eat properly and was perhaps still taking cocaine). It was August, and they began to make plans to meet not long after her birthday. 'Yes,' wrote Kafka, 'it's probably best that we meet. How long would it otherwise take before we could put things straight! Where did all this trouble between us come from? And how you must have suffered from it among all the other troubles.' Those troubles included a strange development. Someone, Jarmila it seems, had been sending letters around Prague which purported to be from Milena. They caused havoc, and Milena enlisted Kafka's help to meet Jarmila and persuade her to stop her tricks. Once the deceit was revealed, Jarmila was terrified Milena would spurn her. It is unclear what lay behind the letters, but they were a mark of the powerful effect Milena had on people.

Milena's twenty-fourth birthday was a strange day. There was no money for a celebration. Kafka sent her his thanks 'that you exist in this world'. In Prague, that day's *Tribuna* included her article 'Kavárna'; it delighted Kafka. In it, Milena summed up her ambivalence about the café society which she frequented in Vienna, not the afternoon cafés of hot chocolate and cakes, but the 'literary cafés',

'cafés with a quite special life which no one understands until they penetrate its depths and breathe deeply of its air.'

She described the prominent guests, famous literary figures

who are revered in the café and whose pictures and caricatures are visible on the walls, who, when they come, sit at their table like capitalists of the spirit with only a few others allowed to sit next to them. These are particularly rare guests. It's strange how as soon as someone becomes sure of himself, either through money or society or creativity, as soon as he finds anchor ... from that moment the bohemian life is flung away almost with scorn ... in a word he becomes respectable. The public division, on the one side the citizen, on the other side the revolutionary, is not quite right. At a certain point even the revolutionary turns respectable ...

Then there are those who create the real foundation of the café, the real atmosphere. The crowd of journalists from all magazines imaginable, famous, less famous and simply unknown. The writers, those who carry their first poems in their wallets and read them wherever they get the chance, and those who have already had something published here or there, who are doing well, and are on their way to capitalism of the spirit. But above all, above all: a crowd of shipwrecked people, a crowd of the strangest characters with the most mysterious lives, people who will never get anywhere and who will never be capable of anything, heroically resigned and silent melancholics, of whom the world knows nothing. Sometimes, buried in these layers is a real genius – those bearers and creators of thought, those who only lack the strength to give it force. Most, however, have a macabre existence like Dostoevsky's General Ivolgin or Korolenko's ex-clerk Voikov, and all those others whom Russian literature treats with such good-natured generosity and delightful humour, while our own writers don't want to know about them, even though they are all about us.

She described the community of life among the café regulars.

People have known each other for years, they know all about each other's lives, their progress, their successes, their failures; they follow each other's doings like neighbours on a porch. The women who are brought here migrate slowly from table to table, whether 'just because', or because of marriage, infidelity, divorce. In the end, they belong to the café, they lose their surname, and they acquire a nickname, transformed into 'chums', and with the growing number of cigarettes and the growing number of lovers, they lose their real womanhood.

Love Letters

The café life which Ernst so enjoyed was for Milena a ghastly substitute for real social life, true interaction between people, authentic creativity.

> The creative person is alone. The uncreative looks for diversion. He looks for amusement, equal to his spiritual level; conversation, literature, something with at least a taste of creativity. And just as illness is contagious, so every spiritual atmosphere is contagious, and whoever falls into the lazy life-dragging tempo of these cafés will rarely force their way to the top. But, but, it is not quite so, since he who is able to force his way to the top will simply never fall in.

She wrote to Kafka to the effect that her situation in Vienna was 'nearing its final end'. He wondered how much this feeling was 'momentary grief and how much lasting truth?'

The promised date of her meeting with Kafka drew closer. 'On Sunday,' wrote Kafka excitedly, 'we'll be together, 5, 6 hours, too little for talking, enough to be silent in, to hold-hands, to look-into-each-other's-eyes.'

Until the very last moment, amidst his worries about timetables and passports, he was not sure Milena would come. She wrote asking his forgiveness for her confusion; perhaps after all everything was over between them. She said that in some ways he was like her father. He could be strict and remote. Kafka feared that, like her father, he would lose her. But he tried to understand: 'Should there be a serious obstacle, by all means stay in Vienna.'

She was nervous about lying to Ernst about a visit to Gmünd. Kafka was chastened. He paid his respects to her 'sacramental indissoluble marriage'. But he was exasperated by some of her attempts to explain why she couldn't leave Ernst; she veered from the depths of the soul to trivial matters: who would look after his boots? Kafka was scathing. 'Should you leave him he will either live with another woman or go and live in a boarding-house, and his boots will be better cleaned than now.' Still, he was the outsider, excluded from Milena and Ernst's 'rich inexhaustible secret' of marriage.

In the face of this 'secret', Kafka and Milena met in Gmünd, a small border town in the hills, with a railway station and a narrow town square enclosed by gabled houses. It was late August. Since their last meeting, less than two months before, their letters had criss-crossed almost daily, they had passed through wave after wave of feeling, of closeness and distance. Now they had less than twenty-four hours together. The encounter was not a success. They went for a walk and lay in a meadow and talked. All the intensity and anticipation of the preceding days erupted in a compressed and difficult day of explanations and misunderstanding. There was too much resentment and, on Milena's part, a mix of uncertainty and frustration about the strength of Kafka's love for her and hers for him. He for his part was tired and nervous from the journey, even less capable of physical affection than before. It was like the first uneasy day in Vienna, without the later days to draw them close. He was beyond the reach of Milena's attempts to 'rescue' him. He considered that 'they talked and listened to one another, often and for a long time, like strangers'.

They parted uneasily, and Milena left for a fortnight's holiday in St Gilgen, a lakeside resort in the mountains near Salzburg, with a cold. She felt uneasy about Ernst, who was ill too. Kafka was afraid he had frightened her away. He wanted to talk the meeting over in their letters.

But her letters to him were fraught, reproachful, guilty and confused. She felt he was repeating the pattern of his previous relationships, drawing close but then finding himself unable to fulfil his desire, not strong enough to love. On the other hand, she was bound to Ernst. It was tired ground, and there was little new to say. It was raining and she was feverish. And yet she needed him, wanted his letters, needed his care. He wanted to nurse her. But he also wanted her to mother him. The cycle continued.

Back in Vienna, Milena worked, delivering fashion pieces, about the usefulness of pockets for example, or what to wear out riding: for the sake of charm she regretted the passing of long-skirted riding habits, but welcomed it for the sake of comfort and safety. Style and dignity could be preserved for 'perhaps the most noble of all sports' by a well-cut jacket and breeches, a cravat and tall boots of 'grey or white buckskin'. The rider could still look like a princess in a fairy tale.

Milena also wrote about her trip to the mountains, with the urbanite's classical nostalgia for the land. She acknowledged the hardship suffered by mountain people, but almost envied them their self-sufficiency and their indifference to the 'bustle and nonsense' of the city. 'Life is dry, hand to mouth, mouth to stomach, straight-forward and terrifyingly simple.'

She described a village feast.

Love Letters

Roast legs of meat and cakes vanish in a twinkling. Cask after cask is rolled into the bar. In the decorated hall, the band settles in and noisily summons everyone into a circle; not for the polka or the waltz – but for real mountain music and real mountain dances. The boys have caps on their heads – that is their custom – with bare knees and studded boots, and the girls wear ribbons in their braids and white, embroidered gloves.

Milena also recalled a visit to the village cemetery, a small enclosure with wooden crosses instead of tombstones, and the occasional bouquet of tin or paper flowers. Funerals were further occasion for ceremony and feasting, 'not necessarily because of joy or sorrow, but rather for the opportunity itself, because it's an event, a change in the endless procession of identical days'. In the city she felt loss and sorrow and death as if someone had seized her by the throat until she could no longer breathe. In the mountains she stood calmly and took death more lightly as part of life. 'It must be.'

She wrote about other trips she made that summer. To the ancient town of Melk, set in a bow of the 'wide, greeny-blue Danube' in the wine region west of Vienna. She admired the town's arched streets and the baroque abbey with its famous library. She moved on through other riverside villages to Krems, which she found even more beautiful, 'perhaps because it reminds me of Prague. A venerable town, a gothic church on the hill, baroque palaces, rococo houses. A fairy-tale square. And the moon wanders over these streets just as over Malá Strana, pensive, wistful, sentimental.'

She sent some of her articles to Kafka and received his praise. They included her translations of some of his early short pieces for *Kmen* and for *Tribuna* his story from 1913, 'A Report to an Academy'. This strange, compellingly imagined work is the dignified, poignant speech of a captured ape who saw his only way of escape through entering human society. To this end he observed and imitated and learnt to speak, to eat with implements, even to drink alcohol. He achieved a way out by becoming a curiosity, an entertainer. But this way out, he explains, is not to be confused with the real freedom he had before. 'In any case,' he ends, 'I am not appealing for any man's verdict, I am only imparting knowledge, I am only making – and even to you, honoured Members of the Academy, I have only made – a report.' Kafka was impressed. 'The translation of the final sentence is very good. Each sentence in this story, each word, each – if I may say so – music is connected with "fear". On this occasion the wound broke open for the first time during one long night and in my opinion the translation catches the connection perfectly, with that magic hand which is yours.'

But away from professional matters their relationship was deteriorating. Each sought pity from the other. He found her letters made him sleepless. She found his unsettling, elusive. What did he want, what was he doing? 'It's more or less like this,' he replied: 'I, an animal of the forest, was at that time barely in the forest, lay somewhere in a dirty ditch (dirty only as a result of my being there, of course). Then I saw you outside in the open – the most wonderful thing I'd ever seen. I forgot everything entirely, forgot myself, got up, came closer – though fearful in this new yet familiar freedom – came closer nevertheless, reached you, you were so good I cowered down beside you as though it were my right, laid my face in your hand, I was so happy, so proud, so free, so powerful, so at home – over and over again this: So at home – but fundamentally I was still only an animal, belonged still only in the forest, lived here in the open only by your grace. . . . This could not last. . . . I had to return to the darkness, I couldn't stand the sun, I was desperate, really like a stray animal, I began to run as fast as I could, and always the thought: "If only I could take her with me!" And the counter-thought: "Is there any darkness where she is?"

'You ask how I live: this is how I live.'

Kafka's impulse to hide ebbed and flowed but never vanished. His vulnerability had in part attracted Milena, but it also drove her to distraction and now even to bitterness. She had to contend with his retreat, his confusion, and his 'terrible' feeling that through her 'I become much more conscious of my dirt'. He warned her that his deeper self would smash anything that the self of Vienna or Gmünd might have created.

Yet Milena could not relinquish her fantasy of escape, and continued sometimes to write as if they might have a common future. Why, asked Kafka. 'Few things are certain, but this is one of them: We shall never live together, in the same apartment, body to body, at the same table, never, not even in the same town. . . . Nor do you, Milena, think otherwise when you examine yourself and me and the "sea" between "Vienna" and "Prague" with its insurmountable high waves.'

It was a sad, wearing time for Milena. She had some sort of influenza or lung illness again and was frightened by thoughts of death. She feared that she hardly deserved a good word from Kafka.

He too was ill and in turn wondered why she didn't feel 'any fear or repugnance' for him. 'To what depths do your seriousness and your strength reach?'

Gradually through the autumn, the frequency and intensity of these letters weakened. Kafka was busy with plans for another visit to a sanatorium, and was preoccupied by a nasty phase of 'Jew-baiting' in Prague; he wrote to Milena of crowds full of hate watched by mounted police on guard.

The more Kafka withdrew, the more Milena fought back, writing of the possibility of a life together, or at least of meeting in Vienna on his way to a sanatorium. But Kafka was adamant. 'No, Milena, the possibility of a shared life which we thought we had in Vienna does not exist, under no condition, it didn't even exist then.'

In Vienna she felt increasingly homesick and in need of money. She advertised in the *Neue Freie Presse* offering private Czech lessons. She asked Kafka to send her prints of works by Mikoláš Aleš, a Czech Revivalist painter who celebrated the Bohemian countryside and depicted heroic scenes from Czech folklore. She also requested a copy of her beloved Božena Němcová's *Babička*. Ernst was again considering moving to Paris.

Kafka's letters brought little consolation. He sensed her disappointment with him. She wrote that she had no hope, that she hoped only to be able to make a break from him. The union which had been based on mutual understanding deteriorated into recriminations and incomprehension. He wanted silence, they must stop writing. In valedictory explanation he wrote: 'What you are to me, Milena, are to me beyond all the world in which we live, cannot be found in the daily scraps of paper that I have been writing to you. These letters, as they are, are good for nothing but to torment ... they can't do anything but produce a day in Gmünd, produce misunderstanding, humiliation, almost perpetual humiliation.'

The prospect of an end to their correspondence terrified Milena. She told Kafka that she needed letters. 'How can I believe that you need letters now,' he replied, 'when you need nothing but quiet, as half-unconsciously you have said so often? And these letters after all are nothing but torture, incurable torture, what's the good of it – and it's getting even worse – during this winter?' It just happened to be he who had finally suggested breaking off the correspondence: 'it might just as well have been you.' They were of course to write in necessity or emergency, but she should stop going to the post office expecting his daily letters. 'I won't say goodbye. It is no goodbye, unless it be that the gravity lying in wait pulls me down completely. But how could it do this so long as you are alive?'

It was not quite to be goodbye. Milena would continue to go to the post office and they would meet again, exchange a few letters and articles, dream about each other. But it was an end of sorts, an end of the internal landscape which they had created and shared for much of the year.

It would be easy to dismiss the relationship between Milena and Kafka as a paper house. Sometimes, reading his letters and imagining hers, it seems they are not writing to each other but simply pouring out their hearts to any willing sensitive audience. Both were people impelled to write out their lives on paper; a correspondence provided an audience for a basic need. Given the people they were, any relationship would have been a highly verbal one, an externalising of the internal. Their correspondence was a reflection of physical separation, but the experience and emotion was no less real.

What drew them together and what pushed them apart? They both knew something of darkness and death. Even though it was Kafka who claimed the monopoly on the word fear, gnawed at it, held it to himself, while Milena tried to prise him away from it, she too knew fear: of loneliness, illness, betrayal. It was a word, an experience, they had in common and it remained part of their vocabulary until the very end of their long conversation. More than any other woman, Milena was not only Kafka's intellectual equal, she was something of his existential equal too. And in their unhappy times they were both drawn to the same fantasy – of a free, healthy, family life away from the corruption of the city. As a boy Kafka loved to swim and walk, and Milena gave him back his energy as she enticed him off into the hills behind Vienna. These were her dreams too. In a letter to Max Brod after the break Milena wrote: 'In me is an unfulfilled desire, a strong, fierce desire for a completely different life from the one I lead or perhaps will ever lead, a life with children, a life on the land.'

But this was the difference. Milena envisaged a family. Although Kafka admired family life, and even yearned for it, he knew it was not for him. He needed freedom to write. He could not offer Milena a life where she could be a woman as well as more than woman. He was not a person of the senses as she was – she loved flowers and music while he admitted that he was unmusical and had no interest in plants. It was as if he was so attuned to the art of words that he had no space left for other sensibilities.

Milena was a free spirit, almost wanton with money and emotions. Kafka was so careful. She could admire this trait, but how different it was. In a letter to Max Brod she wrote: 'Are you saying, as it seems, that Frank is afraid of love but not of life? I think it is the other way round. For him, life is something absolutely different than for all other people, above all money, trade, exchange, typewriters are completely mystical things for him. . . . For him the office – even his own – is something so enigmatic, so strange, as a train engine is to a small child.' She described his behaviour at the post office, passing from one grille to the other, paying, counting the change, flustered, absolutely paralysed when he discovered he had been given too much change. 'Not that he regrets the crown. But it is not orderly.' When she had asked him why he loved his first fiancée, he replied ' "She was so competent" and his face lit up with respect . . .

'When I told him about my husband, who is unfaithful to me a hundred times a year, who has over me and over many other women a kind of strange magic, his face brightened with the same respect. . . . A man typing fast on a machine and a man who goes out with four women at once are all as incomprehensible to him as that crown at the post office . . . incomprehensible because they smack of life. Frank doesn't know how to live. Frank doesn't have the ability to live. Frank will never get better. Frank will soon die.

'Of course we are all apparently able to live, because we sometimes escape into lies, blindness, excitement, optimism, to some conviction, to pessimism or something else. But he never ran away to any protective asylum. He is absolutely incapable of lying, just as he could never get drunk. He does not have the slightest refuge, he has no shelter, he is as if naked among the clothed.

'His books are remarkable. He himself is still more remarkable.'

Kafka too recognised the contradiction between them, almost right from the start. In an early letter he wrote: 'Milena, do understand my age, my being used up and above all the fear, and do understand your youth, your freshness, your courage; and my fear, you see, keeps increasing, for it signifies a withdrawal from the world, thus increase of its pressure, thus further increase of fear; your courage, on the other hand, signifies a going forward, thus decrease of pressure, thus growth of courage.'

Despite their split, and the pain they gave each other, they maintained their love and respect for each other. Milena has been criticised for her relationship with Kafka, for binding him to her and somehow interrupting his creativity. 'With her refined sensuality, her anarchistic lack of principles and her totally unpredictable irrationality, she was like a will o' the wisp who lured people towards the Czech intellectuals and avant-garde,' wrote the critic Rio Preisner. 'Continuing contact between the two would have accelerated the poet's death.' Milena the near murderer. But it was precisely her energy, sensuality and emotion which attracted Kafka, even if in the end he could not manage them. And he was already a willing pupil of Czech culture. If the tension in their relationship did exacerbate his illness, his illness also exacerbated the tension. Milena's 'prey' spent a lifetime trying to understand human agency, responsibility and free will – he was nobody's victim, and after their break he remained loyal to her qualities and to her work. He described himself as her 'best reader' and she told him that she sometimes thought of him as she wrote – the direct personal style of her articles perhaps comes partly from her relationship with him. One of Kafka's biographers described his bond with Milena, fourteen years younger than he, as 'perhaps the one true love affair of his life'.

6

Postscripts

The winter of 1920 was a melancholy time. Both Milena and Ernst were plagued by illness, she troubled by her lungs, he by his heart. She still went every day to the post office in the vain hope of receiving a letter from Kafka. Meanwhile she continued to work on translations of his stories. Stanislav K. Neumann, who also edited the Communist literary and political magazine *Červen* (*June*), had commissioned a selection. The work was not easy: 'It was terrible to be so deserted and to work on his books,' she wrote to Max Brod. But it was a way of preserving some sort of connection with Kafka.

The days shortened and Vienna sank into its third post-war winter. The year 1920 had seen increasing social tension, and there were constant rumours of a right-wing or military coup on the one hand, or a left-wing revolution on the other. The Social Democratic government had done its best to maintain social benefits, but the price had been inflation and debt. The currency had fallen dramatically and the government was still in negotiation with the international War Reparations Commission about a post-war settlement. In October the Social Democrats were defeated in elections and the Christian Socialists came to power. However, the Social Democrats held on in the capital, now dubbed 'Red Vienna'. The contrast there between rich and poor fuelled a feverish political atmosphere, dominated by the language of class warfare. Milena's friendship with Schaffgotsch drew her into these arguments. Every age has its ethos and its slogans, and Milena, with her usual perceptiveness, captured the spirit of hers.

> Look at the election posters of any political party in any town: everywhere stands the worker. Examine the editorials in any newspaper in any country, of any political complexion: the worker, the worker. Look at new art, at new poems, new pictures, new plays: the

worker, the worker, the worker. Today, a man in blue overalls is the axis of the world, and around him revolves the truth, proclaimed by left or right; whatever is said about him, he stands firm and monumental, whether as a symbol of hope, a promise, or a cause for fear.

She did not like 'the worker' as a political stereotype; as she pointed out elsewhere, some were better off than others. But she was sympathetic to those who did live in hardship. The article proceeds to a description of the modern city, not unworthy of the spirit which would inspire Fritz Lang's 1926 film *Metropolis*; Milena finds a reluctant grandeur in the machinery of progress, but in the end, with gentle sarcasm, she deplores the modern city's brutality.

At the edge of the town, by the roads along the foothills – appears the beauty of today. The sober, asphalt streets of the grey suburbs, the glinting tracks of the fleeing railway, the roofs of glass which sparkle in the sun between the straggling workers' homes, stations with thousands of lights and thousands of signals . . . viaducts which arch across field after field, gasworks and waterworks, skeletons of concrete, skeletons of iron; the red caverns of the brickworks behind the town, where children play and the poor make love. Allotments with fences of barbed wire, heads of cabbage, hoses which shoot out fans of silver water, a man in a broad-rimmed hat, who hoes his patch or kneels leaning in the clay . . . if you come here, marvel how quietly thousands of people suffer without making a sound, their own steps heard far along the pavement . . . this is our beauty.

This could be any city: Vienna, or Prague where the growing suburbs had spilled into shanty-towns among the city's industrial buildings. In Prague too, 1920 was an uneasy year. Land reform the year before had not appeased workers in the city and there was social unrest, riots and a general strike. One worker was killed in a clash between strikers and police in Prague, several others died elsewhere. There were also elections, won by left-leaning groups, but their unity was marred by divisions between Czech and German parties and by their differing degrees of radicalism. With hindsight such tensions can be seen as the inevitable ructions of a new country (as well as a reflection of general European social unrest); under President Masaryk's guiding liberal hand, they never spilled over into chronic political instability. But for those who lived through them the talk of revolution was as vivid in Prague as in Vienna; these were unsettling times. Milena could only watch from afar as her friends in Prague participated in the building of the new country, and use her articles

Postscripts

to exhort her compatriots to live in 'goodwill' – for the sake of themselves and for the sake of the new nation.

In Vienna, things were in some ways even worse than in the previous winter. 'Perhaps every town today is a Babylon ... I don't know how it is elsewhere,' wrote Milena. 'But here – God knows – everything is at sixes and sevens, nonsense after nonsense, degeneracy, absurdity, extravagance, poverty, hunger, champagne, one on top of the other, like a carnival.' Unexpectedly early and harsh frosts stripped the trees of leaves overnight, and left the city white by day. 'You hear the word "hurry" everywhere – hurry to pick the frozen apples in the garden, hurry to bring the vegetables to town, hurry to chop the wood.'

New taxes were introduced at the beginning of November, which pushed food and fuel prices up 30 or 40 per cent. Milena felt these taxes lying on the whole city like another 'hard frost'. She was now familiar with the tricks of the freelance journalism trade, and recycled some of the motifs from earlier articles, describing again the crowds at the station, the pervasive smell of cabbage. But, 'Much has changed since last winter. In foodshops you can find anything you crave, but at such prices that no one can afford anything.' Except foreigners and war profiteers.

The city was full of beggars. As a child, Milena had noticed the beggars in Prague, but a story Kafka had told her reinforced their claim on her attention. He had recounted a childhood experience when he had been touched by the plight of a beggar woman. He only had a large coin, which he was embarrassed to give. So he changed it for smaller coins and walked round and round the block, giving the woman a coin each time he passed until, uncertain whether she recognised him, he ran home in tears. With Christmas approaching, Milena now wrote about the beggars' plight and about people's excuses for not giving.

> Yes, yes, I agree, perhaps there are fifty cheats among every hundred true sufferers; perhaps fifty out of a hundred are acting out a comedy of poverty, perhaps fifty out of a hundred could work; still, still, that leaves fifty outcasts from life, fifty in real need; at the risk of giving money to a cheat, at the risk of being conned, give, give! Avoid the greater risk, of not giving to somebody who is really suffering.

She went on: 'I am no politician. I don't know what the best way is to help the poor. I don't know if the best way is called Socialism or

Communism or charity or work. I only know one thing, that as long as there is a single hungry person among us, the world is a bad place.' This posture seems a little naive, even disingenuous, given Milena's interest in social and political questions, her relationship with Schaffgotsch and her politically articulate café acquaintances; perhaps it was an affectation adopted for her role as feuilletoniste for a liberal paper. Later she would take more fixed positions. At this stage her politics were not party-based, and her responses were founded on a direct, humanist empathy for others rather than on political analysis or a programme for action. Her visceral sensitivity to events in her own life extended to a quick sympathy for the underdog.

Milena was not always a melancholy moralist. She saw the harsh side of the modern city, but she was also excited by the 'new industrial epoch' and the resurgence of commerce after the war. She was captivated by the increasingly sophisticated business of advertising and understood at once what made a good advertisement. 'It must be brief, striking to the eye, technically well-produced – even artistically produced – and it must be witty. Above all there must be lots of them.' She scorned the Communists' posters in the recent Viennese election campaign, which consisted of 'endless text in a red frame, the whole programme of the party was explained at length in small print . . . – Nobody, however, ever read it.'

Earlier in the year she had written a piece in a similar spirit, about shop windows. Well-arranged and frequently changed shop displays could promote business and also adorn a street. 'A street is not a dead thing. A street is living . . . it has eyes . . . it looks and listens . . . it is always unique . . . A street even has a costume: its shop windows.'

As Christmas approached, Milena wrote about familiar Christmas topics, what presents to buy, what New Year's resolutions to make. Even in these light-hearted pieces, her tastes emerge, especially her commitment to 'authenticity', to 'real' things and craftsmanship. It was the creed of a generation which rejected the over-elaborate and now mass-produced heaviness of Art Nouveau in favour of a simpler style. She favoured the products of 'Artěl', a group of craftsmen and women in Prague, who championed well-made, boldly decorated products rather as the Arts and Crafts movement had done in Britain. Her taste in decor was informal and contemporary. 'A wide sofa with lots of different coloured cushions, shrieking quite crazily with colour (carefully chosen, however), is enough to change a room into an intimate, warm corner; a few batik lamps are also very beautiful.'

Such tastes reappear in an article on suitable presents for children. She recommended toys that could be enjoyed, rather than beautiful but sterile playthings. She herself liked to give children books. She recommended *Babička*, of course, Kipling, Hans Christian Andersen, Tolstoy's folk tales, even a rather sentimental Dostoevsky story, 'The Boy at Christ's Christmas Tree'.

She was well acquainted with children through her teaching, and through friends. Staša had twin baby daughters, born shortly after her marriage, and on visits to Prague, Milena and she would take turns pushing the pram around Petřín Hill or other parks while they talked. Articles from this time reveal Milena's interest in children, but there was no sign of any of her own. It is unclear why Milena and Ernst did not have a family; Milena's abortion early in their relationship proved their ability to conceive (and her later pregnancy shows that it had not damaged her fertility). Her preoccupation in these articles seems more than Christmas nostalgia, and perhaps reflects her own desire for children.

Her writing about children is remarkably astute and modern. Freud was at this time drawing attention to the importance of our early years; although Milena thought that much psychology was humbug, she nonetheless believed that 'the decisive features of human character are created in the earliest childhood. . . . In essence everyone remains the same as when they were four or five and if they react to something sudden and unexpected, they react in essence with the same internal gesture as when a child.' In a New Year article she wrote that she believed that children should be taken seriously and treated with the same respect as adults. She had no illusions. Children 'are not good'; but they are fascinating, unique individuals who need care and respect. She would continue to develop this philosophy, which proved both a strength and weakness when she herself became a mother.

As the new year began, Milena was still missing Kafka. She felt unsettled and could not sleep. She had not been able to obey Kafka and had continued to write. In January she received a reply, from a sanatorium at Matliary in the Tatra Mountains where Kafka had been staying since December. He commanded her not to write to him. The letter drove Milena to despair, and in a wretched letter to Max Brod she revealed her state of mind.

> I am at my wit's end. . . . I don't know anything, I don't feel anything, I don't understand anything; it seems to me that something completely

awful occurred during these past months, but I don't know much about it. . . . I could tell you everything, how and wherefore and why it all happened; I could tell you everything about myself, about my life; but for what – and then: I don't know, I only hold in my hand Franz's letter from the Tatras, his deadly request and at the same time a command: 'Not to write and to prevent us meeting, only this wish quietly fulfilled, only this allows me to live a little longer, everything else will only reduce me further.' I don't dare to ask him, to write to him; I don't know what I want to write to you. I don't know what – I don't know what I want to know. Jesus Christ, if I could only force sleep upon my brain. Only tell me one thing, you were with him recently, you know: am I guilty or am I not guilty? . . . I am on the edge of madness; I tried to act, to live, to think, to feel correctly, according to my conscience, but somewhere there is blame . . . I want to know . . . I would be very grateful if you could reply. For me it would be a real way out. I would also ask you for news of how he is. It's months since I heard anything about him.

The claustrophobic Lerchenfelderstrasse apartment did not help her mood. There were often extra people staying, friends from Prague sleeping on the couch, colleagues from Ernst's bank or his philosophy seminars, and the frequent presence of his mistress. The distance between Milena and Ernst was becoming ever more apparent. Paní Kohler remained Milena's ally amidst this chaotic hospitality, imposing some domestic order and cheering Milena when she was sad.

One pleasant distraction came in February 1921, when Milena was able to get a press ticket to a masked ball at the Vienna State Opera. The ball was being revived, Milena suspected, to entertain members of the Reparations Commission, and she was fascinated to see this 'official debut of the new rich'.

She received a reply to her letter to Brod, and wrote again, this time more calmly. She said she would stop writing to Kafka. Although she accepted that his fearfulness preceded their acquaintance, she chastised herself for damaging him. She recalled how she had seemed able to help him overcome his anxiety when they met in Vienna. 'If I had then gone with him to Prague, I would have still been what I was to him before. But I was very firmly rooted in this country with both feet, I was not able to leave my husband, and perhaps I was too much a woman to have had the strength to submit to a life which I knew would mean the severest asceticism for ever. . . . I was too weak to be able to do and to complete what I knew was the only thing which would help him. That is my guilt.'

Postscripts

But she assured Max Brod that she retained, despite herself, a will to live, even though at times she sometimes felt she would go mad with grief. She asked him to write if he had time. 'I go every day to the post office, I cannot break the habit.' She also asked him if he would write an introduction for the selection of Kafka's stories for Neumann. She did not have the strength to do it herself. 'Jesus Christ, must I write about him for people? And then again: I simply don't have the ability. Would you like to do it? I don't know if you have any political objections – *Červen* is Communist, but the edition is non-party. Neumann publishes the book with a glad heart and looks forward to its publication. . . . And don't say anything to F. [Kafka]. We will surprise him. Are you in favour? Perhaps – perhaps, it will bring him some joy.' Brod did write an introduction as requested, but the project was never completed.

Milena was also busy with other translations, encouraged by Schaffgotsch, who could help her with the original translation from languages with which she was less familiar before she crafted them into good Czech. In spring 1921 her translation of a story by Jules Laforgue appeared in the cultural weekly *Cesta* (*The Path*), and a serialised translation of a story by Gorky appeared the following year.

Milena's continuing preoccupation with Kafka is reflected in her articles. For example, in one of her pieces about children she cited Kafka's boyhood charity to the beggar as an exception that proved the rule of childish mischief. In an article called 'Secret Redemption', about the silver linings to clouds of melancholy and misfortune, she gave Kafka as an example, describing how his illness had proved strangely beneficial. 'I know someone who has weak lungs. He is tall and emaciated, his face is angular, pointed, beautiful, fierce and good. He said about his illness: "When my heart and my brain cannot endure their burdens, they look for something to rescue them, and for this they engage the lungs." . . . He told it like a fairy tale. As a strange fairy tale from another world.'

Spring came early in 1921 and brought Milena some relief, the greening of the city and the return of the flowers which she loved so much. 'When I glimpsed you in the grey grass along the brook, the bright little heads of primroses, and when I discovered in the wood under the beech leaves the little blue milkworts, and in the green meadows gold celandines, I truly realised that you are here again and I stopped feeling deserted.' It was almost worth the sadness to experience consolation. It was an unabashedly sentimental article, but she was not ashamed: 'after all sentimentality is a gift of God.' It was the other side of her passionate indignation.

But in the middle of April she weakened and wrote to Kafka at Matliary, despite her promise. She told him that she was ill again, this time more seriously, since her lungs were badly affected. Her father was suggesting that she come to stay with him in Prague and later go to the Tatras or Italy to recuperate. She reported all this to Kafka, and in a letter to Max Brod, Kafka wondered what this reconciliation between Milena and her father would mean for relations between Milena and Ernst. He asked Max to keep him informed of Milena's movements, and to let him know at once if she intended to come to the Tatras. He could not face a meeting. 'You are going to see Milena,' he wrote to Brod in May. 'I won't ever have this joy again. When you speak to her about me, speak as you would of someone dead.'

Milena retreated to Prague. The winter's illness had left her worn, she was tired of Ernst's thundering, and although her developing affair with Schaffgotsch was some distraction and comfort, she did not love him as intensely as she loved Ernst or Kafka. He was charming and stimulating but more superficial than either, despite his politics. And there was no money. The reconcilation with her father meant she could spend much of the early summer in Prague. She enjoyed seeing her friends again, but in some ways she was a little out of place. She had not gone through the rebirth of their nation with them, and her Viennese experiences set her apart. The unrest in the new Czechoslovakia was nothing compared to the bitterness of the new Austria, the poverty, soaring inflation, arrests, and talk of putsches. Slávka Vondráčková, resuming the childhood friendship, found Milena had a different sense of humour; hers was 'harder, terser than our naive, but lighter' spirit.

Milena saw her editors at the *Tribuna* offices on Vinohradká Street, and made contact with other Prague publications. Her father and Aunt Růžena encouraged her to look for new outlets, and they gave her an introduction to *Národní listy*, a more conservative paper than *Tribuna*, which her father read and to which Aunt Růžena contributed. Kafka had described Růžena Jesenská in a letter as anti-German; she was of the same conservative, nationalist stock as Dr Jesenský. But she was devoted to her niece and her introduction proved of great help.

Milena also sold *Červen* translations of several more letters from Rosa Luxemburg to Sonia Liebknecht, written in 1916. Rosa wrote frequently and intensely to Sonia, consoling her about her husband Karl's imprisonment, and telling her about life in prison, the other women, the books she read. (Milena would one day herself write brave letters from prison.) The translations were published in the autumn edition of *Červen*.

Milena found Prague alive with energetic new artistic movements, a response to the freedom of independence and to interaction with other European artistic movements, especially in France. A group of young, left-wing artists had in November 1920 founded the Devětsil movement, dedicated to finding modern and politically significant forms of expression. This and other avant-gardes gave a new energy to art, literature and theatre. Milena could only taste what would, on her return to Prague, become her milieu.

She listened to as much music as she could, from the organ at St Vitus's Cathedral, to a band playing foxtrots in a café or the sound of 'black' jazz. She loved Schubert's Trout quintet; Mahler, who could move her to tears (especially his second symphony, written the year before she was born); and Puccini, who could reduce her to laughter.

In the spring she had written an amusing article about the different kinds of concertgoer, contrasting the irritating habits of those who buy expensive tickets and attempt to prove their musical credentials by nodding and tapping their way through the concert, with the genuine music lovers whose tickets may be cheap but who demonstrate their commitment by silent, still attentiveness. 'The higher up near the roof, the more clearly they listen.' Milena always preferred the Gods.

In the same article she extended the principle to a general approval of emotional restraint and composure. At first, this would seem to contradict her reputation for explosive feelings and expressiveness. But it accords with a developing maturity and various testimonies that while she was open and passionate with people she was closely involved with, she was otherwise reserved, especially about her private life. She remained in Prague in July, but did not visit Max Brod as she had promised. 'I don't think that I could have spoken about Franz,' she later wrote, 'and you certainly would not have wanted to talk to me about him.' She also wrote to him asking him to get back her letters to Kafka; their fate is unknown. She then left for a long stay at the Hotel Prokop in Špičák. She had not been there since before the war. Little had changed. 'A whole chapter of huge history lies between this visit and my last. And here I find footpath after footpath, crossroads after crossroads, clearing after clearing, unchanged in their quiet, loving, kind, warm beauty. As if there was no such thing as time or fate.' The place and the fresh air did her health and spirits good.

But on her return to Lerchenfelderstrasse in August, she received an unexpected blow. Her stalwart ally Paní Kohler had gone. In an article she described what had happened:

> In the morning the catastrophe began. . . . Indescribable. Morning – morning – already nine o'clock and Paní Kohler was nowhere. I was still incapable of getting up without Paní Kohler. Half-past nine. Ten. Half-past ten. No Paní Kohler. Someone murdered her in the night, I thought. And I flew downstairs. Paní Kohler was sitting in the kitchen by the stove, crying. Judging by the proportions and coloured tones of her face she had been crying for some time.

Paní Kohler had become engaged, to Josef, who, she stressed, was 'a gentleman'. And Josef would not have her cleaning Ernst's apartment. Josef was jealous.

> I woke my husband. With a pale face I sat by the head of his bed . . .
> 'Friend, we have to divorce.'
> 'Fine,' he tranquilly agreed, to my surprise.
> 'And you will marry Paní Kohler.'
> 'No, that I will not do!' and he jumped out of bed . . . I explained the situation. He was shattered.
> 'I will wash the dishes every day, if you like, but I cannot marry her. I am prepared to make any sacrifice for you. I will divorce if you like. But I cannot marry Paní Kohler.'
> You can never expect a man to help.

Milena made a comic story out of the incident. But her sorrow was genuine. Paní Kohler continued as concierge in the building, but would not help Milena in their flat. A new maid arrived, who was efficient but never received the accolade of being celebrated in the pages of *Tribuna*.

There was another upheaval in her domestic arrangements one night. 'Suddenly something squealed behind the door, weakly, pitiably, like a wet bird. Again and again. And when I opened the door, a little startled, frightened black and white kitten flew into my hands.' Milena took the little cat in, fed her and gently bathed her. She and Ernst, who also liked cats, named her Čička. She became a beloved member of the household, one of the few shared sources of pleasure between Milena and Ernst.

Milena returned to Prague in September 1921, and stayed for several months. On 27 September, her first article appeared in *Národní listy*, on the front page. Like many of her best articles, 'The Window' is about nothing, and about everything.

> You arrive one evening in a strange town, to the slow rhythm of the wheezing train, past the exposed backs of the houses, and you look through the little windows at the winding steps, at a woman making up the bed with a red striped quilt, at a round table lit by a petrol lamp, at a man in his shirt, waistcoat and slippers, slurping soup. . . .
>
> Sometimes in the evening, if you stroll the streets, you stand under an illuminated window, full of eager curiosity. The dwelling which you gaze at seems secret, alluring, the life inside it full of quiet magic. The movements of the person who enters the room are a mysterious secret. You don't know his name, you don't know anything about him, you can see only wrinkles and a smile on his face and the movement of his hands. . . . Outside perhaps snow is falling, or the stars shine or it rains a little. You stand as if bewitched, suddenly conscious of the whole world in the movements inside the unknown room before you . . . Between you and the man inside lies a window. A square tablet of glass. With magic power.
>
> Have you ever seen the face of a prisoner behind prison bars? A face, fractured by the cross of the grille? You will understand that it is the window, not the door, which is a gate to freedom. Beyond the window lies the world. Beyond the window lies the sky . . . at the window lie longings and desires. At the door lies only real life.
>
> I love the windows of trams and trains, the windows of buses, through which flows the noise of the street. . . . To see something through a window seems to me more charming, enjoyable and engaging than to see something directly. To see something through a window means not owning it. Being removed. It means preserving a space for your own longing for what you see. . . . To see countryside through a window means to know it twice: through the eyes and through longing.
>
> Think of the thousands of moments when, having no more strength, you looked at a window. At the moment when you were caught out lying, at the moment when you were hurt by someone who you loved; at the moment when someone died; at the moment when you were exhausted with cares and sorrows; at the moment you said farewell; at the moment when you were terribly ashamed: you looked at the window. It was not the opposite wall or the front of the house, not a

piece of sky or a clump of trees that you looked at, but the only human way of escaping your troubles – this window, leading onto the world.

It was now about a year since the break with Kafka, but Milena still felt bound to him. Kafka had returned from Matliary to Prague and in September he wrote to his friend Robert Klopstock, a medical student with tubercular problems whom he met at Matliary: 'The letter-writer whose sharp and even penmanship you know from her envelopes is in Prague, and so the sleepless nights begin.' Despite all previous intentions, he agreed to receive Milena, in the house on the Old Town Square where he lived with his parents. The reunion went well enough for him to entrust the several notebooks of his diaries to Milena with instructions to pass them on to Max Brod after his death. They met again in November. On 1 December he wrote in his diary: 'After paying four calls on me, M. left; she goes away tomorrow. Four calmer days in the midst of tormented ones. I feel no sorrow at her departure, no real sorrow.' However constrained their meetings, each continued to be in some way an emotional measure for the other. Kafka still felt the agony of his conflicting feelings about her: 'Always M. or not M.'

There was no sign that the relationship bore reviving, but Kafka continued to muse on their conversations. On 18 January 1922 he wrote in his diary: 'M. is right: fear means unhappiness but it does not follow from this that courage means happiness.' And on 19 January: 'The two questions: Because of several tiny things I am ashamed to mention, it was my impression that your recent visits were indeed kind and noble as ever but somewhat tiresome to you nevertheless, somewhat forced, too, like the visits one pays an invalid. Is my impression correct? Did you find in the diaries some final proof against me?' And on 20 January: 'M. is right about me: "All things are glorious, only not for me, and rightly so." I say rightly, and show that I am sanguine at least to this extent. Or am I?'

His diary reveals his respect for Milena's words to him, but also hints at Milena's own confusion. It may have been hyper-sensitivity which made Kafka feel like an invalid in front of her, but it is more likely to have been due in part to her own mixed feelings: admiration, guilt, and in the end retreat. But she wanted to help him as best she could. On another visit to Kafka in late January she tried to ease his self-doubt and isolation and talked to him about 'the joy of merely talking with people'. But they could not connect as they had in the past.

In the New Year, Kafka suffered a near breakdown, extended his sick leave, and went to Špindlerův Mlýn, a mountain resort near the Polish border. On 29 January 1922 he wrote: 'If M., for example, should suddenly come here, it would be dreadful. Externally, indeed, my situation would at once seem comparatively brighter. I should be esteemed as one human being among others, I should have words spoken to me that were more than merely polite. . . . yet I should be plunged into a world in which I could not live. . . . What used to be a dividing thread is now a wall, or a mountain range, or rather a grave.'

This latest parting came as Kafka was embarking on one of his greatest works, *The Castle*, in which many critics see the faces of Kafka, Milena and Ernst in the triangle of K., Frieda and Klamm. K. tries in vain to lure Frieda from the sleek Klamm – Frieda who offers 'strangeness and enchantment'. But as another character points out, perhaps K. is in love with her because he is safe in knowing that he cannot have her.

These last unsettling meetings between Milena and Kafka only made the grey months back in Vienna feel gloomier. Milena found a new distraction, reading detective stories, and consumed several during February. 'From some sort of depression, fatigue or indifference – call it what you will – last month I read only detective stories . . . guiltily, I must make a huge admission: it cheered me up enormously.' She challenged some people's view that such books corrupt and pointed out that in fact good always triumphs and the law is upheld. She scorned what she saw as the intellectual snobbery and amoral inhumanity of her Viennese café associates. It was not these detective stories which were corrupting.

> It is modern literature for the educated which is by nature aggressively immoral. . . . We hear of the suicides of young people under the influence of bad literature, meanwhile our good books pose seriously the question whether life is worth living. We attack immorality while pondering whether morality exists at all. We defend the principles of bigamy, suicide and perversity with the word 'freedom'. . . . The broad sweep of people are perhaps dull and simple-hearted if you like – although this is not really true – but they are never without hope. Hopelessness is and always has been the privilege only of the educated, like liqueurs and clubs.

Kafka, Love and Courage

But even better distraction came in the form of animal company: Čička was a great source of entertainment, tearing around the apartment, tugging at the papers on Milena's desk and the laces in Ernst's shoes, or batting potato peelings around the kitchen floor.

> Čička is an insincere and cheeky scoundrel, like all cats. She does not love anyone, or rather she loves everyone who is nice to her. She thinks only about herself, and does not share in the joys and pains around her, as a dog can. But Čička knows that all is forgiven, because she is so irresistible. Employed from morning to night, she really is an artful piece of nature. Čička the dancer, we call her. . . . I don't know anyone as entertaining, engaging, as ingenious, as my little mottled cat.

Milena remained in contact with Kafka, who recorded thoughts and dreams about her in his diary. During a visit to Prague she saw him on 27 April, and again shortly afterwards, but the visits revived difficult feelings. On 8 May he wrote in his diary: 'M. was here, won't come again; probably wise and right in this, yet there is perhaps still a possibility whose locked door we both are guarding lest it open, or rather lest we open it, for it will not open of itself.' He gave Milena the manuscript of *Amerika*, of which she had translated the first part. It was in effect their last meeting.

Milena's frequent visits to Prague (she described herself as someone who 'returns to Prague from time to time, with overflowing sentimental love') made her reflect on her surrogate home in Vienna. She had lived there now for nearly four years, and had a greater measure of its ways. 'Cheerfulness is the first rule of Vienna. Cheerfulness at any price, cheerfulness in spite of anything. I never understand where people draw it from. The price of food, coal, transport rises daily. No real help comes from anywhere. They have a hard, cruel life full of cares, full of setbacks, full of hopelessness. And yet you never come across despair.'

Milena admired this light touch, the capacity to live for the moment and not worry about the future. But where did it leave her?

> Vienna is a lovely town, and if you know it through and through you return there gladly, with a smile; never with love, but always with sympathy, the sort you show to people who are slightly crazy and slightly ridiculous, harmless and entertaining, people you don't really understand properly. The same way you would love someone who wore a yellow cravat and had a collection of canaries.

Postscripts

She found it a superficial city, apparently full of intellectual life but too comfortable for real originality.

> Vienna crushes people who want to do something, even those who actually have the ability. Precisely because you never come up against a barrier, because it is kindly and good-natured, and there is no danger of starving to death on the pavements. Precisely because it does not whip people until they bleed like almost any other city. Such a thrashing hurts, but believe me, it is healthy. Vienna, however, is a bog; it does not have the strength to bear its weight. And it leads you from your path.

There were many who would have disagreed with Milena's portrait of Vienna, those artists who certainly felt lashed into creativity in the first part of the twentieth century, painters like Egon Schiele and Gustav Klimt, architects like Alfred Loos, or Sigmund Freud. But their golden age was broken by the war, and post-war Vienna was a confused and sometimes torpid city. Its slippery indolence made the more earnest Milena feel left out. After four years she did feel more comfortable, and there were things she loved about the city – the silvery poplar trees along the river embankment, a few friendships. But she still did not feel at home. There was no serious work for her to do here, no real contribution to make.

And her marriage was only nominally alive. She and Ernst continued to share an apartment when Milena was in Vienna, but Ernst's friend Milan Dubrovic noticed that they now used the formal 'Sie' rather than the more intimate 'du'. They had separate rooms. On the left of the apartment Milena had two spacious rooms with light, colourful furniture. To the right were Ernst's two darker rooms, with heavy furniture and tall bookshelves. They now knocked before entering each other's domain, where Milena entertained Schaffgotsch and Ernst his mistresses.

Milena reflected on marriage, and in the summer she put some of her thoughts on paper. In an article called 'Superficial Talk about Serious Things' she began with reflections on the over-analytical nature of the times and the fashion for explaining everything with reference to the new concept of 'the unconscious'. 'If you say to someone for example that his subconscious inclination to homosexuality puts obstacles and pressures in the path of a straightforward life and forces him to steal silver spoons – it seems impressive. If he says feebly: but sir, I simply am not homosexual; you answer: but friend, what do you know about your unconscious?'

But it soon turned into an article about the failure of marriage.

> I have been thinking about why modern marriages are so problemati-
> cal, so short and so unhappy.... If a marriage does not end after two
> months with divorce, it trails along with a whole crowd of problems to
> a terrible internal catastrophe. I don't believe that marriage is any
> different than it used to be. But people are different. Perhaps cleverer
> and more intelligent. But decidedly worse.

These reflections were of course general, and inspired by what she saw around her in her small world of indulgent bohemians. But the relevance to her own situation is clear. She blamed, first, the fact that people expect marriage to bring instant happiness, second, that they tend to treat marriage as 'an experiment', when it is a responsibility based on the 'sexual secret of two people ... a secret with a deep moral purpose: children.' Third, people confuse 'being in love' and 'loving'. Marriage should be about the latter and requires 'good will and above all, firm determination'.

Was it Milena or Ernst who lacked these qualifications? Certainly Milena can be charged with mood swings and will o' the wispishness, and her own affairs; Schaffgotsch was now her regular escort. But her brief affair with the writer Hermann Broch and her involvements with Kafka and Schaffgotsch started after Ernst had already betrayed her and broken her illusions about the joys of marriage. For all that, she still clung to the dream of lasting love, a marriage of understand-ing, and children. It was a theme she would return to again.

But there were happier topics to explore. In one long feuilleton, Milena, an early fan, celebrated the work of Charlie Chaplin. She had two postcard photographs of him on her desk, one of his face, 'quite white with powder', the other full-length, showing the same pierrot face but also the big boots. The shots came from the film *A Dog's Life* which Chaplin made in 1918. (By 1922 the films he had made included *The Tramp*, *Easy Street* and *The Immigrant*.)

Milena admitted that when she had first seen Chaplin's films she did not know what to make of them. 'They were so completely different from anything I had seen before. So much headlong foolery together with the most subtle tenderness from this grotesquely faced little man.' The blend of smiles and tears, of humour and sentimen-tality – the pathos of the hungry vagrant and his dog united in their search for food – was bound to appeal to Milena, and all those 'who cry as quick as lightning and laugh as quick as lightning ... those who love fairy tales and love grotesques.... I still don't know if I like Charlie. But I do love him.' She considered him a true artist of the new medium of cinema, one of the first who 'mines the given material – movement and light – honestly, and shows that wordless expression is sometimes more than with words.'

The summer of 1922 was uneventful but more tranquil than the previous year. In early October she sent a letter to Kafka via a friend. Kafka replied with news about his summer in Planá in south-eastern Bohemia, where he had been staying with his sister Ottla and working on *The Castle*. He was now fully retired from the insurance office because of ill health. He wrote that he gathered from her letter that Milena had had a good summer. The situation in the Lerchenfelder-strasse apartment was, if unorthodox, at least more stable, and once again Čička provided more entertainment. In October, Čička gave everyone a surprise. She was a he, and the romping kitten became a father. One night, as Milena recorded in an article for *Národní listy*, Čička had escaped out of the window across the rooftops.

> Not long after, Čička returned home. But in what a state! His muzzle covered in blood, his white silky fur dishevelled, matted, and full of dirt.... But he did not return alone. Behind Čička, a gentle little slender black cat with green eyes leapt into the room. Miaow, this is my wife, explained Čička. And Murli – so we called her – made herself quite at home in a couple of hours. But for Čička a new era had begun. ... Poor Čička! In a week he changed from a cat with freedom to a cat with slippers. But love is blind.... Today, Čička is the father of three healthy strong black and white kittens.

The cat cemented another friendship for Milena, with the Jewish writer and cat lover Jiří Weil, who was part of Prague and Vienna café life. He became a firm admirer of Čička, and of Milena as well. His fascination with Milena, and with her relationship with Ernst, stayed with him and he later drew on their story for a play.

As well as writing long feuilletons, Milena filed regular fashion and culture pieces to *Národní listy*. A November article confirms her liking for things English. In a piece entitled 'Paris or London' she paid tribute to French elegance. But she concluded that the plainer English style was better suited to Czech women, who tended to be more like the 'tall, thin, straightforward and sporty' Englishwoman than the 'slender, petite, intriguing Frenchwoman'. She also described a visit to Berlin where she enjoyed a Russian-German cabaret, Der Blaue Vogel.

The arrival of winter again brought illness. Ernst was seriously ill, probably with heart trouble, which left him weak for some time. Milena cared for him, while she tried to work on a translation of a story by Leonhard Frank, a German expressionist writer who attacked bourgeois society. But, as she wrote to the cultural editor at *Národní listy*, Karel Scheinpflug, the work was not going well, partly because she was also beset by the demands of her fashion work. 'When that is a bit in order, out in the world, and on its legs at least a little, I will return to translation. It's very hard, I spent a whole afternoon on a page.'

Nonetheless she had another suggestion to make, a translation of a novel by R. L. Stevenson. She had already translated one of his stories, *Will o' the Mill*, which appeared in instalments in *Cesta* in Prague. She described the story about Will, adopted son of a village miller and now an innkeeper, as 'clear and crystalline . . . all you need'; her choice of this tale of countryside love is also intriguing because of the reasons Will gives for withdrawing from marriage to Marjory, the parson's daughter. When all assume the betrothal is arranged Will changes his mind: ' "I have been thinking about getting married," he began abruptly; "and after having turned it all over, I have made up my mind it's not worthwhile. . . . I hope you don't mind . . . You ought not. We should never be one whit nearer than we are just now, and, if I am a wise man, nothing like so happy . . . As to whether I have ever loved you or not, I must leave that to others. But for one thing, my feeling is not changed; and for another, you may make it your boast that you have made my whole life and character something different from what they were. I mean what I say; no less. I do not think getting married is worthwhile." ' It is hard not to hear echoes of Kafka's ambivalence about the married state.

Now Milena suggested to Karel Scheinpflug a translation of Stevenson's *The Master of Ballantrae*. 'There's no translation yet. Do you want it? We would have to announce in the paper that it's coming so that no one would steal it. It's subtle, beautiful, vivid, fresh, and wonderfully written.' It's not difficult to see why Milena should have been drawn to this novel from 1889, not only as a mystery of adventure and suspense, but also for its investigation of the nature of good and evil through the characters of the Master and his brother; perhaps also because it contains an acute, painful portrait of a triangle of love. She told Scheinpflug that she could do it in a few months, since she had already started, convinced he would want it. 'Translation – sometimes I know everything perfectly and find it all excellent, sometimes it is torture and full of cruel new words until it hurts.'

Milena's translation, itself probably based on a German translation, cannot always capture the Scottish flavour of the dialogue, but it conveys the novel's clarity and drama. In an article about Stevenson's life and work, Milena described *The Master of Ballantrae* as Stevenson's best novel, and praised the vivid descriptions and subtlety of characterisation. 'I, who with pen in hand, for hours and days and weeks followed the struggle between the two brothers, crafting a word here, a word there, I love them both, I understand them both and I feel sometimes as if I am in the presence of two friends.' The novel eventually appeared in instalments in *Národní listy* from November 1923.

But alongside her enthusiasm for new projects, Milena continued to brood on her failed marriage. In the New Year of 1923 she took up the theme of her article from the previous summer ('Superficial Talk') and developed it into what became one of her most famous articles. 'The Devil at the Hearth'. It is worth quoting at length.

> Why is it that all – or nearly all – modern marriages are unhappy (as if it would be 'unmodern' to be content)? ... This question always amazes me. Not that I would not be able to tell you why modern marriages are unhappy – is there any question a journalist would leave unanswered? But again and again I ask: why should a marriage be happy?
>
> This is the point. Two people – two small, lonely, human fleas, exposed to so many moments of helplessness and hopelessness, so many sorrows in life – two tiny people on this huge globe, so unimaginably, terrifyingly and distressingly vast, both by every law of nature unhappy – find themselves all at once, at half-past nine in the morning, shut in the same flat, sharing the same name, the same property and the same fate, all in a moment. And you expect them to be instantly happy, simply because there are two of them? ...
>
> There is only one sensible reason for two people to get married – that they simply cannot *not* get married. That they cannot live without each other. Setting all romance, sentimentality and melodrama aside, it does happen. It happens every day and call it love or what you will,

it is certainly the strongest and most legitimate feeling in the world. A feeling which most people in life push aside and pass by.

Two people marry to live together. Why on top of the huge gift of this opportunity do they demand happiness? Why can't people be satisfied with this true unadorned greatness rather than choosing lies bedecked in ribbons? Why do they make promises which neither they themselves, nor the world, nature, heaven, fate, or life itself can keep and which no one, ever, anywhere can fulfil? Why do they add to a real, actual and practical contract conditions worthy of the most fantastical literature – like happiness? . . .

If we examined marriage more carefully before tying the knot, we would understand quite naturally a few things we didn't think about before. For instance, that living with someone is not easier but rather harder than living alone. There are many compensations for loneliness – freedom and independence, fewer responsibilities, or perhaps simply the option to go to Australia on your own. Marriage is difficult because the minute you get married you have to give up everything it does not offer. And this is the second reason modern marriages collapse: people marry without really making a decision one way or the other, without making the decision to give up everybody else.

To know someone really well is an incredibly difficult thing. I don't think it is an exaggeration to say that in a way it is possible to know someone as well after half an hour's conversation as after ten years of living together. I also think that it is almost impossible before the wedding for two people even to guess who it is they are marrying. Even if they know all their doings, their ideas, enthusiasms, convictions, faith and religious beliefs, they are not familiar with their socks, their sleepy eyes, the way they gargle when they do their teeth in the morning or the way they tip the waiter. Someone can deceive others about the depths of their soul, but they will give themselves away in superficial matters. . . .

Usually people reproach themselves for precisely the things which are in their very nature, and they do not realise that it is exactly the task of marriage to support each other to the point where each feels the right to be as they are. In the end, it is always confirmation of the self which one person prays for from the other. Proof that they are loved 'despite' . . . To have, in this lonely world, someone who confirms their right to exist with all their failings and weaknesses – because what is friendship anyway if not support for paralysed self-confidence? To have someone to defend them from punishment, revenge, judgment, a bad reputation and pangs of conscience. . . .

So, briefly, it seems to me that our marriages are so unhappy because we make them so easy. It is very comfortable to accept from someone a promise which they cannot keep and in a year, when it is not kept, to jump up and run away. I think it is much harder and also more honest to make promises which it is possible to keep and really fulfil. . . .

Why don't people promise that they will never be remiss in coming home with oranges in their pocket, or a bunch of violets or a bag of raisins? Why don't they promise to appear at breakfast already washed, smelling of soap and water, fresh and scrupulously dressed even on the day after their golden wedding, as well as every day until then? . . . Why don't they promise that they will always take an interest in each other and in each other's interests, be it history or art, football or butterfly collecting? Why don't they promise to allow each other freedom to be silent, freedom to be alone, freedom to enjoy privacy? Why don't they promise all these 'trifles' which it is possible to fulfil and yet which never are fulfilled, instead of something so unimportant as happiness?

All Milena's longing, all her realism, all the painful wisdom gained during the four and a half years of her failed marriage to Ernst and the two years since the breakdown of her relationship with Kafka, are here.

7

Transition

Milena's fifth New Year in Vienna, 1923, found her calmer, more independent, with an increased authority in her writing and a greater emotional detachment after the storms of the past few years. If 'The Devil at the Hearth' was a last cry from the heart for all that she felt she had lost (or never had), its tone of realism revealed that she was learning to move through her imperfect world more calmly.

Such articles were popular with her readers at *Národní listy*, and during the year she delivered several pieces on relations between men and women. In February she tackled the topical theme, 'The Emancipation of Women', with the sub-title 'Some very old-fashioned thoughts', exploring one of the great modern conundrums: how to reconcile calls for equality with the implications of the undeniable physical difference between men and women, 'the great, unchanging and terribly simple natural law, that a woman needs nine months to bear a child, and a man only a few moments to engender a child.'

Readers had written to her accusing her of being too progressive. So in this article, with her tongue a little in her cheek, she was more cautious. She acknowledged that men and women are different and have different spheres, but she rejected any notion of male superiority. She questioned the emphasis which some of her contemporaries put on equality in the workplace since this ignored the importance of women's work in the home. 'This call for equal rights and equality always seems to me to undervalue women. I don't know anyone in the world who could decide who is more able, men or women, and how foolish to undertake such a contest.'

The importance of a woman's work in the home should not be dismissed.

> To bear children is not hard. Any cat can do it – and more bravely, naturally and wisely. To bring up children, however, is a huge thing . . .

Transition

To bring up a child does not mean smacking him when he dribbles on your apron. To bring up a child means first being firm, decent, fearless, hardworking. It means having a huge heart. Is this a small thing?

One of the noble characteristics of women is that they will become what it is necessary to be. If they need to earn money, to feed the children, their husband and themselves, they can do it.... They can manage factories, drive cars and trains, they can study, they can hold office, they can fight for life courageously, as we have proved countless times during the war, and as we will prove again. But all these jobs remain just that – jobs. They are not – for the real woman – a calling. At bottom her heart remains always that of a woman and mother. It remains so through all the slogans about the women's question, and that it stays so is her highest value.

It was in some ways a conservative view and would have suited many of her readers. But it also reflected her own view as, at the age of twenty-six, she celebrated the state of motherhood which she had not yet reached but for which she seems to have longed. Her work gave her confidence as a professional woman, but she had still not found the emotional stability and acceptance which a family would offer. Not that she had any illusions about the difficulties women faced. Men were undoubtedly freer and more self-sufficient. And she resented the fact that in Vienna, and even more so in Prague, modern women who thought nothing of going to the theatre or the café alone found it impossible to stand waiting in the street for even two minutes without attracting unwelcome attention. She advised men who wanted the respect and admiration of women to dress and conduct themselves in a way which made them look like the sort of man who would leave a woman alone!

Where did Milena's brand of feminism come from? She had no doubt that men and women were different, with different preserves. Some of her views would not be contradicted by more conservative women, but this is a reflection of her understanding of the reality for many of her readers. What is radical is the honesty and openness with which she discusses these issues, always supporting women's independence and happiness and encouraging a more balanced and healthy life, where women could express themselves freely in how they dressed, what exercise they took, what work they did, how they loved. She was always close to strong, creative women like herself, in work and in friendship.

In part her attitudes were a reflection of the times. Her education and the philosophy of the new republic emphasised the importance of women's emancipation. (T. G. Masaryk's wife Charlotte was an American and a feminist, and there were more Czech women in higher education than in Germany or Slovakia and several women in parliament.) Czech history and tradition offered plenty of role models, from Libuše, the prophetess and mythical ruler of Prague, to Vlasta, the warrior who led the war of the maidens against their menfolk after Libuše's death; or more recent heroines like Božena Němcová.

Added to these legends was Milena's own experience. She had seen, within her own family and then her own marriage, the ways in which a woman's life could be disappointed. Her own independence, the product of both necessity and temperament, made her a champion of independence for all women. But she did not see women as victims or men as villains. She was a humanist who understood the complexities of life. She needed men, and their affirmation of her womanhood; but her natural sympathies were for women, and her insight into both the riches and trials of their lives never faded.

In mid-February Milena went to Prague again, but she was unable to see her editor Karel Scheinpflug and found her father ill. It was not a successful visit and she quickly returned to Vienna, feeling depressed. Her friend Wilma Löwenbach reported catching a glimpse of her that winter from her car as Milena hurried down the street. 'Her eyes were blank, her face pale and drawn, and she seemed unaware of her surroundings.'

Milena and Kafka corresponded tentatively and irregularly during these months. In one letter, Franz explained that by and large he hated letters. Letter-writing is 'in fact, an intercourse with ghosts, and not only with the ghost of the recipient but also one's own ghost which develops between the lines of the letter one is writing. . . . How on earth did anyone get the idea that people can communicate with one another by letter! . . . Written kisses don't reach their destination, rather they are drunk on the way by the ghosts.' He soothed these barbed comments with the remark that Milena was the person 'to whom I perhaps enjoy writing most'. In the same letter he mused on how modernity was trying to compensate, inventing the railway, the car, the aeroplane, to bring people together. But 'the opposing side is so much calmer and stronger; after the postal service it has invented the telegraph, the telephone, the radiograph. The ghosts won't starve, but we will perish. I'm surprised that you haven't written about this yet, not in order to prevent or achieve something with its publication, for that it is too late, but in order at least to show "them" that they have been recognised.'

This letter may well have been the inspiration for a March article by Milena, which took up exactly this theme. On 8 March an article appeared in *Národní listy* called 'Letters'. Letters must once have seemed a marvel, a miracle of rapid long-distance communication.

> Today? The speed of our century passes nothing by. We write letters easily, sometimes daily, urgently, rather mechanically, and in a few years, I prophesy, we will write even love letters on typewriters. . . . It's already a law of this century, which is founded on the machine, that originality, individuality and idiosyncrasy are pushed to the back. . . .
>
> If I get a letter from a friend, written on a typewriter, it irritates me immensely. A letter written with a pen conveys much more than what is written in it: it reveals haste or care, energy, order, it betrays lies, hints at truths, brings laughter, and commands reflection, sympathy or resistance.

This article reveals something about Milena's attitude to a defining question of her time, man's relation to the machine. Like the Russian revolutionaries, or the Constructivist artists across Europe, Milena could relish the machine as an engine of modernity. She felt the excitement of the new century, and she loved analysing the changing moment. But while she embraced the new, she could not forget the price to be paid in human terms, or simply the loss of what had been before. Her prophecy was right; in a decade or so, she herself would be using the typewriter for the most personal of correspondence.

For now, she and Kafka used pen and ink. He had finally read 'The Devil at the Hearth'.

> I still often think of your article. Strangely enough, I believe – to let the fictitious dialogue enter into a real one: Judaism! Judaism! – that there are such things as marriages that are not based on the despair of being lonely and, what's more, superior, conscious marriages, and I think that essentially the angel believes it too. For those who enter into marriage out of despair – what do they gain? If loneliness is joined to loneliness it never leads to a being-at-home, but to imprisonment and exile. One loneliness reflects itself in the other, even in the deepest, darkest night. And if one joins a loneliness to a security, it will be even worse for the loneliness (unless it be a delicate, ado-

lescent, unconscious loneliness). Marriage means rather – if one is to define the condition sharply and strictly – to be secure.

This is precisely what had attracted but also terrified Kafka. He finished the letter:

> But at the moment the worst thing is – not even I would have expected it – that I can't go on writing these letters, not even these important letters. The evil sorcerer of letter-writing begins to destroy my nights – which anyhow destroy themselves on their own – more than ever. I must stop, I can no longer write. Oh, your sleeplessness is a different one from mine. Please let's not write any more.

Spurned yet again, left with her own denigrated form of nocturnal suffering, and even her denigrated realism (had she given up too soon her dream of a 'superior, conscious marriage'?), Milena more or less obeyed. She distanced herself with her relationship with Schaffgotsch and with the demands of *Národní listy*. She wrote about fashions in underwear, what to wear to a tea dance, the pleasure provided by a vase of fresh flowers, the importance of fresh air, exercise and hygiene, and why water was as good a cleanser and tonic as any salon product. She turned out her particular blend of good sense, tinged with puritanism and a trace of snobbery. Simple ways were best, but even in simple matters good taste must rule. Her goal was beauty – not artificial beauty, but beauty in terms of health, spirit and a cared-for body.

Cinema continued to be another of her favourite distractions. Was German or American cinema better? American films embraced the new medium, and were full of verve and humour. But they were sometimes too simple and basic. German films tended to be more sophisticated, with more complex plots, but she found them less at ease with the power of the new medium. She recalled a famous Swedish film of the period, *Erotikon*, which she had seen in Vienna, an erotic comedy by Mauritz Stiller about a woman who leaves her husband to be with her lover, while her husband marries his niece. It was sexually audacious, but Milena found it 'crystallinely chaste and pure – I mean pure in thought'. The whole film had a rare intimacy and realism, which Milena detected and which inspired contemporary and later film-makers (including the Czech director Gustav Machatý, who made his own *Erotikon* in 1929 and then in 1933 the daring *Ecstasy*, both of which Milena may have seen in Prague).

Such articles were typical of Milena's prolific, eclectic output. What made her readers keep looking for her byline was their confidence that whatever subject she tackled she would bring her fresh, humane, questioning voice to bear.

But her work could not eradicate her continuing preoccupation with Kafka. In May she sent him greetings, to which Kafka replied with a brief postcard from Dobřichovice. He followed this with a letter thanking her for her kind words. She had been working on the translation of his story 'The Judgment', concerning a young man's fantasy about his relationship with a friend abroad and his real, uneasy relationship with his father. Her translation appeared in *Cesta* in the middle of 1923 (entitled *Soud* which translates as *The Court*. Later translations used *Rozsudek* – 'The Judgment'). It was the last of her translations of Kafka's writing to be published. Other Czech translators were beginning to tackle Kafka. But Milena was the first person to introduce Kafka to non-German speakers. Her translations are not always precisely accurate, but even her critics concede that she was a sensitive and impressive translator; Kafka himself certainly found her so. (Her translations of other writers continued to appear in *Cesta*, stories by Gustave Flaubert and R. L. Stevenson in 1923, and by Edgar Allan Poe and Stendhal in following years. Schaffgotsch may well have helped her with some of these. The end of her relationship with him coincides with the end of her contributions to *Cesta*.)

As summer came, Milena took refuge as usual in visits to Prague. She found it easier to find subjects there. She watched summer celebrations along the River Vltava, relishing the crowds and the flags. Rather sentimentally, she described how much she loved her home city, and how much it was changing in her absence.

Prague, my golden little town, my wonderful, beautiful, beloved home, my heart is in your stones, how suddenly you have become a metropolis, full of variety, joyful, living, how beloved you are to me, suddenly new and full of surprises. I stand on the bridge and I look at you and I see already how you change, how you grow, how you stretch and reach out. What a great, immeasurable city you will be.

The pull of home was becoming stronger and stronger, and the question of where to live and what to do about her marriage pressed on her. It was one part of the broader question which emerged in her letters and articles: how to live, how to be a good person. In an article in June she included an examination of human responsibility.'Cause or Effect' was her strongest attack yet on psychoanalysis. In the post-war climate, she wrote, people were searching for certainty and asking 'how to live'. Psychoanalysis seemed to offer some answers. 'Today it is the property of us all, even those who don't believe in it.' She summarised the work of Freud as she (not always accurately) understood it. She believed that psychoanalysis was the study of the unconscious as the foundation of all human behaviour, and that it argued that 'People are not free. People are bound a thousand times over by early ties and ballast, inherited from their ancestors. People are even more bound by sexual instincts, on whose influence – in earliest youth – they themselves have no influence. . . . What is mirrored in someone's conscious is only a weak reflection, an unclear, unwitting, imprecise propulsion to act.' But, Milena claimed, there was nothing new in this. Dostoevsky, 'the great psychoanalyst', had already described more simply what happened to characters who succumbed to the painful pressures of life. 'He hates, he steals, he loves, he kills, he acts, not because of his own decision, but because of a drive; it is not I myself who act, but this "I" created by foreign hands, hands of fate, circumstance, experience, inclination. It is not I who steals, but my unconscious I which forces me to do it.'

Even if she accepted Freud's description of unconscious drives, she was sceptical of what she believed psychoanalysis claimed could follow from this, that by shedding light on the unconscious causes of action someone could be 'cured'. 'Identifying the cause does not remove it.' Milena believed it is better to accept responsibility for who you are, better to live as a person who simply is, rather than be dissected and reduced to nothing but a powerless tool of the unconscious. What a loss to concede responsibility! 'It is the human tragedy that we are responsible for things we cannot control.' But this is the challenge and the duty, to be responsible for the effects of our actions, if not the causes.

Her own sense of responsibility was very strict on some matters, less so on others. In personal relationships, her sense of obligation was strong. Her articles stressed the responsibilities of marriage, and her letters to Max Brod brooded on what damage she might have done to Kafka. Her behaviour could be impetuous, but the remorse if she thought she had done wrong was genuine.

Her attitude towards money, however, was cavalier. Between 1921 and 1923, for example, she incurred large debts at a Vienna fashion house, Zwiebackers, ordering goods for which she could not pay.

Transition

Back in 1921 she had written an article about the case of Georg Kaiser, a German expressionist playwright who had fallen on hard times, sold his rich wife's estate and rented a villa. He was charged with theft. At his trial, Kaiser gave an impassioned defence, appealing for the artist's immunity from the mundane practicalities of life. But the court, and a large part of the public, regarded him as nothing but an egotistical thief, and he was sentenced to six months in prison. Milena characteristically saw it differently. She deplored the nature of his behaviour but scorned people's outraged reactions to the case.

> The press blamed Georg Kaiser because with the money that he gained improperly he bought not bread, but oysters.... That he was not satisfied with two rooms but wanted a palace. They forget one very important thing in this world: life is not logical. There would be no luxury if there were no hunger.... People who have known hunger for a long time have a cold fear of it, a fear of such proportions that it hurts not only their stomach but also their spirit, their heart, their mind. To satisfy someone who once really looked poverty in the face is terribly hard, perhaps an impossible task.... I cannot believe that anyone would prostitute themselves from hunger. But I can believe that from hunger they drive themselves to become a millionaire. Georg Kaiser needed tens of thousands of marks because of hunger, because of hunger he suffered delusions of grandeur, because of hunger he shouted at the judge: 'I am a great poet to whom everything is permitted!' Not from immediate hunger. From the hunger of years before.

Milena did not think of herself as a 'great poet' whose stealing should therefore be excused, but she did regard money as an irritation rather than an obligation. She could, in the end, afford to. Although Ernst had little money, her father continued to support her.

She began to plan her summer travels. In May she had written an article about the joys of window shoppping on Na příkopě. Apart from beautiful suits and exquisite orchids and camellias she dreamt of 'a matt black car; if I were rich I would buy such a car, settle my beloved inside it and take off for Rome, drive to the Italian sea ...' And in another article she described sitting in a café reading American magazines, full of photographs of different people and places. 'The whole world is in them.... You turn the pages and think about the world.'

Now, part of the dream was about to come true and she left for the Italian sea. It is not clear who she travelled with, probably with

Schaffgotsch. It was an adventure, a pilgrimage, a welcome interruption to her unsatisfactory Vienna life. She was also hoping to find some sort of resolution about her future.

She went to Viareggio on the coast, where she admired the health and beauty of the unselfconscious Italians on the beach, one sunned family in particular. 'They all had slender, bronzed bodies, well-kept hair and hands, beautiful skin; they all moved with animal elegance.' She went to Venice and enjoyed 'the fairy-tale palaces, the water, ships and golden sun'. She went to Pisa and inspected the tower. She particularly loved Padua, with its white streets and galleried arcades, and was struck in particular by one 'wonderful, light, singing street'. But she found the ceaseless train journeys rather tiring and disorienting, and in Padua her suitcases went astray, fortunately not for long.

She returned to Vienna at the end of September. She had sent Kafka a postcard from Italy, wishing him well since she had heard he was planning to move to Berlin, and she received a reply from his new home in Germany. He half-explained his situation, and his move from Prague.

> So far, things in Berlin are not so bad as you seem to think. . . . I live almost in the country, in a small villa and garden, it seems to me I've never yet had such a beautiful apartment. . . . And you say even less in your letter. Is the general condition a good, a bearable one? I cannot unriddle it. Of course one can't even do it in one's own case; that's what 'fear' is, nothing else.

This letter is the penultimate one published in *Letters to Milena*. (In December he sent his 'kindest regards'.) To the very end, their debate about fear, their own relation to it and their attempts to deal with it, continued. The openness between them remained. But in one crucial way Kafka was reticent. Although Milena must have known the truth from other sources, Kafka said nothing of the fact that he was living in Berlin with Dora Dymant, a young Jewess from Berlin whom he had met on the Baltic coast during a summer trip with his oldest sister Elli. His union with Dora brought him a kind of peace and a new world at the end of his life.

Milena's own travels had not brought her peace. She returned from Italy 'full of excellent resolutions'. She does not elaborate much, beyond the intention to 'tidy out the left drawer of my desk'. But life back in Vienna swept even this practical goal away, as well, it seems, as more fundamental desires; perhaps even to leave Vienna. The warm glow of the Mediterranean sunshine faded. She sent *Národní*

Transition

listy an article about the limitations of travel, the impossibility of solving life's problems by seeking a new life elsewhere, beyond the window.

To close the door here and start anew somewhere else. Completely, from the beginning, away from the new tear in the soles of your shoes, soup in the afternoon, the same old pillow under your head; here everything is falling into ruin, there it is possible to escape everything. So it seems to your heart, one evening at the window as summer turns to autumn; suddenly you can say nothing but 'Away, away, away . . . Into the world!'

But the journey is disappointing and you lose sight of what you are looking for. And when you return home, a little homesick, nothing has changed.

Through all your homesickness the house stood standing with its four walls and geraniums flowering at the window. You fly up the steps, terribly afraid of what you will find inside. But when you open the doors breathlessly, there is your quiet, trustworthy beloved room, the same unchanging corner of home . . .

The first thing you do: look out of the window. There over the roofs, beyond the sky and the streets lies the world. Just as unfamiliar, tempting and alluring as the day you left. But here at the window you stand, poorer through experience, robbed by knowledge: the world out there, even if it was ten times as big, does not hold a new beginning. The way to a fresh start cannot be found by taking a train into the world.

She needed to find another way out of routine life in Vienna and her provisional marriage with Ernst. But leaving him would be a huge risk, as she hinted in an article.

Men have a much easier time than women! They are so self-sufficient and so free! . . . If they lose everything they hardly lose anything, they can always begin again; and they are not abandoned if they are alone, since the world of deeds and work is open to them; quite different from the world of women which is always instinctual; men's work suffices to fill up even a disappointed and lonely life. For a woman the unhappiness of separation is a living calamity, for a man it is the unhappiness of a natural sorrow. For a woman, loneliness is a catastrophe, for a man it is something unpleasant but never fatal.

An article just a week or so later paints a more complex picture. It was a response to a reader who enquired, 'How should a woman feel if her husband is unfaithful?' There is no simple answer, says Milena, no rulebook. Every case is different. But there are common themes.

> Above all, I think it is necessary to recognise that an unfaithful woman and an unfaithful man are not guilty on – let us say – the same level. Not just because of physiology. But because a woman has other responsibilities and duties towards her sexuality than a man; a woman can become a mother; motherhood is her calling and task. Motherhood imposes on woman the duty to be faithful and sexually honest, however hard. Man is free. . . . All I mean is that an act which is full of serious physiological consequences for a woman is physiologically insignificant for a man.

Her stricture to women was not one she was able to follow. She would not defend infidelity; marriage makes sense only with sexual fidelity. But people are not perfect. And so her advice to the woman is this:

> Look at yourself. Above all, understand your man. . . . Perhaps you did not show enough interest in his little wishes and cares which you have listened to day after day, year after year? Perhaps you did not do enough to show you loved him? Perhaps you were always in a hurry, full of worries, and forgot to be pretty and charming? Perhaps you were so exhausted that you forgot to find a patient smile. Men are great big boys and it only seems as if they understand life. In reality they only understand themselves. But if you love him, is that not enough? . . .
>
> An indulgent smile and patience would soon cure your husband of his romantic notions. Tragic gestures, scenes, reproaches and threats often make a mountain out of a molehill. . . . Either a woman must manage to be such that her husband wants to be faithful to her, or she must bear his infidelity if she does not want to lose him. Every crime needs two people; the one who perpetrates the crime and the one against whom it is perpetrated.

These articles, which pander to her conservative audience with some commonplace agony aunt advice, are given bite by the shadow of irony. They show Milena's feel for the complexities of relationships and her inability to see anything, even her relationship with Ernst, in black and white. She returned to the theme in the New Year.

> If I can wish you anything for the New Year, young and old, rich and poor, it is: more inner honesty and more broadmindedness . . .
>
> After my article about unfaithful men, I got many letters from alarmed women: how could I excuse such a thing . . . I did not excuse

anything, as I did not judge anything. It is not a question of criticism, but of reality. In real life there is no shared life which would not lead to a similar conflict. The central motive of the whole world, all history, is the erotic struggle between people. Every marriage is traumatised by it like a forest by a storm, every person is engulfed by it like the land by a flood. . . . Is it therefore possible to criticise the flood, the lightning, the earthquake? Of course not. But one thing I can do: I can look them in the face, I can fight against the dangers, I can deal with them, bear them, run ahead of them, I can take shelter. But I must know them, their nature, their cause, their possibilities and prospects.

It is not only unfaithfulness. All human characteristics. Someone stands before you, like a tree in a wood . . . look him carefully in the face; look carefully at his hands, movements, smile, at the expression of his face, the lean of his shoulders. Listen carefully to what he says and you will understand him. You will understand what he can and cannot do. Live next to him, not cursing what he cannot do, but praising what he can . . .

Suddenly you will see that he is as poor, weak and lonely as you. Suddenly you will see that he has a sleepless face, suddenly you will hear what he says. Before your eyes appears another, quite different pain from yours. And without knowing how, you say something which helps you both, you and him. Something simple, clear, right . . . Face to face, a quiet, honest word.

A strange New Year's wish; perhaps she and Ernst had spoken honestly or she had glimpsed his own emotional desires and pro-fessional frustrations with sympathy. But if the deterioration of their relationship had not destroyed her affection for him, her capacity to see him clearly, it was increasingly obvious to them both that the marriage was hollow. The arrival of warmer weather could not ease her restlessness. She liked the slowly ripening northern spring; the heat and brightness of Italy had been wonderful the summer before, but she was by nature a creature of a more subdued clime. She kept at her writing for *Národní listy*, providing articles on fashion, the pleasures of dancing, the train journey from Vienna to Prague. But none rose above the routine. She was perhaps more preoccupied with thoughts of how to leave Vienna.

In Berlin, meanwhile, Kafka's health was deteriorating. On 14 March 1924, Max Brod brought him back to Prague, only six months after he had left for Berlin. Three weeks later, Dora came and took him to the Wiener Wald Sanatorium in Austria, where complications of his tuberculosis were diagnosed for which no effective treatment existed. Kafka was moved to the University Clinic in Vienna and then to the small Kierling sanatorium in the countryside outside Vienna, where he could see the hills from the window of his room. Dora and Robert Klopstock, Kafka's friend from Matliary, watched over him. The lesions in his throat made swallowing and speaking painful. Even drinking a glass of water became agony. It was clear that he would not recover.

There is some uncertainty as to whether Milena visited Kafka during these last few weeks. It is unimaginable that she did not know of his presence; she was closely in touch with friends of Kafka's such as Max Brod, Jiří Weil and Franz Werfel. And there are two references suggesting that she did visit him. According to a writer on Milena's life in Vienna, Marta Marková-Kotyková, Schaffgotsch claimed that he and Milena visited Kafka in Kierling in May 1924. Marková-Kotyková doubts Schaffgotsch's reliability and points out that in neither Kafka's diaries nor other accounts is there any reference to a visit from Milena. But Kafka was in no condition to write his diary, and why should Schaffogtsch have invented the visit?

There is also a reference from Milena herself. In a letter to a close friend in 1938, she wrote: 'I sat next to Kafka when he was dying in Vienna, and waited until he died.' There is no suggestion that Milena was actually with Kafka when he died – this was Dora's sad privilege. But given that Milena and Kafka had remained in touch, however awkwardly, and given that they had continued to regard each other with affection and respect, it seems highly likely that she would have visited him.

As May came to an end, Kafka faded further. Nothing could obliterate the pain. He extracted a promise from Klopstock to give him morphine if the pain became unbearable. On 2 June he demanded the drug, and Klopstock complied. Kafka died at noon on 3 June.

Among the German-Jewish community in Prague, Kafka's death was mourned. There were obituaries in the German press, including one by Max Brod; S. K. Neumann, for whom Milena had translated *The Stoker*, wrote a tribute for the *Communist Review*. But among the Czech community there was scant attention to his death. Milena's dignified tribute and farewell, published in *Národní listy* on 5 June 1924, was an exception.

Dr Franz Kafka, the German writer who lived in Prague, died the day before yesterday in the Kierling sanatorium at Klosterneuberg near

Transition

Vienna. Few people knew him, because he was a recluse, a wise man frightened of life.... [His illness] gave him an almost miraculous sensibility, and a terrifyingly uncompromising intellectual refinement; on the other hand, he was a man who unloaded the whole weight of his fear of life onto the shoulders of his illness. He was shy, anxious, gentle and good, but the books he wrote are cruel and painful. He saw the world as full of invisible demons, which tear defenceless humans to pieces and destroy them.... He understood people as only people of great sensitivity can, people who stand alone and can tell the whole person from one glance at their face. He understood the world to extraordinary depths, as he himself was an extraordinary and deep world. He wrote the most remarkable books of modern German literature; they embody, in an untendentious way, the struggle of a generation. They are true, naked and painful, and even where the expression is symbolic they are also naturalistic. They are full of the dry smiles and second sight of a man who saw the world so clearly that he could not bear it and had to die.... All his books describe the horrors of the secret misunderstandings, the guiltless guilt between people. He was a man and an artist so painfully conscious that he heard even where others, the deaf, felt safe.

Milena Jesenská

The obituary is proof, if any is needed, that Milena had the intelligence to recognise Kafka's genius as a writer and the sensitivity to discern and describe the traces of his extraordinary personality. Despite the painful passage of their relationship, she also had the grace not to feel bitterness. Later in life she would not speak of Kafka much; when she did it was always with great respect.

Kafka's death coincided with (and perhaps sealed) the end of Milena's time in Vienna. It was clear by now that very little held Milena and Ernst together. Milena was involved with Schaffgotsch and Ernst was busy with his philosophical studies and with his circle of café friends and lovers. They decided to separate. Despite Milena's article about the risks for women of standing alone, she had grown up enough no longer to need Ernst as a defining principle, nor to need Vienna as a place of exile from her difficult adolescent home. She had discovered work by which (along with help from her father in times of need) she could support herself. And she was no longer dependent on Ernst for emotional satisfaction.

In the spring of 1924 Wilma Löwenbach had visited Milena and found her much healthier and happier than earlier in the year. Wilma was impressed by Schaffgotsch and thought him handsome (he wore his hair combed back and carried a handkerchief folded in his jacket pocket), well-mannered and attentive to Milena, who had always approved of a little chivalry, even towards the most independent woman. (In some of her articles she includes tips for young men about how to behave with proper gallantry; she advised that a real gentleman, while in general standing back to open doors for women, would always lead the way if entering an unfamiliar restaurant or bar.) After Ernst's sometimes cavalier behaviour she enjoyed the care Schaffgotsch gave her. They also shared their political views, and were able to work together. Now that Milena had separated from Ernst, Schaffgotsch was prepared to go where Milena wished.

There was nothing to keep her in Vienna and, with Kafka's death perhaps, nothing to complicate a return to Prague. She had been spending as much time as possible in Prague anyway, and her relationship with her father, while still uneasy, was much improved. So finally, after more than five years, Milena left Vienna for good, in the company of Schaffgotsch. They took rather dingy ground-floor rooms in a house in Zborovská street in Smíchov, the industrial quarter of Prague which spilled along the river from Malá Strana. Milena's father now lived in an elegant town house in the expanding New Town to the east of Wenceslas Square, at Dittrichova 17. He did not take Milena's latest partner to heart; a Communist was a Communist, however good his table manners.

Milena had hardly begun to pick up the threads of life in Prague, before she and Schaffgotsch were invited by their friends from Vienna, Alice Gerstlová and Otto Rühle, now married, to stay with them in Germany where they had moved. It was a comradely invitation which postponed the uncertain business of reintegration into Prague, and Milena and Schaffgotsch accepted.

They spent the last months of 1924 and much of 1925 with Otto and Alice, at their large house on a hill near Dresden. Otto had been a founder member of the German Communist Party, although he left not long after the war because of the party's increasingly rigid ways. He now ran a publishing house in Dresden, Am andern Ufer (On the Other Bank). He and his wife Alice, twenty years his junior, were a cultivated pair and Milena and Schaffgotsch enjoyed their company. Here was a friendly intellectual environment where Milena felt accepted, in contrast to the cafés of Vienna. The two couples were in accord on political matters, and Milena learnt a great deal from Otto and Alice. Given her views on psychoanalysis, however, a discipline

Transition

Otto and Alice were both enthusiastic about, there must have been some lively arguments as well.

There were other diversions: visits to concerts and plays in Dresden, as well as musical evenings at the house when Milena played the piano. There were excursions and tennis matches. A photograph from 1925 shows Milena and Schaffgotsch as a tall, elegant couple in the leafy garden of the house.

It was a peaceful place to work. Schaffgotsch was writing a play and also tried his hand at some fairy tales. Milena delivered articles to Prague as usual, some on serious, some on trivial matters. An article on underwear became a plea for patriotism: why buy fashionable French underwear when Czech lace and appliqué work was just as good? She was more lenient towards England. In an article called 'In Praise of England' she quoted from Karel Čapek's delightful book *Letters from England*, and praised English tailoring. She also returned to the theme of infidelity, in an article composed as a reply to a letter from a man torn between his wife and his lover. 'With two women you have two worlds, and it is not by chance – such an instinct for balance is human – that they are opposite worlds, that they complement each other. If you decide on one woman you will lose the other; that is, you will lose the other world, that which complements the first.' (Schaffgotsch was certainly a different world from Ernst.)

But if something must give, her advice is this:

> Remember an important thing: marital love differs fundamentally from other love. Marriage is, so to say, an official arrangement for eternity. . . . An affair cannot provide the same common ground for life. . . . Between the old and the new life, my boy, there is a terrible barrier: divorce. When you look into the face which guided your days for years, which smiled and cried together with you, you will find memories of everything that you lived through with her; but this familiar face no longer belongs to you, you will never speak your private little language again, and you will never again return home, up those steps, to her welcome. . . . If, despite all this, you have enough strength to leave, you will fall into the other world exhausted, like a wounded animal.

On 30 May 1925, her divorce from Ernst came through; the appendage to the marriage certificate lays the formal responsibility for the separation on Ernst Pollak. Milena was twenty-eight and had been married for seven years. Their relationship had flourished in one city only to fade in another; the age difference, the difference in sexual experience and attitudes, as well as the divergent paths they chose, Ernst towards philosophy, Milena towards journalism, drove them apart. Despite their eventual incompatibility and unhappiness, Milena is said to have written later to the lover of her friend Staša, Ada Hoffmeister, that Ernst was her greatest love. He was certainly her first real love, and she continued to regard him with affection and respect. He proved to be the man she spent longest with.

The loss was real, but divorce did not leave her 'exhausted, like a wounded animal'. It was as if she had already paid the emotional price long before the divorce actually came through. Now she was enjoying life at the Rühles' house, and working well. She wrote a moving article called 'A Great White Silence' on a film about Captain Scott's Antarctic expedition. She described the explorers' bravery, their eventual failure and senseless death, and pondered the meaning of heroism.

> When you emerge from the cinema onto the lively street, your thoughts naturally turn to your own safe evening ahead, when you think of your supper, the book lying on your table, the peaceful four walls of your room, hidden from the world; your head spins, because you don't know which is more senseless: the quiet life which you lead and the quiet death at home in bed, or that death out in the snow which no one can ever explain. Because it is wrong to say that he died for science, for his nation, for an idea; in the depths of his heart he died only for his own heart, for some excitement.

These words read as a prophetic gloss on her own later bravery.

She also found ways to broaden her work. She edited a selection of recipes sent in by readers of *Národní listy* from all over Czechoslovakia. The book, *Milena's Recipes*, offered a selection of traditional Czech cooking, including a long section on cakes. It was a paradoxical picture of Milena; she was not a good cook. But the image of 'Milena', the all-knowing wise woman of *Národní listy*, was stronger than the reality: the book sold out.

She also talked to Otto Rühle about collaboration, which later bore fruit when she translated his book *Jak zacházeti s dětmi* (*How to bring up children*). (It was published in 1928 for the Žena imprint which she was then editing for the Topič publishing house.)

Her main project was an illustrated edition of *Peter Pan* to be published in time for Christmas 1925 by the Akciová Press Children's Library. Milena could not speak English, but she worked with a young Czech woman, Jiřka Malá, who did the basic translation.

na by the River Vltava, aged 13 *(Museum of Czech*
ature, Strahov, Prague)

Milena on the tennis court in 1911, aged 14 *(Museum*
of Czech Literature)

na in 1915, taken to mark her graduation from
rva *(Museum of Czech Literature)*

Milena in the mid-1920s
(Museum of Czech Literature)

Jan Jesenský, Milena's father *(Museum of Czech Literature)*

Ernst Pollak in 1938
(photo: Hartmut Binder)

Franz Kafka i
1923/24

Arco in Prague *(Museum of the City of Prague Photographic Archive)*

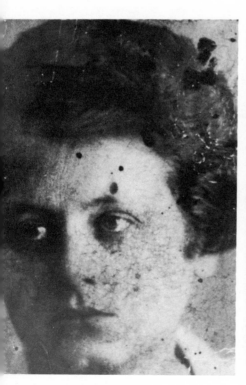

's identity photograph taken for *Národní listy*
(National Museum Newspaper Archive)

Milena (centre), Otto Rühle, Alice Gerstlová and
Franz Xaver Schaffgotsch (right) in 1925

Front page of *Kmen* with Milena's
translation of Kafka's story *Topič*
(National Museum Newspaper Archive)

Illustration to one of Milena's fashion articles in
Národní listy (National Museum Newspaper Archive

Milena with Staša Jílovská in summer 1925
(Staša Fleischmann)

Slávka Vondráčková in her textile studio

ír Krejcar in the 1940s
Fleischmann)

Milena and Krejcar at the sanatorium in Piešťany in
the Slovak mountains *(Museum of Czech Literature)*

on of Milena in *Národní listy* as patient 'No 20'
d the time of her confinement (see page 139)
nal Museum Newspaper Archive)

Milena and Honza in the early 1930s
(Staša Fleischmann)

The flower market near Milena's childhood home *(Museum of the City of Prague)*

Prokopovo náměstí 4, Milena's first home in Prague

Lerchenfelderstrasse 113, Vienna, where Milena lived with Ernst Pollak

Maltézské náměstí before the Second World War

zské náměstí 13, Malá Strana where Milena
on her return to Prague

Interior of Maltézské náměstí, with cushion fabrics
by Slávka Vondráčková and armchair designed by
Jaromír Krejcar (*Museum of Czech Literature*)

Spálená Street 33 (now 35), where Milena and Jaromír lived when they were first married

Francouzská 4; Milena and Jaromír lived on the top floor

Cartoon in *Žijeme* of the modernist interior of the Francouzská apartment with Milena, Jaromír and Honza *(National Museum Newspaper Archive)*

Kouřimská Street

The Topič publishing house which published books by Milena in her mid-twenties

Milena at Dobřichovice in the early 1930s

Milena's article in *Přítomnost* about the German occupation of Czechoslovakia, March 1939 (see p. 186) *(National Museum Newspaper Archive)*

(see p. 186)

Willi Schlamm by the River Vltava *(Steffi Schlamm)*

Steffi Schlamm *(Steffi Schlamm)*

Joachim von Zedtwitz

Lumír Čivrný around the time of Milena's arrest
(*Lumír Čivrný*)

Aero coupé in which (sometimes accompanied by Milena) von Zedtwitz smuggled refugees
he border (*Joachim von Zedtwitz*)

Ravensbrück concentration camp *(Wiener Library)*

The last known photo of Milena in the late 1930s *(Joachim von Zedtwitz)*

Transition

Milena's skill was to transform this into rich, harmonious Czech. She loved J. M. Barrie's stories and wrote an enthusiastic introduction for Czech children. She explained that these strange events took place far away in England, in the beautiful Kensington Gardens. 'But don't think that mysterious things don't happen in our Prague parks when the gates close ...' Her daughter later treasured a copy of *Peter Pan*, and of the sequel *Peter Pan and Wendy* which Milena edited in two parts for publication in 1926 and 1927.

She spent July 1925 in the Czech countryside, milder terrain than the hills around Špičák but also beautiful. She wrote a series of articles under the title 'Letters from Arcadia'. She walked in the woods, enjoying the different foliage of the trees, the oaks, with strange ancient gnarled faces, and the more delicate poplars. She watched the deer graze and then, startled, leap away:

> Each leap has its own natural music, the deer runs like a wave on water, like a wave through corn, beautiful as only an animal can be ...
>
> After a long search I found a bare place which is higher than the other parts of the wood. When you stand on a tree stump, you can look out across the countryside, to right and left, across the green velvet weave of hundreds of different greens.

At dusk she recalled her childhood fears that the world around her would vanish when she was not there, or vanish after dusk, 'a strange moment, when you are left exposed'. One night there was a thunderstorm, and she awoke to the rain. 'I like the rain. An indescribable but vivid liking. In the woods a million tiny pearls appear in the little clearings, droplets form into great drops on the leaves and fall heavily onto the sodden ground, pattering on the earth. What a sound!' She felt invigorated and refreshed by the holiday.

Milena was ready to return to Prague. She and Schaffgotsch had stayed with the Rühles for ten months. Living together had been pleasant, but not always easy; Schaffgotsch could not always match Milena's moods and passions. She did not want to commit herself to a life with him. She did, however, want to commit herself to Prague. She had been circling around the city of her birth for so long, it was time to engage properly, to go home.

8

Prague

Milena found herself welcomed in Prague in a way she could not have expected. She had made a reputation for herself as a journalist, and a glamorous one at that. People hung on her tales of Vienna and Dresden and looked to her as a fashion-conscious, worldly-wise writer on women's issues. The scandalous aura of her youth was forgotten, at least by most, and she received invitations from Prague's establishment, the readers of *Národní listy*. She preferred, however, the company of other writers and artists.

Prague was an exciting city to live in. The Devětsil group of artists and architects was well established, as a left-wing avant-garde drawing on other movements abroad – the rational spirit of Constructivism and the subjective excesses of Surrealism. While designers and architects tended towards a blend of beauty and utility (which they shared with the Bauhaus), painters and poets added traditions of Czech lyricism and came up with their own 'ism', Poetism. Poetism was, according to one art critic, 'an attitude to life, a hedonistic philosophy and a celebration of modernity which obscured all the contradictions of human existence with a fragile illusion of happiness.' Devětsil's young leader, the artist and critic Karel Teige, wanted to combine these two apparently opposing spirits: 'Constructivism is a method with rigorous rules, it is the art of usefulness. Poetism, its living accessory, is the atmosphere of life . . . the art of pleasure.'

The unifying spirit, perhaps, and one which animated the circles Milena moved in, was the energy of the new Czechoslovakia's younger generation. On the one hand an energetic desire to improve society for all, through artistic as well as other means, and on the other an energetic impulse to enjoy life to the full. The city was bursting with the spirit of its avant-gardes, from cabaret, vaudeville and puppet shows to montage, experimental films, poetry readings and new modernist buildings. This on top of the creative output of more established artists like Jaroslav Hašek, Karel Čapek, Leoš Janáček (whose operatic works included *The Adventures of Mr Brouček*, which drew on the post-war spirits of absurdist surrealism and social satire).

The artistic spirit was supported in part by the political and economic confidence of the new republic. After a temporary sharp recession in the early 1920s, by the middle of the decade the Czech economy was going from strength to strength and Czechoslovakia was an established country on the map of Europe. The political parties, although fragmented and at times quarrelsome, maintained political stability under the guidance of President Masaryk and by resorting at times to governments of experts.

On her return to Prague, Milena found an apartment, probably with Schaffgotsch, in a three-storey house in Maltézské náměstí in her favourite quarter, Malá Strana. Maltézské náměstí, a charming square (or asymmetrical triangle), was (and still is) a jumble of small palaces and lesser buildings including pubs. In the middle stands a baroque statue of the Shepherd Christ with sheep at his feet. This was the magical Prague of Milena's childhood, the world of red oil lamps and river reflections. But the square had a different side, and at night Milena listened to the tread of the lamplighter and the police, the chat of the local prostitutes and feline caterwauling.

She furnished the apartment in her own informal and colourful style. There were rugs and cushions, some covered in fabrics designed by Slávka. She found a huge sofa, put pictures on the walls, draped a shawl over the standard lamp and kept a bowl of apples and the teapot or wine bottle on a trolley. (It is not difficult to understand why Gauguin was one of her favourite painters.) There were always piles of newspapers, such as *Národní listy* and the more liberal *Lidové noviny* (*The People's Paper*), left-wing cultural magazines like *ReD*, the monthly journal of Devětsil, and Vienna papers including the theatre critic Karl Kraus's *Fackel*. Journalism in the new republic was a lively world, with writers and editors believing that they had an important role to play in shaping the new country.

There is a photograph of Milena from this period, taken in 1925 at the Fotostudio Praha on Wenceslas Square, possibly as an official photograph for *Národní listy*. It is signed with a flourish by Milena herself. Her wavy hair is pulled back from her face and she is wearing a simple white V-necked shirt. Her complexion is good, her eyes are warm, her lips are full and the dimple in her chin adds softness to her well-structured bones. She is undoubtedly beautiful. It is easy to see why she was so admired, for her looks and her style. After the illness and fatigue of Vienna, the stay near Dresden and 'Arcadia' had restored her health. Now back in Prague, she did exercises in her flat and took every opportunity to renew her walks in the nearby countryside. She wrote articles about the importance of fresh air and exercise, and explained with unembarrassed frankness how a woman could not dress herself to her best advantage if she did not know and care for her body.

An article that summer outlined her creed: 'I don't like people who never think about clothes, who regard fashion as something unimportant. . . . But even less do I like people who judge others only by their dress, who live by the conventions of well-cut clothes.' Her own style was distinctive; she wore good fabrics, usually in plain colours, made up carefully into simply cut dresses, often with a plain white collar. It was not an affectation when, in an article, she compared good fashion to architecture.

Prague kept her busy, writing, attending editorial meetings, seeing friends. Her flat became a centre for her circle, and she often invited friends there to talk, discuss articles, answer the readers' letters with which she was inundated, and imagine a new world where everything old, claustrophobic and fussy would be replaced by their fresh, open style. Milena knew and collaborated with many interesting women, most of whom would write for the various newspapers and magazines with which she was associated in the following years. There was Běla Friedländerová, who had travelled to the United States to study physical education and returned with new ideas about the importance of bodily health to mental health. There was Milča Mayerová, a dancer who had studied in Germany with Rudolf Laban, a leading figure in modern dance who believed that dance connected human beings with the dance of the cosmos. Milča now had her own school of dance in Prague. Another of the circle was Marie Fantová, also known as Ma-Fa, the daughter of an architect, and a satirical journalist whose ironic style contrasted with Milena's more sentimental tones.

There was also Slávka Vondráčková, Milena's childhood friend with whom she had explored the Old Town Square Christmas fairs, who was now increasingly successful with her textile work and travelled abroad a great deal; she was a diminutive and high-spirited woman, a bisexual, who was an enthusiastic member of Devětsil and the Artěl arts and crafts group. Then of course there was Staša, now established as a journalist and translator, as well as looking after her family. She had formed a long-lasting attachment outside her marriage, to Ada (Adolf) Hoffmeister, who had trained as a lawyer but was now known as an avant-garde artist famous for his caricatures. There are happy photographs from the summer of 1925, showing Milena and Staša laughing in the countryside around Prague, in linen shifts or shirt-waisted dresses, with their hair cut in short bobs, the preferred style of any woman who thought of herself as 'modern'.

Milena loved her work, but she had a healthily wry attitude towards journalism. 'Being a journalist is a strange business, it is not a talent, it is hardly serious. Perhaps journalists are the sort of people who never learnt anything else properly – I at least was so completely hopeless at my studies that I quickly forget everything, useful and useless.'

This new life altered Milena's relationship with Schaffgotsch. In Vienna she had relied on him and he had drawn her into a new world; in Germany they had been welcomed together by mutual friends. In Prague it was different. Milena belonged; Schaffgotsch, although he found translation and journalistic work, did not. Perhaps there were political arguments; although Milena and most of her friends were left-wing, she was not amenable to a strict party line or a constrained set of views. (She seems not to have been troubled by the contradiction in having a Communist lover and writing for the conservative *Národní listy*; the rebel and the snob had long lived side by side.) While she rushed around Prague, Schaffgotsch often did not know where she was. He would wander from café to café looking for her, until some of their acquaintance nicknamed him rather cruelly 'Where's Milena?' In time they ended their relationship, although he continued to live in Prague, in an apartment in Újezd, not far from Maltézské náměstí. His own divorce, after several years of separation from his wife, came through in 1926.

Milena savoured Prague after the years away. She told her readers how much she appreciated life in Prague anew. In comparison to post-war Vienna, Prague was a city of well-being. 'We perhaps do not see it, but for visitors Prague is first a city of exquisite romantic streets of olden times, and then a town of salami, sausages, smoked meats, bacon dumplings, crisp bread and whipped cream. Nowhere else can people eat so well and so cheaply, nowhere do they eat so much.'

She loved shopping at Pan Myšák's, a large store with an ice machine, an ice-cream machine, a sugar-grinding machine and a coffee-grinding machine. Cakes of all colours, with jam and nuts and cream, were spread on the wooden counters. Little things revealed to her the life of the city, and the spirit of the age.

She enjoyed her first winter back in Prague, experiencing once again the pleasures of snow on the red roofs and the strange glow over the city cast by lights shining through the wintry dampness above the river.

> Nowhere abroad does such a light shine as over Prague. The evenings are soft and the light has an orange tinge. The whole town, even the river and the embankment and all the illuminated windows, has an orange glow ... I had not seen it for years, and when I saw it again, it seemed to me as if I had found something I had lost.... By the National Theatre the night fog is like the thick top of milk, and through the creamy crust blue and brilliant lights shine suddenly, and golden lamplight streams clear ...

As if writing herself back into the city, Milena wrote not only about the city as a whole, but about her particular corner of it. She wrote a tribute to Malá Strana, its hidden corners, its curious, roughly built houses, its flowering gardens, the sticky horse-chestnuts along the river. It was a world from her childhood, her 'first love and first happiness'. But then she had gone abroad, learnt to see other cities with other buildings, other advertisements, other light. Now Prague was no longer a fantasy refuge but the real world, of work and food and sleep. 'The town stopped being a fairy tale, emblazoned with blue mist and planes of snow, and began to be what it is: the habit of living people. Now I am living in Malá Strana. In an old building, above an arcade in a strange little crooked square, and my joy knows no bounds.' She felt a strong 'local patriotism' for her street.

But in reality Malá Strana was no paradise. People lived crowded together and there was little light or air. Milena pointed out that while there was a society for the protection of Old Prague which attended to the buildings, there was no such organisation to protect the people, to put up street lighting and repair collapsing roof tiles.

Milena was better off than some in the district. She had a cleaner. This was a mixed blessing. Her maid brought an orderly but deathly atmosphere to her two rooms, and had a habit of lining up the chairs and putting the three cushions in a row on the sofa. It was a constant battle. 'I imagine a language in which I could explain that I want everything informal. Once I said as much. Please, leave the chairs crooked. When I came home I despaired. All the chairs stood in a line, one next to the other, perfectly, geometrically crooked. She had arranged them askew!'

One of the pleasures of Prague was that Milena could at once feel at home in her little corner of Malá Strana, and feel part of a cosmopolitan European capital which attracted people from across the continent. She was particularly interested in the Russian community. There were Russians preaching the revolution and other Russians who were refugees from the revolution, happy at least still to be in a Slav country. The poet Marina Tsvetaeva, for example, came to live just outside Prague with her husband Seryozha, a white Russian in exile who was studying in Prague. (Masaryk's government was hospitable to foreign students and immigrants.) Tsvetaeva gave readings, and moved in the Czech-Russian circles, which drew people like Vladimir Nabokov who visited Prague in 1923. Traces of Prague appear in her poems, even after she left towards the end of 1925. Her stay overlapped only briefly with Milena's return to Prague, but Milena was friendly with other Russians and described one of their parties. The gathering reminded her how she had seen a production of Chekhov's *Three Sisters* at the National Theatre and thought how difficult it must be to write a three-act play where nothing happens. But at the party she saw that something was happening: life.

> When you enter a room where ten Czechs sit at tea, you have to make an effort to get anything to happen. You see clearly that everyone is trying, everyone is energetically thinking what they should say not to be boring, and somehow everyone is constrained and uneasy.... The Russians, however, sit at the table, drink tea and discuss a pale blue silk cap. The cap passes from one to the other and everyone says something about it ... I remembered that I don't understand the language and yet it seemed to me that I understood everything. I tried on the pale blue cap and it was lovely, I spoke some Czech and no one understood but I cheered up ... I felt at home.

Milena shared her generation's search for authenticity, in relations between people and in art and fashion. When Slávka returned about this time from a trip to Paris proudly wearing a showy coat with a red rose at the collar, Milena was appalled: 'Jesus Christ, what are you wearing ... and here I am striving for simple lines, we stand against all artificiality, against imitation, fakes, cheap junk.' Enraged, she tore the rose from Slávka's lapel and threw it on the stove. The gesture illustrated her rallying cry for the era, 'the way to simplicity'. This was the title of an article written in May 1926, which became the title piece of an anthology published later that year. In the article, Milena explored the contemporary creed of simplicity, a concept which could include anything from the design of a chair to a spiritual attitude. Milena's article reflects perfectly the paradox that the taste she had acquired, the simplicity favoured by Prague's bohemians, was a fairly elaborate and elite notion: 'simplicity simply is not simple'.

> Moderation is a complicated characteristic and the hardest virtue, since it requires internal certainty. However, no one is certain by nature, the beauty of certainty is conquered, earned, purchased, and it belongs above all to a conscious and proper appreciation of all values. People gain strength from certainty, and it belongs to people who learn to lose without despairing. . . . The deeper it goes, the more concentrated and dense becomes the circle of knowledge, and in the end, like a magnet, it strikes what is really natural and simple. . . . To start with, everything whirls around, like crystal dust in a slanting sunbeam. It hurts, and above all brings pain. But if you don't slacken, everything finds its level, everything in you is subject to some centrifugal force, and everything falls into place. Your heart begins to look like a simple heart . . .
>
> Whoever once learns moderation in the deepest sense of the word will never love, for example, fake pearls. But more than that, it will never even occur to them that they could love them and they will never be proud that they do not. . . . Fake pearls are a trivial matter. However, if our relations to the tiniest things are not in order, how can our relations to important things be right?

Vienna had taught Milena the hard lesson of how to lose without despairing, and now, perhaps, her own crystal dust was falling into place.

In the summer of 1926 Milena was invited to join an excursion of Mánes, the Creative Artists' Association, a group which included some of the most exciting artistic figures in Prague, and had commissioned for its headquarters the white, glass-fronted modernist building which stands on the Vltava today. The party embarked on a steamer for a river trip. The boat left the city and Hradčany behind it, passed the other rocky fortress hill of Vyšehrad, into more open country. Poplar trees lined the bank and the steamer passed the quarries of Braník, a little hilltop church and open meadows until it reached Zbraslav, a riverside village with a baroque palace. The group settled in the garden of a pub. Milena knew some of them, especially Ada Hoffmeister, Staša's lover and a member of Devětsil. Other famous names she was meeting properly for the first time included Karel Teige, the young pipe-smoking art critic, leading theoretician of Devětsil and editor of *ReD*.

Another was Jaromír Krejcar, a brilliant young architect. When he and Milena were introduced they began to talk, and did not stop. They talked about design and interior decoration and found they shared a taste for the sophisticated simplicity which was the holy grail of the Czech avant-garde. She told tales of Vienna, he of his country childhood. He was a handsome man, tall with good bones, and they were immediately attracted to each other. The day became a legend between them and among their friends. Some said they did not return to Prague that night but that Jaromír took Milena to an inn in Zbraslav. Others that they drove all the way to the Hotel Prokop in Šumava. Others that they returned on the steamboat and then went together to Maltézské náměstí. Whatever happened that day, they were soon inseparable.

Jaromír had been married before and was involved with another woman, Jarmila Fastrová, an old acquaintance of Milena's. Jarmila always said that Milena stole Jaromír from her, for which she never forgave her. But Milena claimed that the relationship was already floundering, and that she tried to effect a reconciliation between them. Whatever the truth, it seems that yet again Milena fell in love with a man at least nominally involved elsewhere.

Jaromír was a year older than Milena, the son of a forester who had died when Jaromír was a boy but bequeathed to him a deep knowledge of the countryside. Jaromír's original plan was to enter the building trade, but with the support of his mother, who bought a sweetshop in Prague, he was able to study architecture. Mother and son lived above the little shop, in Spálená street off Wenceslas Square. Jaromír, an early admirer of the work of Le Corbusier, was regarded as an excellent student. In 1922 he edited *Život* (*Life*), the first journal of modern architecture in Czechoslovakia, and was invited to join Devětsil; he became the group's leading architect. In 1923 he designed his first major building, an eight-storey reinforced concrete structure, known as the Olympia building. His brilliance and radical credentials were sealed by the friendship of Karel Teige. In 1923 Jaromír founded his own studio and he took part in the Bauhaus exhibition in Weimar in the same year. Later, he became the Bauhaus representative in Prague. Through the 1920s he designed several villas for people from Prague's artistic circles. With these buildings, he established a reputation as one of the creators of Czech modernism, committed to simple lines, blocks of space combined in a pleasing and functional way. He also had an eye for detail, carrying the line of a windowsill on round the wall to create a shelf, or building shelving into a bedhead.

Jaromír had a vision of the modern city, and in Milena he found someone to share it. She had no architectural training, but she combined a practical sense for real people's needs with an aesthetic sense. It is easy to imagine that an article she wrote in July about Prague arose from an enthusiastic conversation with Jaromír. Prague had grown, as Milena had seen during her visits from Vienna, and needed a new sense of its future, new roads, better public transport, better communications.

> The further development of Prague will require a fundamental change in the whole plan of the town, finally sorting out the stations and in future also the airports, their connection with the centre of the town, which will then no longer be a historic reservation as it is today, but the real centre of a big city.... We need to plan its development, by looking at the basic modern technical construction of a town, and – and I'm not being sentimental – at today's technical utopia. Yesterday's technical utopia has been fulfilled today – why should today's utopia not be realised tomorrow?

Milena and Jaromír were 'modern people'. 'If someone asked me who I would describe as a modern person,' Milena wrote, 'I would say it is someone who has mastered a perfectly modern technique for living. Someone for whom the telephone is as natural as his own voice and for whom swimming is as simple as walking. Comfortable and exemplary clothes are natural and fresh air is a must. A modern person uses aeroplanes and express trains without their nerves fraying from fear that they will die or lose their luggage.'

They could believe that they embodied the new age. Prague was at the crossroads of Europe, with influences coming from east and west. They went to theatre performances at the National Theatre but also attended the fringe theatres, where cabaret and nascent performance art flourished and Mayakovsky and Pirandello were the

126

latest thing. They enjoyed classical concerts but they also loved the jazz music which was sweeping into Europe from America. They were captivated by the black jazz singers who visited from New York or Paris, and Milena had a favourite record of negro spirituals. They were both good dancers and graced the floors of Prague's smoky cellar jazz clubs.

They also enjoyed excursions into the countryside with their friends. Photographs show Milena lying on the grass with her head in Staša's lap, or lazing in a flat boat among the reeds. The group clusters around a large open-topped car, with wild flowers trailed around the dashboard; or Milena and Jaromír sit at a table on the terrace of a country pub, she looking happy and even bashful, he loving.

Milena and Jaromír were an attractive couple, both tall and handsome and elegantly dressed (although Milena was not as slim as she had been). He admired her way with words, her intellectualism, she was impressed, by his charm and visual brilliance. Milena's flat soon had photographs by Jaromír on her walls and his dressing gown in her bedroom.

Milena and Jaromír belonged to the new left wing, committed to radical politics in the arts and in society. Since the war the country had been governed by and large by a 'Red-Green' coalition of Social Democrats and Agrarians. But by the middle 1920s this stability was breaking down. The left-wing parties began to quarrel more and more, about how radical to be, which other parties to work with, what form of socialism to support. Criticism of Masaryk, the guarantor of the country's political identity, intensified. Eventually the socialist divisions split the coalition; there were elections in 1925 and Prime Minister Antonín Švehla of the Agrarians formed a new governing coalition, this time excluding the left, who dubbed the new government the 'gentlemen's coalition'. (The political fissions also led the following year to some of the German parties taking a part in the government of the country.)

The exclusion of the left meant that Milena and her friends no longer belonged to a coalition that had combined readers of left-wing magazines like *ReD* or *Kmen* with readers of the conservative *Národní listy*. They were now definitely part of the opposition. But there was intense debate about what the left should be, and for Milena, Jaromír and their circle the defining question was what attitude to take towards Communism. The Czech Communist Party had been formed in 1921 by a group which split away from the Social Democrats. It was not a hardline party, and had tended to support cooperation with the democratic parties in the interests of the new state. But that was beginning to change. The inspiration of Soviet Russia, and the political polarisation across Europe as workers struggled for greater rights and the world economy came under increasing strain, gave the Communist Party new momentum. Milena had been introduced to Communism in Vienna by Schaffgotsch and she and Jaromír belonged to a circle whose artistic radicalism and internationalism brought them close to Czech Communists. But she was not interested in joining the rigid cadres of young radicals who showed a rather earnest face at their tables in the Café Metro. For now, she was a sympathiser but kept her distance from the Party.

However, there were individual Communists she did become close to. One was the journalist Julius Fučík. He was a few years younger than Milena, and had grown up in Plzeň (Pilsen), an industrial town west of Prague. He was determined from a young age to be a journalist, and soon moved to Prague where he became a literary and theatre critic. He joined the Social Democrats but when the Communist Party split away in 1921 he went with it. He was eighteen. From then on he dedicated all his energies to radical journalism, writing for various publications, not least *Rudé právo*, the Communist Party organ. (From 1927 to 1929 he was editor of *Kmen*, the magazine in which some of Milena's translations of Kafka had appeared, and in 1927 he also became editor of the Communist critical magazine *Tvorba*, along with F. X. Šalda, the most distinguished critic of the time.) Fučík was handsome, charismatic, passionate about his work, his country and its people and arts. He read widely, in Russian, French, German and English literature (especially Kipling, Wells and Shaw), but he was also a fervent champion of nineteenth-century Czech writers. Milena and Fučík had a great deal in common, from their passionate personalities to their love of Czech literature. Like Fučík, Milena saw the nineteenth-century Czech man of letters, Jan Neruda, as the father of Czech journalism. In his essays and humourous stories he used small details to tell a bigger story, as Milena liked to do. She equated journalism's eye for detail with another developing profession, photography.

> The journalist is interested in tiny details, but from these builds something important. It is not possible to leave out the photographer's

subjective opinion when the lens is pointed at the object – this is what makes a film good or bad. And it is not possible to exclude philosophy when the pen is directed at its object. . . . From attention to detail we draw attention to great things, and through love of little things we stop being petty. . . . I would almost say that the poet is a creator and the journalist a technician of words.

Fučík encouraged Milena's belief in journalism as a craft with a social purpose, and their shared work, political direction and enthusiasms soon cemented a deep friendship which developed alongside her relationship with Jaromír.

Milena's appetite for friendship was always intense, whether with men or women. Slávka Vondráčková gave this description of Milena's effect on people: 'She fixed her eyes on you, quite concentrated, as if she wanted to penetrate deep, deep inside you. As if – as she threw questions at you – she wanted to unsettle you, to make contact, to bind you. All her life she extracted people's experiences from them, and filed them in her own dictionary. She documented you.' She needed attention.

Milena and Slávka had become close since Milena's return from Vienna. They enjoyed talking about their work, the articles they might write, the people they knew in common. The friendship was intimate enough for Slávka to make some sort of declaration to Milena. Milena wrote to Slávka:

I do not know how it is with you, Sláva, I don't know whether you loved me and I don't know what love between women is, although once I perhaps understood it, it was too late, and even if I had understood it earlier, I perhaps could not have done anything different, because I really do not understand it. Somehow I am passionate only for myself, and I would terribly like to find someone who could unbind the ability for passion in me, and lead me to act, so that I would suddenly know how to bear it. Perhaps men do not know how, perhaps I am not brave enough, I don't know anything, God, really I sometimes know nothing . . . before you, I simply know nothing, I am confused and I lose certainty . . .'

It is a strange letter which hints at a great deal. On the one hand Milena's own sense of sexual ambivalence, an awareness that passion of one sort or another was as much part of her relationships with women as with men. On the other, a sense of unfulfilment, as if her relationship with Ernst, perhaps even with Jaromír, had not brought her everything she desired. It suggests something withdrawn, a parallel with the reserve which people often identified in Milena. She wanted much from people and life, and believed in her right to demand and to give; but she never quite found what she was looking for.

In typical fashion, this emotional letter moves on to more practical matters, and she asks Slávka for a loan. 'We have debts and I don't have enough for them. There is the office and rent and Bauhaus, and Jaromír is starting out and money does not flow in. I, however, am not able to earn from the newspapers more than what goes on housekeeping and a few absolutely necessary rags and instalments for the furniture and office – simply, I need help.'

Milena was finding that even being a well-known journalist did not bring riches. But she did her best. She was involved in helping edit a series of books, Žena (Woman), for Topič; and she gathered together some of her articles for an anthology, *The Way to Simplicity*, also for Topič.

Several articles were from her Vienna days, but the end piece seems to have been written for the collection. 'The Curse of Excellent Qualities' describes Kafka, although without naming him. 'I think that the best person I knew was a foreigner, whom I often met.' She described his modesty, his humility. 'Later I realised that he is the most remarkable man I ever met, and nothing so changed my life as the little glimpse into his heart. . . . He was too good for this world and I am not afraid of the phrase, it stands true.' She referred again, rather sentimentally, to the story about his agonised childhood experience with the beggarwoman. Milena had not forgotten Kafka.

But her Prague now bore little relation to the Prague of Kafka. Few of her friends knew much about him as a writer, and even less of their affair. Once when Slávka was visiting, Milena came across some of her letters from Kafka and started talking about him; Slávka soon got bored. The darker Prague, whose shadows contained Kafka's – and Milena's – fear, seemed to have faded.

She dedicated *The Way to Simplicity* to her 'Dear Father,' an acknowledgement of their reconciliation. She had finally been accepted back into her father's city. But her new life and new friends made contact with her father's world harder to sustain. She was writing less for *Národní listy* and she wanted a broader canvas. In the autumn of 1926 she and Staša and other friends began to plan a new magazine, which would embody their vision of the new world, *Pestrý týden* (*The Motley Weekly*). Staša was the editor, backed by Milena, Ada Hoffmeister and the cartoonist V. H. Brunner, a former member of Artěl, a serious and gentle man of an older generation who became a great friend.

Pestrý týden is reminiscent of the American magazines which Milena so enjoyed, full of the world in all its variety. The team threw themselves into the task of filling the large pages with articles, columns, photographs and illustrations. Their friends were called on to contribute. The first edition came out on 2 November 1926. The front cover was a montage of photographs from the celebrations of Independence Day on 28 October, with President Masaryk prominent. The magazine declared its hand as a proud organ of the First Republic and its social and democratic ideals. Inside were poems by Vítězslav Nezval, photographs of life in Central Africa, cartoons by Josef Lada, photographs of sportswomen accompanying an article by Běla Friedländerová. Ma-Fa contributed a piece about whether men and women can be friends, concluding that they can although they are different creatures. Milena wrote an article about the need for women to demand more of themselves, as men do, to strive for their own sake if they are to succeed in the battle for equality. 'Women, however, usually only measure themselves against others.'

The magazine was soon in full swing. The 1927 New Year edition, for example, carried a cover photograph of two mountaineers on an icy peak. Inside were an article by Karel Teige giving an introduction to Bauhaus; a cartoon by Ada Hoffmeister showing a man causing a car accident as he stands in the street absorbed in his copy of *Pestrý týden*; an article by Jaromír about the time-saving and hygienic advantages of a modern bathroom, with photographs of white baths and gleaming boilers.

Further editions reveal more about the interests and Utopian spirit of the age. Slávka wrote about oriental textiles. Milena's friend from Vienna, Gina Kaus, wrote about childcare, and erotic freedom, Willy Haas wrote from Berlin about films. There were reports on the fighting between revolutionaries and nationalists in China, on Hollywood, the Russian shipbuilding industry, George Bernard Shaw, Harley Davidson motorbikes, peasant life in Slovakia, how to furnish a small flat, callisthenics: a litany of the interests of the young left-wing avant-garde. Milena wrote occasional pieces, on how kitchen appliances were making the lives of working women easier; on the growth of Prague; on the value of friendship and how the older you become, the harder it is to make friends. But she was kept occupied commissioning articles for each week's edition. She proved an energetic and political newspaper animal, wooing, pleading, manipulating articles out of people; she hated to be defeated.

Milena and Jaromír's relationship flourished in this active, creative climate. Jaromír too was working hard. In 1927 he was commissioned to reconstruct the Odeon publishing house, and his design for the Olympia building was finally completed. He was well known now for his modernist villas, plain, perhaps with split levels on a slope, a corner balcony, a nautical feel. He sent contributions to exhibitions in Moscow, wrote for *ReD*, and entered the competition for a new stadium to be built above Prague. But he did not make much money, and both he and Milena freely spent whatever they had. Nonetheless, they decided to get married. The witnesses at the civil ceremony in Prague on 30 April 1927 were Ada Hoffmeister and Karel Teige. Milena's father approved; here at last was a respectable – and Czech – son-in-law.

Milena left Malá Strana. An article later that summer perhaps describes what she felt about the day she moved. 'That day a piece of your life dies. . . . When everything is happily packed, your flat, which until yesterday was a familiar, homely shelter, a refuge in moments of hunger and sleeplessness, seems like an unfriendly warehouse.' But if she was sorry to leave Maltézské náměstí, she loved her new home. No. 33 Spálená Street was a small, four-storeyed house tucked in between two taller buildings on a busy but friendly street with shops, pubs and a church. On the ground floor was Jaromír's mother's sweetshop, and in the passage behind was a set of spiral stone steps, leading up to several flats. There was a nook halfway up the stairs, just the right size for a vase of flowers. Jaromír refurbished their apartment, which looked onto the street at the front and over a little yard at the back. (The following spring Milena wrote an article lamenting the grey shabbiness of many of Prague's courtyards; why could the brick and concrete enclosures not be made into gardens?) Milena began to furnish the flat in her usual simple but colourful style. She later claimed that at a house-warming party one of the guests knelt down before her and declared, 'Many thanks, Milena, for not transforming this apartment into a model of hygiene and antisepsis.'

Spálená 33 became a well-known and well-frequented address among different groups in Prague. Milena and Jaromír managed to bring together artists, architects, journalists, conservative associates from *Národní listy* and left-wing political figures. Their Saturday evenings became famous, when they served sausages and Viennese coffee (as well as beer and red Beaujolais) to their various friends. Fučík visited, always bringing Milena flowers. Once the distinguished man of letters F. X. Šalda came; he was infirm and had to be helped up the spiral stairs. Later Jiří Weil wrote: 'In that time, when people gathered at Milena's for those Saturdays, it was beautiful, not the beauty of a picture magazine, but the beauty of life, bright and colourful.'

Not everyone liked Milena's affectionate, demanding ways. Evžen Linhart, another Devětsil architect, did not. But there were plenty of people who did, and Milena flourished. There is a description of her at this time from Marie Husníková-Kvasničková (who worked as a nursemaid for one of Milena's friends, Zdenka Wattersonová): 'beautiful blue eyes, a glorious head of wavy blonde hair, standing full of energy and grace and a smile full of life.' Milena later remembered this period as perhaps the happiest of her life.

Work was going well. Following the success of *The Way to Simplicity*, Topič published another selection of Milena's articles in 1927, *Člověk dělá šaty (The Person Makes the Clothes)*. It was a selection of Milena's lighter pieces, on what to wear when skiing, the pleasure of gossip, the value of a good dressmaker, and her enjoyment of the current fashion for light, comfortable clothes. Milena was a frequent visitor to the offices of the Topič publishing house, behind the beautiful art nouveau mosaic facade on Národní třída (formerly Ferdinand Avenue). She also contributed to a 1927 Topič anthology on the theme of travel, *Šťastnou cestu (Happy Journey)*. Ada Hoffmeister wrote the introduction, and Milena included several articles, old and new. One described the ideal suitcase, another the joys of standing in front of a travel agency and letting the posters of Greece and the bright blue sea transport her far away, another the pleasures of driving in an open sports car through the mountains, dressed properly in dust-proof overalls, tasting the spirit and freedom of the road. But perhaps the most delightful article is one celebrating a new fashion, 'The Trench-coat or ten in one'. As so often, Milena writes more than a fashion article, making of the all-weather trenchcoat a revealing cultural artefact.

> This miraculous coat has another characteristic [besides versatility], a
> sign of the simplicity of the new world: it makes it possible for a poor

man to become a gentleman. It rages against the injustice that a gentleman is measured by having ten coats or more ... America is a democratic state. When I looked at this coat, for the first time a notion of what America's democracy is coursed through my veins. America rightly recognises that among the people who do not have ten coats are many brave, talented, honest, active and physically well-groomed people who are locked in an iron cage of poverty; such people have no access to spas, hotels, theatres or society in general, because they cannot afford the high-class qualifications for entry.... America cannot provide all poor men with ten coats; so it creates a fashion which indicates riches with only one coat. Good God, how simple!

In October 1927 Milena and Jaromír visited the international architectural exhibition of housing in Stuttgart, which Milena reported on for *Národní listy*. Milena reflected first on the host country, Germany, soon to cast its shadow over Czechoslovakia. She was not impressed.:

Why is this land of such remarkable diligence, such a sense of right and wrong, so infinitely unlovable, ugly, grey and sad, despite the praise we must give it? Perhaps because nowhere else is there such a big difference between ordinary people and the elite of the nation.... None of the magic of German greatness, the range of its spirit, falls on the people: they are without song, without sadness and passion, without thought and tenderness. They are sentimental and brutal. Order stops being a gift of God if a person lives to be orderly rather than being orderly to live.

But the exhibits of modernist housing for workers were inspiring. She particularly admired Le Corbusier.

Corbusier is the pioneer of modern living, as Baudelaire is the pioneer of modern poetry. His family house is lofty, light, full of movement and rhythm with views to the outside.... There are no square rooms, walls, roofs and floors in the usual sense of these words. On the first floor the whole area of the house is dedicated to living space. Instead of walls there are windows from floor to ceiling along the height of the whole house. You are surrounded by gardens, light, infinite space. From this room steps lead to a floor which hangs over half the living room, like a balcony. You must literally imagine a balcony, whose side does not reach to the ceiling. It is just high enough to conceal a bed behind it, or a desk.... Standing in the first-floor bedroom you can lean down over the living room. All is open, all is full of space ...

The Gropius house next door is quite different, although not from a completely different world. It is more practical perhaps. Everything is logical, subtle, tasteful. The division of the inside is more normal, more sympathetic to Central Europe, its weather and conditions, more friendly . . .

From Czechoslovakia, let it be noted, there is not a single house in the exhibition. In the exhibition hall of drawings and models a little display of the best known of our modern young group cowers in the corner, sent in disorganised haste of course, even though this group competes with dignity with foreign modern architects. It is incomprehensible that we take so lightly and casually such an important opportunity, and it is even more incomprehensible that we do not have an organiser who could send representative drawings to such an important exhibition – on time.

The New Year of 1928 brought a new happiness: Milena was pregnant. She had written so many articles about children and how to bring them up, given her readers advice about maternity clothes, and expressed her view that motherhood was a fundamental fulfilment of a woman's life; her second marriage now offered her the chance to put her ideas into practice. They included some distinctly modern notions. In September 1927 she wrote an article on the ideal school for children. Given, she wrote, that many people are unsuited (either because of bad character or poverty) to parenthood, children should be entrusted to modern, hygienic and progressive schools for the whole week, where their minds and bodies would be developed under scientific tuition. 'I could write pages and pages about the advantages of bringing children up among other children, the psychological and social advantages and the benefits for the whole of their lives. They seem to me so obvious that I don't want to think that anyone today does not believe them.'

She continued to work through her pregnancy. She wrote a series of articles on the modern home, how to open up the space in an apartment, the benefits of the latest modern conveniences to a working woman, why ornate plates and cutlery are inappropriate. She was also busy with *Pestrý týden*, to which she contributed a serialisation of a detective story by Sven Elvestad. But Milena and Staša's radical approach and support for revolutionary Russia brought trouble. In the spring Milena was sacked for 'unconsidered propaganda in favour of the Soviet Union'. Staša resigned in solidarity.

In the spring, Milena and Jaromír went skiing. Milena was in the early months of her pregnancy and was an excellent, practised skier.

But it proved a foolish risk. She had an accident and broke her leg, and the couple returned to Prague. The medical history of this year is hard to disentangle. Milena was back on her feet and apparently back to normal for the later stages of the pregnancy, but the accident may have contributed to later problems. (Milena's daughter Jana later blamed her mother's problems at the birth on the broken leg, but she also claimed – incorrectly – that Milena was in bed all summer.)

Milena was soon well enough to continue writing fashion pieces for *Národní listy*, anything from two to six pieces a month until July. Several draw on earlier themes and she was clearly marking time. In the summer she and Jaromír went to Špičák, and Milena sent *Národní listy* an article about Šumava, 'the most beautiful corner of the world'. She loved it in the summer as much as in winter, with the distant views of hills and bilberries to pick. Milena wrote to Staša saying that she was healthy and active and enjoying the holiday. But then something went wrong. In her book about Milena, Margarete Buber-Neumann describes how Milena swam in an icy mountain lake, eager to prove to herself and Jaromír that she was well and in good spirits. 'Soon afterwards she was taken with chills, fevers, and a kind of paralysis.' She was rushed back to Prague, where septicaemia was diagnosed. Another account, by Slávka Vondráčková, says that Milena had ankylosis (stiffness) of the knee of gonorrheal origin. Gonorrhea was common enough; Milena could have caught it from Jaromír, who was no saint, or from one of her earlier liaisons.

Whatever the precise cause of her collapse, she was taken to hospital for the last weeks of the pregnancy and given morphine for the pain. Her father and Jaromír feared for her and the baby's life, and they spent long hours at her bedside. No other visitors were allowed, and her friends were very worried. But on 14 August 1928, after a long and difficult labour (and perhaps a Caesarian operation), Milena gave birth to a baby girl. Like her father before her, she is reported to have wanted a boy. She named the baby Jana, but from the beginning called her Honza, a nickname derived from her father's name, Jan. Jana later wrote about the labour: 'Milena spent the entire thirty-two hours wishing for a boy and gripping her thumbs for luck. Instead, I was born, apparently clenching my thumbs too. Later, Milena would often ask me who or what I had been wishing for.'

9

Motherhood

The successful outcome of the birth did not mean that Milena could go home. Her right knee was still completely stiff and the doctors were making various unsuccessful attempts to loosen it. She was often in excruciating pain and only found ease in the morphine injections she was given.

Her husband and her father argued about caring for the baby. Dr Jesenský did not trust 'that ladies' man', as he called Jaromír, and Milena too was reluctant to leave Honza with her busy husband. But she trusted her father even less, and for a while kept the baby with her in the sanatorium in Vinohrady. She later claimed that she had told her father: 'Rather than give you this child, dear Father, to make it as unhappy as you succeeded in making me, I'd have it thrown in the Vltava.' Milena's resentment of her father was still strong. But as always she could not do without him. He was very attentive in this period, dealing with the doctors and bringing specialists who would try just one more time to manipulate her knee.

News of Milena's illness spread in Prague and once visits were allowed, friends like Staša and Slávka came to see her. So too did Ernst Pollak, who, after travels abroad, was now living in Prague once more. Milena was glad to see him. But much of the time she was alone. She worried about work and money. She wrote notes or sent telephone messages to friends asking them to write articles for her column in *Národní listy* so that her position would not be usurped. One article by her, about cosmetic surgery, appeared on 28 November. It seems likely that it was something left over from before her illness.

Her worries about work are clear from a letter to Slávka in December. It is written on lined paper from an exercise book, in an eager hand with anxious underlinings.

Again you must help me. Things are in chaos at *Národní listy* and I must sort it out, I must not lose my job and I know that I must work more. I need to send them some nice things soon and you must help me. I want to start a column: women in art, work and sport . . . please deliver something which I can use early on . . . Write me an article about:

1. How you got involved in textiles.
2. What you most like about it.
3. What goal you follow . . .

I am still lying here just the same and my leg hurts just the same, progress is at a snail's pace, I can only manage to be patient with help from morphine, I feel that I'm at the bottom of something which I can't even properly see, I have forgotten what the world looks like from a vertical position. Unhappiness is not the right word, but I appear and am very low . . .

P.S. Please, ask your friend the gardener to write some answers to my three questions as well. Please. You know, as I lie here, these requests for articles are like an SOS for my job.

Slávka and others contributed something. But many of Milena's friends were reluctant to write for the non-progressive *Národní listy*, and anyway their own work and preoccupations made it impossible for them to satisfy Milena's demands. The need for money was real. Jaromír was busy, but projects went slowly and were not well paid. He diversified and put an advertisement in *ReD* offering well-designed kitchen units, chairs and lamps in Bauhaus style, but he could not pay for all Milena's care. Inevitably, Dr Jesenský contributed generously.

After some weeks in Vinohrady, Milena was moved to a sanatorium at Piešťany, in the Slovak mountains, which offered a famous mud bath treatment that her father hoped would help. Some movement returned to her knee, but Milena suffered a great deal. She later told Margarete Buber-Neumann: 'The pain was indescribable. Not only during the treatment but afterwards, without interruption, day and night. To bear it, I needed more and more morphine. Jaromír, who had to buy it for me, was in despair. I began to despise myself. Where was my character? What had become of me?'

Jaromír's visits from Prague were increasingly uncomfortable. Milena's pain, and the veil of morphine behind which she hid, put a great distance between them. They would sit out on the terrace of the sanatorium, with the hills behind them and Jaromír's hat resting on the table between them. Milena wore a white blouse with an open collar, a pleated skirt and a hat low over her brow. A walking stick was propped by her wicker chair. She was no longer the energetic, free-spirited creature he had married.

Even at a distance Milena tried to fulfil her wifely duties. She worried about the apartment, which they had still not finished furnishing. She wrote to Slávka asking her to visit the apartment and see what was needed in the way of curtains and carpets, and what the room for the baby needed. She instructed her to send fabric samples and then get things made, but not at great expense.

As her strength returned, Milena was able to fill some of the time writing articles again. At Christmas she was saddened to hear of the death of the artist V. H. Brunner, her old friend from *Pestrý týden*, and she wrote obituaries of him for two magazines. She mourned him as a good Czech, a man with a 'beautiful heart'. She turned to other articles, and after several months her name at last appeared in *Národní listy* again.

She wrote a review of a book of modern photography, praising the art form; a means to see the world anew. She also gave a wry account of her recent experience of being reduced, as a patient, to nothing but a number. She had become 'number 20' rather than Milena, or at best 'she'. 'Two lads carried me on a stretcher up some steep steps and shouted at each other: "Go carefully – it won't do her much good if you drop her!"'

She also turned to the 'women's question' again, joining a rather pompous debate in the paper about whether men or women were responsible for a perceived 'moral decline'. Claiming to be no 'expert', Milena declared that generalisations were inappropriate; there were good and bad men and women. But there were nonetheless differences in power and responsibility. The current laws on equal rights and marriage, for example, were inadequate, and double standards applied to the conduct of men and women. But women enjoyed much more freedom than their mothers and grandmothers. They could not have it both ways, demanding (and beginning to get) equality but still looking to men and marriage for protection.

The article provoked critical letters from readers to which she replied the following Sunday. Relationships should be founded on love, not financial convenience. 'A man who stopped loving me and wanted to leave would not offend me. I would be more offended by a man who stopped loving me and wanted to stay. I am not afraid of being deserted, the only thing I fear is being judged as weak, wretched, incapable of standing alone. In this way I defend women. ... Man does not exist to defend and protect woman and woman does not exist to be defended and protected.' As in her articles about marriage written at the time of her separation from Ernst, Milena maintained that divorce often left a more painful legacy for women than men, and that many ordinary women were not in a position to support themselves. But her idealistic belief that marriage must rest on love, while causing much pain when the foundations crumbled, gave her a true strength to stand alone and remain friends with her former partners, rather than cling to an unhappy relationship. She would need this strength again.

Despite these few articles, Milena's connection with *Národní listy* was withering. She was not able to contribute her best, and she had become uncomfortably radical for the paper. Already in 1928 she told the editor of one left-wing paper that she found *Národní listy's* nationalism 'unbearable'. Now she made efforts to develop other outlets. She contacted the respected *Lidové noviny* newspaper, more liberal than *Národní listy*, and was invited to submit articles. The editor was the esteemed First Republic intellectual Ferdinand Peroutka, who regarded Milena as a talented, spirited journalist; he would prove an indispensable ally in future years. (Her connection with the paper also renewed her acquaintance with Karel Čapek, whom she had known during the war. He was more famous than ever since the worldwide success of his play about robots, *R.U.R.*, in the early 1920s. He was a friend of Masaryk and a stalwart of the paper.) Milena was soon asked to edit as well as write for the Home–Fashion–Society page, work which she began from the sanatorium, bombarding her friends yet again for help.

In June 1929 she pursued Slávka in England, where she was staying with Mica Weatherall, a Czech who had married a teacher at Eton College. Milena knew that Mica had literary connections with people like Stephen Spender and Rosamond Lehmann. After dealing with money matters with Slávka, perhaps left over from the flat furnishing, she asked her to lobby Mica for help.

> You are right that I have many rich acquaintances, but I am in debt to them all and we have a dreadful time trying to find money to pay for my treatment here ...
>
> The main thing is for Mica to write. I need clever articles. She can write about whatever she wants, as long as it has something to do with women ...

Motherhood

> I'm still in pain, terrible, agonising pain, but I think there's hope. It wouldn't bother me at all to have a stiff leg. But they don't want to leave it alone and they make me exercise it. Certainly I will be glad if they succeed.

Eventually, after nearly a year, the doctors decided there was nothing more to be done. They had restored some movement to Milena's knee but she would have to resign herself to being lame for ever. In late summer 1929 she returned to Spálená Street. She was at first fairly immobile, dependent on crutches, and otherwise spending a great deal of time on the big sofa in her room reading detective stories. She had put on weight and her strong-boned face had become puffy. She looked more and more like her father with his heavy brow and dimpled chin. Her return did not make things easier with Jaromír. She felt ashamed and anxious; Jaromír, like Ernst, enjoyed the company of beautiful women.

There are few clues about Milena's initial feelings towards her baby. From the start she employed maids and nannies to help care for Honza. She must have felt a mixture of love and resentment at the child's arrival coincident with so much pain. Her sentimental attachment to the idea of motherhood as the most natural fulfilment for a woman was severely challenged.

As always she turned to work to carry her through. It was at once an absolute financial necessity and a vital source of self-respect. She was not mobile enough to wander the city or do much research, so her articles for *Lidové noviny* at first tended towards the personal or developed old themes. An early piece considered café life, this time with more sympathy than in Vienna, perhaps a reflection of longing, now that she was unable to go out much. She described an archetypal tale of a young man who turns away from home and his mother's love, to sit in cafés with his friends and dream about the future. 'The café table marks the start of the night, which seems a waste of time from the mother's old-fashioned point of view. In fact, these nights are full of work, full of important conversations and debates, full of exciting contact with the world.' This world does not last. The boy grows up, finds a job and gets married. This is real life.

> Life where work is not about promise and stimulation, but labour and wages, where money is not something to be sweetly lost, but something to pay taxes with, where free time is like a will o' the wisp, ever in the future, never present. . . . Life is not serious, it is only wearying

and full of dull cares. The light-heartedness of youth is one of the few serious things in life. But people only realise that when they lose it.

It must have seemed to Milena as if she had lost all her light-heartedness. This article was followed by another in which she explored the importance and the scarcity of unconditional love. Both partners in a couple are like 'fragile glass', and it takes a great deal of strength and generosity to preserve the relationship from fatal disruption from outside: 'As soon as the relationship is invaded by anything which it is not possible to speak about, it loses honesty and therefore viability. This is the chemical process of love, jealousy, secret battles and uncontrolled nerves.' Milena's relationship with Jaromír was like fragile glass. She was often alone at home, and the money worries continued. It seemed to Slávka, who would visit and sometimes encourage her to go out more, that she lived only for the child.

Milena wrote an article about her family life at this time, and revealed, perhaps unwittingly, her painful receptivity to nuances of feeling in herself and those close to her. The article was about Honza, now more than a year old, and her love for the three most important people in her life – Milena, Jaromír and the maid, Jája. Jája, whose full name was Marie Pěničková, was an efficient young blonde woman from Moravia, 'unsentimental and precise', who looked after Honza. She wore a blue striped dress with a white apron and cap, and got Honza up in the morning and fed her. 'Between Jája and Honza there is an almost instinctive understanding. To say that Honza loves Jája is an understatement. . . . Her love for Jája is like the air she breathes, the cereal she eats, something eternal and omnipresent, enduring, unbreakable, firm and trustworthy.'

But as Honza's horizons grow, another creature comes into view: her mother, Milena.

> If Jája stands at one end of the room and Mama at the other, Honza is always confused about who she wants to go to. In the end she lifts up her arms and runs to her mother with a little cry, which reveals her brief internal struggle. But Mama's hands are quite different from Jája's. Above all, they are a source of entertainment. As soon as Honza arrives, Mama can find some game, perhaps with her fingers, or with a shoelace, a book, the telephone, a dictionary. She can make Honza laugh until she almost chokes with unpractised little giggles.

Milena relished Honza's bedtime.

Motherhood

When Honza goes to bed, she cannot sleep until Mama comes to say goodnight. These moments after dark by Honza's little bed are the time when the power of the mother's magic wand over Honza's heart is clearly visible. Perhaps Honza vaguely remembers the moment when she belonged completely to her mother's body and when her mother's breath and blood were her breath and blood.

But Honza has another love too, for her father.

Daddy is something rare, he seldom comes into her room, he is rarely at home in the hours when Honza is awake. He usually goes into Honza's room when Honza cries. But as soon as Daddy comes, everything is fine . . .

If Mama is amusing company, Papa is a comrade in adventure. Daddy is a rascal, he sprinkles Honza with little drops of water, he ruffles her hair, he blows smoke up her nose and Honza loves all this mischief. . . . When he telephones, Honza presses the receiver to her face and shouts into it: 'Hello, daddy, papa, ata, ada, tata, child water shoe.' This is the longest sentence Honza knows, a mark of the greatest respect.

On one level the article is a charming description of family life. But there is a nervous thread. It reveals Milena's early detachment from her child as, like many women of her class, she left her to another's care. This distance can only have been exacerbated by her illness and her continuing reliance on morphine. The three adults love the child, but are separate from each other. Jaromír is portrayed as absent, involved with Honza but not with Milena.

Milena's awareness of the mixed blessings of motherhood, the delights and dilemmas of being a woman, also lies behind another article written in the same month, 'Civilised Woman?'. It is a wry look at the precarious freedoms that women had won. The new age had rejected the 'humbug' of the 1890s and a woman could now be 'civilised', sporty, economically active, clever, witty, and above all independent. 'I am not sure whether we properly realise the significance of this fact. Independence is the ability to support oneself. It means literally that dusk has fallen on an age when we gazed with sentimental pity on the prostitute, or when we sympathised with the suffering of uncomprehending women living in degrading marriages. It may be very hard, but it is now possible to support ourselves.'

But the world of fashion was taking its revenge. After several years of giving independent women independent clothes, comfortable, unrestricting outfits for work and leisure, fashion had dealt a 'pestilential blow'. 'Paris threw us a diktat of nonsensical trailing dresses, unpleasing lines, skirts short at the front and long at the back. These fashions, covered in pretty-pretty and useless trimmings, are expensive, unnecessary and ugly. They force us to a slow walk, they turn us once again into sedate matrons.' Milena watched in despair as the new styles took hold: could it be that the liberating clothes of previous years, which had seemed the external expression of a vast social change, had been after all 'only fashion'? She would continue to write about fashion but with less enthusiasm, partly because it came to seem increasingly frivolous but partly because she had lost her figure. She no longer took pleasure in finery and gradually retreated into plain, dark dresses or suits.

Although Milena's articles at this time were largely about personal matters, she was not unaware of the outside world. After a halcyon period of economic boom and political stability Czechoslovakia, like the rest of Europe, was beginning to be affected by the looming world economic crisis. In 1929 there was a miners' strike in the north of the country. Milena was back on her feet by now, although sometimes leaning on a stick, and she helped to organise holidays in Prague for the miners' children, 'distributing' them from the railway station to her friends, including Staša. The strike was bitter, and the government and the police became increasingly repressive. Solidarity meetings in Prague were broken up, and press coverage watched and censored. The government had since 1923 had resort to a Law for the Protection of the Republic, which was used to censor anything regarded as undermining the country. It would later be used against fascists (small groups of whom were beginning to emerge in Czechoslovakia), but at this stage the main targets were Communists. Julius Fučík set up an underground paper to cover the strike. Milena was beginning to be part of a world regarded as subversive, a world of illegality, confiscated identity documents, a world prepared to go underground. Elections at the end of 1929 reflected the growing economic and political tensions, and the Social Democrats made a comeback.

Although Milena worked hard for *Lidové noviny*, she never gained the pre-eminence that she had enjoyed on *Národní listy*, in part because the paper had other established women columnists, including Milena's acquaintance, Ma-Fa, a highly intelligent and popular journalist. In June 1930 Milena stopped writing for the paper. There are suggestions that she was sacked when she wrote, anonymously,

Motherhood

some frank articles about drug abuse. But it may have been because she had simply lost some of her inventiveness and nerve. Her attempts to build a new life after the illness were proving precarious.

She retreated for the summer to the village of Dobřichovice on a tributary of the Vltava outside Prague, with Honza and Jája. She kept the morphine tablets on which she was dependent in the laundry cupboard, and told Slávka that without them, 'Life is terribly hard, it is unbearable.' With them, life still meant mood swings and depression, and in July 1930 she returned to the clinic at Veleslavín for two weeks.

There is very little concrete evidence about her activities in the following months. There are hardly any published articles; having lost her job on *Lidové noviny* and become too radical for the mainstream and liberal press, Milena would need time to build up her position as a journalist again.

One consolation was a summer holiday in July 1931 on the Belgian coast, at La Panne, a small town just across the border from France. Milena and Staša took their children and a maid, and Milena was accompanied by a young architect she knew through Jaromír. They cycled around the countryside, sunbathed on the beach and swam. Milena wore loose trousers and a T-shirt, or her swimsuit. While the children built sandcastles, the adults discussed the political situation in Europe and their shared interest in Communism. It would be Milena's last real holiday abroad.

Back in Prague, Jaromír had prepared a new home for the family. He had been commissioned to build a large apartment block at 4 Francouzská Street, in Vinohrady, and he reserved the top-floor apartment for himself. The family moved in, probably in 1931 (they were certainly there by 1932). The flat was wonderful, high up and looking down over a large square with a church onto the city. It was distinguished by a long balcony which ran the length of the apartment. Behind the main room, which opened onto the balcony, was a corridor with smaller rooms including, naturally, a spick and span bathroom. Milena gradually filled the terrace with great flowerpots of shrubs and even small trees, and smaller pots and baskets of flowers. The terrace became known as Milena's hanging gardens. It provided room for a sandpit for Honza, and somewhere for Milena's several cats to play.

From Jája's perspective the household was an erratic one. The flat was chaotic, and when a visit from Dr Jesenský was threatened,

Milena would bustle round and chivvy Jája into tidying up. At times the money ran out and then Milena would send Jája to Dr Jesenský's clinic to borrow more. If there was money, Milena and Jaromír simply spent it; one friend recalled how he happened to be visiting when Milena came across a large banknote forgotten in Jaromír's coat, and promptly took everyone out for dinner. Milena and Jaromír filled the Francouská flat, as they had filled the Spálená apartment, with friends and visitors, perhaps as a distraction from their own halting relationship. Their popular Saturday gatherings resumed, but their flavour was increasingly political. Staša and Slávka were there, but some of Milena's other friends from the days of her return to Prague, for instance Wilma Löwenbach, who had not joined in the group's move leftwards, were no longer included.

With Jaromír often busy elsewhere, Milena's friendship with Fučík (now editor of the Communist paper *Rudé právo*) deepened and they embarked on an affair. He would arrive at the flat with a huge bunch of flowers and Milena would send Jája and Honza off for a walk on Petřín Hill. They were a dynamic couple. Milena's health and moods varied, but although she would never recover her former slender self, her strength and confidence were returning and she was a match for the charismatic Fučík.

Her intimacy with a leading Communist was matched by her connections with the party itself. She attended mass meetings and demonstrations, and hosted small left-wing gatherings at the new flat. A snapshot of her involvement is visible at the end of a notice in *Rudé Právo* in the summer of 1932 about an anti-fascist conference of workers, where Milena is listed as a contact address.

But it was not all work. The avant-garde of politics was matched by a cultural avant-garde which flourished in an atmosphere that, while not entirely uncensored, was freer than in most surrounding countries. Milena enjoyed visits to the radical theatre of E. F. Burian, or the cabaret act of Voskovec and Werich. (She once, in jest, threw eggs at them for an anti-Communist jibe.) Sometimes when Slávka arrived early for a meeting at Francouzská, Milena played records, of tangos or songs like 'It's a long way to Tipperary'.

And she continued to enjoy the cinema. Staša's young daughters, Olga and Staša, recalled how Milena took them to see all the Eisenstein films: *Strike* and *The Battleship Potemkin* (both released in 1925), and his account of the Russian Revolution, *October – Ten Days that Shook the World*, which was released in 1928, revolutionary in its story and its cinematic technique. She even took them to a Sunday morning showing of a Russian film about the orphans of the revolution; in the foyer, Milena was greeted by the Soviet ambassador. This was all part of their Communist education. Milena once visited the family with Julius Fučík. Staša recalled how she and her sister greeted him: 'Good day, Sir.' Milena corrected them: 'This is Julius Fučík and you do not say Good day, Sir to him, but Honour to Labour, Comrade!' They also remembered sitting with Honza when she was a toddler, entertaining each other with copies of left-wing newspapers provided by Milena.

Milena's immersion in this world brought her something as important as friends, it brought her journalistic work. The strength of the Communist Party in Czechoslovakia was reflected in its burgeoning press. There were several magazines and newspapers serving the cause, often staffed and written by the same people. Milena's connection with some of the luminaries of this world gave her new outlets.

One was the Communist cultural magazine, *Tvorba* (*Creative Work*). Julius Fučík, Záviš Kalandra and Kurt Konrad (a young Communist with whom Milena had a flirtation) were its leaders, and other friends of Milena's wrote for it. Milena began to contribute to the paper, reporting on the effects of the Depression. The collapse of international trade had devasted Czechoslovakia's economic base, and unemployment rocketed (to well over a million out of a population of about fourteen million by the winter of 1932-33). There were strikes, lockouts and clashes between workers and police which resulted in twenty-nine deaths between 1930 and 1933. The political struggle between the left and the liberals intensified. In the severe winter of 1932-33 Milena used the pages of *Tvorba* for a battle with her old boss at *Lidové noviny*, Ferdinand Peroutka, now at the prestigious liberal weekly *Přítomnost* (*The Present*). He was an acerbic critic of Communism, and in an open letter to one of the paper's other senior figures Milena showed how far she had moved from the liberal position, in her new identification with the Communist cause.

Dear Mr Kocourek
I spoke some time ago with Mr Peroutka about the conditions in which the unemployed live, even the unemployed in Prague; I spoke to him about rock dwellings and leaky cellar rooms, about mouldy wooden huts, about the holes in which mothers and children live – he

could not believe his ears! And I offered to show him or anyone from
the editorial team of *Přítomnost* the human burrows...

She wrote that she had accompanied Mr Kocourek to the rock
slums on the edge of the city, but that she had been appalled by the
articles in *Přítomnost* which followed, describing the terrible conditions but also focusing on the fact that 'help came' from the
newspaper's readers.

Help came in the form of 'financial and material gifts from Prague and
beyond', and in the name of *Přítomnost* you thank the donors and
propose organising a private society, to be headed by some distinguished person, such as Karel Čapek, under the auspices of *Přítomnost*. You go even further, Sir; you will get a photojournalist to
photograph a human lair of stone in Prague with some lucky woman
receiving your charity in front of the 'doors' of this home, and you are
so crude and you have such a rough heart that you will stand this
woman in the cold, with her children in her arms, in front of the bare
dwelling in the rock, to smile into the camera with joy at the 'help
from rich people who still have a conscience': ... clearly things are not
so bad.

I know already, Sir, what you will reply. You will reply that a little
help is better than none, that these are human, not political matters.
You will tell me that this is why you are not a Communist, because
you are annoyed by the way Communists 'agitate with poverty' and
use it politically.... No hole in the rock, no child in a pigsty, no sight
of ragged, hungry and sick people will force you to feel shame. Not
even the huge unemployment figures which you hear every day on the
radio will persuade you to realise that to feel and act charitably is
beautiful perhaps, but a completely private thing; it is simply insuf-
ficient for the help for which the workers' movement struggles.

She defended by contrast the work of radical journalists.

You claim that red journalists agitate with poverty. In reality red
journalists work from morning to night to prepare a way out of poverty
and to stop the capitalist system making the oppressed people evaluate
charity as help, but instead demand their rights ... As a red journalist
you would have 1,400 crowns a month, work morning to night, and
within a week you would lose your sentimental attitude to help,
because you would see how it *doesn't* come.

Kocourek did not let the charges go. A following issue of *Tvorba*
carried both his reply and Milena's riposte to it. As Milena had

Motherhood

predicted, he said that the left-wing press used such topics for political agitation, while the article in *Přítomnost* had drawn sympathy and help from the readers, from offers of rooms and medical help to money and shoes.

> Should I refuse the thousands of crowns which readers of *Přítomnost* sent, simply because it is 'alms', or because someone could throw the discredited word 'charity' at it? ... Should I help the poor to keep their heads above water, and so further the continuance of the capitalist system, or should I leave the poor to their poverty, and perhaps even sharpen it, to encourage people to throw off their proletarian humility and catholic education, and storm against further sacrifice?

He defended himself against the charge of naivety, and agreed that the situation had arisen from bad and unjust economic organisation, 'of which Marxism and Russia are good critics'. But given that there was no guarantee that neglecting poverty would lead to revolution, help must be given. Finally he defended himself as an independent, even socialist journalist, but not a 'red journalist' with a cause. Milena's reply concentrated on his point about the best way to treat poverty with regard to revolution. She did not deny his or the donors' concern. But:

> Human love is like some white flower, growing in hotbeds of stinking dung. Mr Petschek [an industrialist] for example certainly gives a lot of money to the unemployed, even though he was previously prepared to sack them. He evaded his duty to employ his workers, yet he gives charitably to the sacked men. Is it not cheaper to be charitable? This is the logic behind bourgeois charity. If you go to the root of the matter, you always find that bourgeois charity is a matter of money. It would cost much more not to be charitable, and besides, it would not have the glory of service.

Milena had become a fervent polemicist for the revolutionary cause.

What is not clear is whether Milena's close ties to the Communist Party led to her becoming an actual member. There is no official record of her membership and some of those who knew her say that she was not the joining sort. But given the newspapers she was beginning to work for and the people she consorted with, it seems highly likely that she was a member. Margarete Buber-Neumann certainly believed so. Whether Milena was technically a member or not, she became increasingly close to the party and its activities. Buber-Neumann writes that Milena told her that her illness had made her think; that she had shed her old superficial habits and wanted to work to build a better world. It is true that Milena's life and writing is shorn of any frivolity in this period, but the notion that she had previously been nothing but a gadabout does not ring true. Her social and political concern had long been there, founded on her humanist instincts. What was new, no doubt influenced by her illness, was the resort to a clear political programme, a secular creed, a mission. The Communist Party, in its indignation at social injustice and its concern about events abroad, was a natural harbour for people like Milena and her friends.

Milena was watching events over the border in Germany keenly. The European Depression had contributed to the rise of Adolf Hitler, and the left wing in Czechoslovakia was increasingly alert to his presence. Hitler's Nazi party had done well in the 1930 elections, becoming the second largest party in the Reichstag, and in the 1932 elections it became the biggest. In January 1933 the leadership of the Weimar Republic capitulated and handed the chancellorship to Hitler. In Czechoslovakia, with its substantial German minority, alarm bells sounded. What was the proper response? Milena, again in *Tvorba*, argued once more against the approach of concerned liberals like Peroutka, who had written appealing for a united front against fascism.

'Only a strong and united democracy can defend us,' appeals Mr Peroutka. That's clear.

The question is, who does today's democracy defend and who does it give freedom to? Workers know: not them. A democracy which trails a million unemployed and three million hungry, a democracy which sends the police in on striking workers fighting against falling wages, a democracy in which the representative of the League of Human Rights is not allowed to talk about fascist terror, a democracy which imprisons people for high treason if they protest against war – that's not democracy. It's only a protector of capital, a capitalist democracy . . .

A capitalist democracy shows endlessly how undemocratic, how belligerent, how dictatorial it is. Hitler would never have come to power in Germany if his rise had not been 50 per cent a legal rise. If he had not been installed by capital, nationalism, the police and, yes, a capitalist democracy, which is like 'a door into the room' of fascism.

Peroutka was wrong to say that the left wanted to defend freedom with dictatorship. 'Wrong. Their programme is to replace a capitalist democracy with a socialist democracy . . . the socialist democracy which will eventually come, fighting for the freedom of workers, that is, most people.

'This front we want.'

As well as writing for *Tvorba*, and for a while editing it, Milena was also on the editorial board of *Žijeme* (*We Live*), a non-political magazine published by the Union of Czechoslovak Crafts (Svaz Československého díla). As before, she rallied her friends and acquaintances for contributions – Karel Teige, Ada Hoffmeister, Slávka Vondráčková. She herself wrote about more personal things, but not without injecting a political message. She described the daily life of a secretary, afraid to have a child because of the expense, or wrote about the life of a 'liberal capitalist'. One of her articles is on a favourite theme, childcare, taking her previous suggestion of communal childcare to a logical if disturbing conclusion. In 'Is it possible to bring up a child well at home?' she evaded the 'huge question' of whether the mother is the ideal carer of a child. The main thing is to ensure that a child's physical, intellectual and social needs are met, and the parents may not be the best guarantee.

> And now, imagine a large and spacious house, full of light, clean, orderly and tidy. Somewhere outside the town or at least in the middle of a garden. A house where we could take the child in the morning and collect it in the evening. Or, once a week on a free day, it would belong to us. A world of children, where children would live with one another. With their own concerns, their own mentality. Under the care of educated and capable people. Under the care of good doctors and good teachers. Away from all the troubles of home, the sensitivities and emotions, the poverty or even the luxury, away from things which don't serve children. It is possible that there are still women who would regard such an institution as a cruel arrangement which steals their children from them. But how many hundreds of others, how many thousands, how many millions, would welcome such a place as the saving of their children?

The article, as well as demonstrating Milena's enthusiasm for current radical left-wing ideas (such institutions existed in the Soviet Union), perhaps also indicates her ambivalence about her own position as mother. She loved Honza intensely, but seems almost puzzled by her new role. Her attitude to childcare was erratic. She left Honza to maids and nannies, but when the child contracted scarlet fever she insisted on nursing her herself; her own experiences had left her with a strong antipathy to doctors and hospitals. She had her daughter's hair cut very short and dressed her in plain jumpers and shorts (some of which she knitted herself), almost like a boy, as if the practicalities of caring for a little girl should be minimised.

Articles like the one on childcare eventually became too much for the Union of Czechoslovak Crafts, who felt she was using their non-political organ to preach her own message. Yet again she lost her job. But her views on how to bring up children were never pure ideology. When a chance came to prove her loyalty to Soviet ideas on childcare, Milena baulked. During a visit to Moscow, which he wrote about in *Tvorba* at the end of June 1933, Jaromír was commissioned to build a convalescent home for workers and party functionaries in Kislovodsk in the Caucasus. He and Milena discussed whether she should accompany him, which would have allowed them to educate Honza in the Soviet Union. They were not alone in regarding non-Soviet Europe as an increasingly corrupt and dangerous place to be, especially given events in Germany. Other architects, including Le Corbusier, had visited the Soviet Union to help build a better life, and Jaromír, who needed work, was keen to go.

In the end, however, Milena decided to stay behind in Prague. This decision reveals her renegade views (which would emerge more fully later), as well as the strength of her attachment to Prague – her instinct, this time, to stay at home and keep her child there too. It was also a reflection of her failing relationship with Jaromír.

With Jaromír away, Milena threw herself even harder into her journalistic work, running between home and the offices of the various publications for which she worked. She joined an earnest Communist photo-journal, *Svět práce* (*The World of Labour*), which was launched in the spring of 1933. Dutifully, she wrote about the sombre side of things which, earlier, she had seen in a more romantic light, motherhood again for example, or her beloved Malá Strana. She described some of its beauties and its popularity with tourists. But in fact the old and crowded quarter was a breeding ground of poverty, prostitution and disease, with tuberculosis and other illness caused by bad housing.

> It is a poor quarter, hopelessly ugly, beautiful only to those who can cause misery but can't bear to look at it, who need to hide the hardship of poverty behind a romantic veil, who need for their own peace of mind to see poverty as good-humoured and picturesque . . .
>
> There is only one country today which looks to the future and the present instead of the past – the Soviet Union. There gradually they

are putting history where it belongs: in museums. No one goes to look at it. Instead of musty relics, the Soviet Union can show the magnificent constructions of the most modern technical progress. Instead of crooked streets, workers' modern quarters. Instead of dreamy gardens, great green areas, accessible to all. Instead of decorated poverty, the sober, clear-cut reality of today.

Milena later told Margarete Buber-Neumann how her phase as a Communist journalist destroyed her writing and turned her into a manufacturer of slogans. Certainly, these articles are dreary compared to her previous (and later) writing, and the constant praise of the Soviet Union feels in part dutiful. But the work did not completely destroy her spirit. Her eye for atmosphere and detail remained, and the dreamy gardens refused to be completely eradicated.

Her flat became a forum for party discussions, informally or at more formal meetings. When Bohumír Šmeral, one of the founders of the Czechoslovak Communist Party and a moderate, returned from a visit to the USSR, he encouraged a gathering at Francouzská to organise and fight for the revolution. In particular he imparted his knowledge about life underground and gave his audience ideas about how to run an underground press. These lessons would prove useful later on. Milena also offered the flat as a refuge for people on the run, even hiding the more hardline Klement Gottwald, who later became Communist Party Secretary, Prime Minister and President of post-World War II Czechoslovakia. She paid the price for her open identification with the party, and lost her passport.

But the party was not unified, and arguments about the way forward turned into bitter divisions. Some argued that the threat of fascism required ever tighter party discipline, others, including Milena (like her heroine Rosa Luxemburg), were disturbed by the cruder, more dictatorial elements in the party who followed Moscow blindly. In his autobiography the writer Fritz Beer, then a young man, describes the factionalism and intrigue in the party (and also reveals something of Milena's impulsive intensity). He was an admirer of Milena's and was present at several private, frank discussions about the shortcomings of the party. Somewhat foolishly, he let slip traces of these conversations to party functionaries. ' "If you can't keep quiet," Milena said, "then *we* can't speak openly in front of you." ' Fritz wanted to make amends; he tried to undermine the credibility of a real traitor to their cause by denouncing him to a party official as an active member of the opposition. Milena was furious.

She would not have him countering the party's dirty tactics with more dirt. As quickly as she had befriended Fritz, she broke off with him. Fritz defended himself in a letter, in which he apologised, accused Milena of pride and intolerance, and regretted the loss of their friendship. He heard nothing in reply.

Fritz Beer continued to admire Milena as a woman of intelligence and integrity who, in her relationships, could be 'honest to the point of self-destruction'. As a sensitive person who had faced difficulties in her life, she protected herself behind a hard shield. But behind the carapace was a woman who took every friendship seriously, 'an eternal romantic'. It was as if she was searching for something, some intimacy, immersing herself in one intense friendship after another (often with younger men) in the hope of finding gratification.

Milena's life was filled with meetings, gatherings in shabby pubs in Vinohrady, manifestos, magazines, the language of class struggle. There were associations in Prague for every conceivable subgroup – doctors, journalists, artists, and of course women's groups, such as the Ženský Klub (Women's Club), or Syndikát ženské pracující inteligence (The Syndicate of Women Working as Intelligentsia). There is no sign that Milena was a formal member of any of these, but she was close to women who were, such as Staša and Slávka, and other friends from the *Národní listy* days who had moved left, such as Milča Mayerová and Běla Friedländerová. She also got to know Jožka Jabůrková, a Communist journalist and tireless campaigner on behalf of working-class women.

Around this time Milena was asked to care for a sick member of the party who was living underground. Evžen Klinger was a Hungarian Jew from Slovakia who had been Secretary of the Slovak Communist Party. Milena knew his name from articles in *Tvorba* about the economic and political situation in Slovakia, which were often printed with bare spaces stamped 'censored'. Now he was in Prague, living in a cellar flat under another name, and like Milena working for *Svět práce*. Milena took him to a good, and discreet, doctor, who insisted that Klinger move out of his damp flat. He became Milena's lodger, and, as had happened before, her lover. Klinger was a large, bearlike man, of great intelligence and kindness. He was a few years younger than Milena, had a good sense of humour and was a popular story-teller. He was a deeply political animal but, like Milena, wary of some of the party's harshest excesses and rigidities. (In 1935, the authorities in Prague stopped regarding him as suspect.)

Motherhood

Their affair must have been some consolation for the news from the Soviet Union that Jaromír had fallen in love with another woman and wanted a divorce. Riva (her full name was Rebeca Hozova) was a Latvian who had been working as an interpreter. Milena accepted the need for a divorce, which finally came through on 15 October 1934. No reason is given in the note attached to the marriage certificate; who was to blame for Milena's illness and her drug dependency, her moodiness or Jaromír's wanderings? Jaromír returned to Prague with Riva as his wife in 1935, and Milena's second marriage, which had begun in such joy, was over. She and Jaromír remained friends, and not only for the sake of Honza, whom Jaromír adored.

Milena, Evžen and Honza left the luxurious Francouzská apartment, and went to an attic flat in a tiny street on the far side of Vinohrady, Horní Stromky 9. Dr Jesenský shrugged his shoulders: another Jew. After a few months they moved round the corner to a modern apartment house at Kouřimská 6. The flat's kitchen and balcony were small. The main furniture was some modern armchairs and the typewriter. Milena's mother's crucifix hung over her bed. Jája had gone.

Times were again very hard. Milena continued for a while to work for *Tvorba* and *Svět práce*, but, having lost her job at *Žijeme* because she was too left-wing, she now lost her job at *Svět práce* because she was not left-wing enough. The editor, Kopřiva, objected to her relationship with Klinger, who was regarded by an increasingly hardline party as a Trotskyite. After a row about the matter, Milena is said to have slapped Kopřiva in the face, slammed the door and never returned.

Milena's disenchantment with the party grew. Jaromír returned from the Soviet Union not only with a new wife, but also with enormous scepticism about the way of life there, the pettiness and corruption of the party apparatus, the failing economic model and the suppression of citizens' rights. Milena and Evžen listened sympathetically and drew their own conclusions. This lost them many friends among those who regarded any questioning of the Soviet way of life as treachery. Fučík had himself left for an eighteen month stay in the Soviet Union in 1934 and would remain loyal to the party. Milena's relationship with her childhood friend Staša was damaged by their diverging political attitudes. With Staša's daughters, Milena now tried to persuade them against Communism as fervently as she had once preached in its favour. A few others who were regarded as renegades by the party, such as the doyen of Prague's avant-garde theatre, E. F. Burian, and the journalist Stanislav Budín, provided friendship and support. But Milena and Evžen felt very much on their own.

They lost not only a community, but work. They managed to make a little money cooperating on translations of Hungarian books, Evžen sitting in his spectacles preparing a literal translation, Milena turning it into Czech. Honza later wrote a description of their enthusiasm for their work. 'Milena would literally weigh every word, turning it over and over; sometimes it would take her days to find the right one. There were times when we were lunching out somewhere – Milena hardly, if ever, cooked at home – we all three sat at the table and suddenly the word they were searching for would come to Milena or Evžen. Neither of them had to make a note of it: if it really was the word they had been hunting for, they would not forget it.' Milena also worked occasionally as technical editor on *Stavitel*, the magazine of the Architects' Association, and contributed to the women's page of *České slovo* (*The Czech Word*).

Such work brought in a pittance. Milena turned as before to her father. Every Saturday she insisted on sending the reluctant Honza to visit her grandfather, and the child would often return with a cheque. Sometimes Milena sent Honza to Ernst Pollak with requests for funds. Honza recalled her mother making the best of their poverty, sticking candles into bottles when the electricity bill could not be paid. Milena's drugs were another drain on resources. She was now using morphine-like dicodeine tablets known as 'Dicodit', available with difficulty on prescription. She loathed her dependency on the drug, and would try to wean herself off it, with wretched consequences, as Honza witnessed.

> The 'Dicodit jug' stood on the top shelf of the sideboard. It was yellow and formed part of a tea set – I think it was originally a milk jug. We all knew about it, it was part of our daily lives and there was nothing mysterious about it except the speed with which Milena could empty it. As soon as it was empty, it meant endless traipsing round chemists' shops for Evžen and me, arguments with chemists and wrangles with their assistants, assuring them this was the last time and quite exceptional – anything, in fact, to get Milena her fix . . .
>
> I shall never forget how once she decided to give up morphine. She did not want to go to hospital but to do it herself, ending her addiction to Dicodit in her own way at home. At first things did not go too badly.

Motherhood

Both she and we were kept going by the euphoria of her tremendous decision, so somehow we managed to cope with her nervousness and physical exhaustion. But the withdrawal symptoms gradually grew stronger and Milena locked herself in my room.

Eventually she started screaming for drugs, and Honza went off into the night to find some, only to discover Evžen at the chemist's, already getting Milena a new supply. When Slávka, who was still attached to the Communist Party, nonetheless visited her old friend, Milena described her 'hopeless, stupid feeling, such an irremovable feeling'.

Her own sense of darkness was matched by the darkness around her. The journalism of the past which found riches in ordinary life seemed inappropriate as the decade progressed. As Hitler consolidated his power in Germany and brought in ever more restrictive laws against Jews and other 'enemies' of the Reich, there were some anti-semitic and anti-immigrant protests in Prague too; the resignation of Masaryk in 1935 because of illness seemed to mark the end of a gentler era. Fascism took hold in Spain too, and Milena, like left-wingers all over Europe, was horrified by the Spanish Civil War. Then, in the same year of 1936, came news of the Moscow show trials, as the Soviet Communist Party turned against its own. Milena's last drop of faith in Communism was drained. She later explained to a friend why she had severed all connection with the party: 'With those kinds of people, with so many bad characteristics – egoism, philistinism, deceitfulness – it's impossible to imagine building a socialist future.' She had no more illusions about the reality of the world around her. From now on she rejected any political ideology, left or right.

10

Munich

By all accounts, Milena was in a deplorable state in the middle 1930s. Around this time, her old friend Alice Rühle-Gerstlová asked her for help. Alice and Otto had already fled Germany; now Otto's colleague Henry Jacoby and his wife Frieda also needed a refuge from fascism. Milena agreed to rent a room to them, but she was really in no condition to have strangers to stay. The Jacobys were distressed by her cursory domestic arrangements, her carelessness with her own health and appearance, and her mood swings. In the end there was a row about money, and the Jacobys left. Henry wrote to Alice and Otto in September 1936: 'It is a great shame that no one is concerned enough to get her to a sanatorium, where she could perhaps overcome her dependence on drugs – if not, it will certainly lead to catastrophe one day.'

Some were of course concerned, not least Evžen Klinger. His support and affection were fundamental to Milena. But the will on Milena's part to break her habit was not yet there, and she remained mired in self-loathing. She was self-conscious about her limp and about her weight, which New Year's resolutions and diet plans did little to help. The glory and vanity of her younger days had gone, and she wore nondescript, self-effacing dark suits. Her relationship with Klinger was sorely tested, but survived. Outsiders felt that he was more in love with Milena than she was with him. But she was very dependent on him; he was intelligent and devoted, and very attentive to Honza. Without him life would have been far more miserable.

The Jacobys were not alone in their distress at Milena's condition. Others included Willi and Steffi Schlamn, former Communists and Jewish émigrés from fascism in Austria, who made Milena's acquaintance in the mid-1930s. Steffi was appalled by Milena's shabby clothes and careless hairstyle. Out of doors she would go bareheaded or at best wear a beret. Nor could Steffi understand why Milena had newspaper instead of lavatory paper in the bathroom; even if times were hard, this was not necessary.

Steffi and Willi came to know Milena well. Willi, a left-wing journalist and editor of the Vienna *Weltbühne* had moved to Prague in 1933. His wife, a Montessori teacher, followed a year later. Milena enjoyed their company. She shared their left-wing but not obsessive politics; they were, like many émigrés, intelligent and courageous people; and she knew what it was to be in a kind of exile. Willi and Milena were both journalists and became close friends. Steffi, warm-hearted and good with children, was a great success with Honza.

Despite her wretched personal situation, Milena was as attentive as ever to political developments. She listened to the émigrés' tales, of Hitler's tightening grip in Germany and his influence in Austria, of the increasing repression of those who did not 'belong', left-wingers, homosexuals and of course Jews. In the mid-1930s it had become clear that Hitler was rearming Germany again; the battle was clearly to be about extending Germany's dominion in Europe, especially over areas with German inhabitants. Hitler's eye was turned on Austria and on Czechoslovakia, with its large German minority in the Sudetenland. Sudeten Germans had followed the triumph of Hitler in Germany with interest; in achieving self-determination from the Austro-Hungarian Empire, Czechoslovakia had failed to give its own minorities a sense of equality and many Sudeten Germans had experienced petty oppression from local Czech officials. Inevitably, they saw in Hitler's rise a chance for their own advancement. From 1933 the main Sudeten German party was led by Konrad Henlein, a young instructor with one of the German gymnastic associations. He was a charismatic although not particularly brilliant figure; as the 1930s progressed and his vague championship of the German nation clarified into calls for autonomy, Hitler kept a close eye on him as a possibly useful pawn in his greater game.

Hitler's belligerence was watched with unease by the European democracies, and many Europeans came to regard war as inevitable. The Czechs watched with particular nervousness, and put much store by a mutual assistance treaty with France, signed in 1924 as part of a broader French policy to deter Germany from any expansion east-wards. The Czechs expected Britain to back up any French support. A Czech–Soviet pact had also been signed in 1935. But it was hard to discern the depth of commitment of these allies.

Milena seems to have felt that the times called for all her attention and powers. Her rejection of Communism and all ideologies had not been a rejection of politics or engagement; if she was to resume a more active role as a journalist, she must drag herself out of the dilapidated state into which she had fallen and cure herself of her drug addiction. Early in 1937, with the assistance of her friend from adolescence, Jiří Foustka, she attended a clinic in Bohnice on the outskirts of Prague. The treatment was intensive and painful, but Milena had recovered the willpower to regain her health and strength and the cure was successful. She returned home to a beautiful Prague spring, with the fruit trees in blossom on Petřín Hill, the song of swallows and blackbirds and warm sunshine. Despite the looming anxiety about war, there was plenty of life and colour in the city, with peasants from the country dressed in brightly patterned headscarves selling radishes and embroidery, and people boating and swimming on the Vltava.

Milena was rewarded by an opportunity to channel her new energy into worthwhile work. Salvation came in the guise of her old sparring partner Ferdinand Peroutka. He was now more than ever a grand old man of Czech journalistic and literary circles, and editor of the respected liberal paper *Přítomnost*. He had always admired Milena's writing and spirit, and now that she was no longer a Communist he harnessed her talents for his own newspaper. He invited Milena to join *Přítomnost* and gave her generous space for articles. Evžen wrote for the paper too.

Milena went to work eagerly. She had no difficulty finding subjects, or finding a voice. Without the shackles of Communist jargon, with subjects which engaged her more deeply than the froth of fashion, she was soon writing long, powerful articles which combined an eye for detail with broad political understanding. One of her first articles, printed in October 1937, was about refugees, not only about those like the Jacobys and Schlamms who had come earlier and in relative comfort; but about the several thousand who had more recently flooded across the border in disarray.

> There are workers and craftsmen, clerks and intellectuals. Most belong to the first category, and among these there are functionaries of the socialist parties and trade organisations. . . . About a fifth of them are women and children. . . . They came without money, without papers, on foot, after several days without food . . .
>
> Then the Jewish emigrants began to come, and people who were in danger because of mixed marriages; and then the economic refugees,

mostly Jewish shopkeepers and businessmen. These last brought money with them and they live here without support. But money cannot overcome loneliness in this outpost of exiles . . .

Although the number of political refugees has recently stabilised, there are marked changes. Many leave here for other lands as soon as they have the chance, above all a chance to work. But the stream does not dry up completely. One goes, another comes, since the causes of emigration are ever more serious and urgent.

She praised those who gave help to the refugees, both individuals in the border areas offering food or some small paid work, and the networks in the cities which organised shelter and provisions. Milena saw the work of these committees for the protection of refugees at close quarters, through a new friend. Mařka Šmolková was chairwoman of the Jewish Aid Committee, and Milena met her through Wilma Löwenbach, with whom she was friends again now she had turned away from Communism. Since 1933, Mařka had been involved in helping refugees and campaigning to find them more permanent refuge outside Czechoslovakia. Milena was impressed both by her dedication and by her warmth and wit. Mařka took Milena to visit one of the émigré refuges, where she put all her reporting skills to work again.

An empty factory, half derelict, a cold hall with blocked windows . . . bare rooms with six or eight iron bedsteads without mattresses or linen . . . a pathetically humble library, a tiny room with torn books, carefully ordered and numbered, all of course presents from people. There's a bathroom, if you can call a broken shower a bathroom, but only the sick are allowed to wash, because there's little fuel. In the kitchen they prepare cabbage, and goulash once a week . . .

I cannot, however, rid myself of the feeling that there is something still worse than their daily poverty. I looked into their faces, I spoke to them. They talked about their fates, as people speak to the healthy after a hard illness, they smile and don't say anything: because what can they say and where can they find the words?

Some of the people she spoke to had been interrogated, tortured or imprisoned in Germany. Milena was moved.

I think I will never forget the young woman with lovely hair and a beautiful smile, who stood a little defiantly in front of me and said: Yes, I was arrested and in prison a long time. Did they torture her? No, no, only a few little things. What little things? Well, blows on the head, blows across the knuckles. Those are little things? Well – and again the indescribable smile – Well, in Germany they're little. Do you have children? Yes. The word rang quiet clearly and firmly. Where? In Germany. Are you fearful for them? She shrugged her shoulders. Isn't it horrible knowing that Nazis are bringing them up? How could I have brought them here? How? Where to? She was almost shouting, almost crying. How do you imagine the future? The bent head of the young woman straightened, she looked at me quite directly and quietly: We wait until we can return home!

Although these people were foreigners, Milena wrote, they all shared a horror of the swastika. 'This handful of exiles can teach us what the swastika is. They are living witnesses to its great strength and the power of its lies. They carry the evidence on their own skin, and those of us who are like Thomas, who would not believe until he had tangible proof, can go and touch them with our own hands.' She ended the article with an appeal to people to give money, and to the government to offer work and guarantees of safety.

Although the style was fresher, many of Milena's articles for *Přítomnost* shared some of the spirit of her Communist journalism, in her sympathy for those in distress and her ability to draw people out so that she could pass on their stories. She was, like many sensitive journalists, ambivalent about this skill, as the preface to the article about refugees shows:

> The task of the reporter is sometimes similar to that of a hyena. The journalist travels with a notebook and writes about people's troubles to make news. If he does it without some hope that his words might help, he deserves our scorn. It's because of this hope that I ask to be excused for the eagerness of my questioning, which must have been painful and tiresome. Inevitably, I must seem like someone from another, safer world, who comes pen in hand to write of their suffering.

Despite her proper unease, or perhaps because of it, she was good at her job, and Peroutka was pleased with her work. Her name was soon being used in an advertisment as one of the paper's attractions. Milena sometimes found Peroutka a difficult, distracted boss, but she admired his commitment to the paper and to the ethos of the First Republic. The death of Tomáš Garrigue Masaryk in September 1937, which provoked collective grief as thousands of people queued to pay their respects at his bier, served to remind people like Milena and Peroutka of the values on which their peaceful new democracy had been built, and which were now threatened by instability in Europe.

Not all her early articles for *Přítomnost* were directly political. In December 1937 she wrote a detailed, affectionate feuilleton about the grocery industry in Prague, in which she also recalled her stay in Vienna; the passage of time allowed her to be nostalgic about the city's charms even if it had been an unhappy home. 'Vienna in spring, when the chestnut trees are in bloom, when the whole of Vienna smells of lilac and when they begin to open one swing boat after another in the Prater . . . the vast aspens on the violet-filled meadow-banks of the Danube, the ashes and silver poplars which line the whole Prater and which, on spring nights, conceal lovers.'

The silvery magic of Vienna or even of Malá Strana was missing from her current corner of Prague. Another article from the same month, about the increasing mobility of people in the modern world, began with a description of the quarter where she lived, the further reaches of Vinohrady not far from the Olšanské cemetery and the Jewish cemetery where Kafka was buried.

> In Vinohrady in front of the Olšanské cemetery stands a wayside inn. Time has forgotten it, although it stands in the middle of the town, a long, modern street runs past it, and there are tram lines and taxi stops. Not far away there is already a snack bar and a modern café, a cinema, a sweetshop and a wine bar with a gypsy band, in short all the pleasures of a dissipated Sunday for the locals. But the inn is still just as it was thirty years ago – a spreading chestnut tree stands in the garden, hung with lamps, and some walking group plays music above the din of skittles. On a summer Sunday afternoon it is packed here.

This quarter had in its own way become home.

Now that Milena was working again, there was a little money to spend and it no longer went on drugs. She bought pictures for the walls of the little flat, and seeds and plants for her window-boxes. Sometimes she appropriated plants from elsewhere. Honza later described one such escapade in the Lobkovic gardens.

> One night the park-keeper apprehended us cutting roses; we already had a nice bunch. But Milena managed to convince him that we were in fact pruning the bushes and removing excess blooms, which would have sapped the plant's strength. She gave quite a performance; it is by no means easy, late at night, to convince a man entrusted to keep order that at that hour you are caring for the well-being of the public

gardens and that your bunch of half-open buds were really superfluous and were cut for the good of the bushes. It took time enough, but in the end she managed, and when we left, the foolish man even thanked us and remarked that really there were too few people like us in the city. . . . I realised what is meant by the 'art of dealing with people', and from that time on I knew that Milena had completely mastered it.

Milena's social life was busier, meeting friends from the world of journalism, attending émigré parties, and having friends round (although there was no improvement in her cooking). She continued to keep open house for those in need. She even gave hospitality to Jaromír's wife Riva for several weeks in 1937, when Jaromír returned from a trip to the Paris World Fair with heart trouble and had to go into hospital. Honza regarded Riva as rather helpless and found the interlude taxing. Milena had remained friends with Jaromír (as she had with Ernst) and she often found herself helping him out, sometimes with money. After the war, Jaromír, then living in Paris, wrote to his daughter: 'I know how Milena was glad that, even after our divorce, I stayed friends with her, how it often helped her, and then how I too had some internal support from it.'

As Milena's connection with *Přítomnost* strengthened, she introduced Willi Schlamm to the paper and translated articles by him from German into Czech. He was highly regarded as a political commentator. The two became very close, in one of several intense friendships which Milena enjoyed with younger men in the latter part of her life. Willi, born in 1904, was a handsome and intelligent man who shared Milena's political interests and her concern for the future of Europe. He was also amusing, with a fund of Jewish jokes (some of them risqué) which Milena loved. He teased her for her earnestness; once she told him off for talking when she was listening to a classical record. They would meet for coffee at the Café Bellevue by Charles Bridge, with a view across to the Castle, to discuss their work and the future for themselves and their countries. Milena was fond of Steffi too, and Steffi knew that despite Milena's near infatuation with her husband she did not really have anything to fear. (Evžen seems to have felt the same, and shared the friendship with the Schlamms.) Steffi was put to the test sometimes; she was close to Honza, and often took the child off Milena's hands. Once Milena even asked her to take Honza away on holiday for a few days, while she and Willi remained in Prague. (On other occasions Milena went away with

Honza herself, and took her to Špičák, as her father had done when she was a child.)

Steffi found Milena a moody but also a very generous-hearted woman. She regarded her as an unorthodox mother, sometimes strict, sometimes lenient, perhaps treating Honza too much like an adult. Certainly, Milena talked openly to Honza about her personal life and appealed for sympathy for her difficult childhood and unhappy marriages. This made the mother and daughter very close, but sometimes bewildered Honza. Yet Steffi never doubted that Milena loved her daughter, and that in her own way she was a good mother.

Honza's education was a tricky matter. She went to school, but was not a disciplined pupil. In an effort to keep Honza at her studies, and given that the kind of communitarian childcare centre Milena had preached about did not in reality exist, she decided to hire a tutor. A student she knew referred another student to her, Lumír Čivrný, and he began to give Honza lessons at home. He found it hard to keep her attention. 'Honza was already too mature in her experience of life, she knew well how to make the most of being a child: to get her to do something you had to accept the rules of her game, her ironic smile in the face of authority. She was in this a smaller version of Milena.' Čivrný was impressed by Milena; looking back, he sees her as a 'crystalline type of the New Woman, formed by different and sometimes antagonistic streams of life and thought'. He admired her writing, her 'feeling for good, precise Czech, for an unaffected style, for concrete precision. But at the same time she brought something unique, something uncompromising, the ability to feel.' Milena too was taken by the young man and kept him on as a tutor.

One world that Milena found time to share with her daughter was her old love, the cinema. Sometimes they went to Walt Disney cartoons, which Milena enjoyed as much as Honza; sometimes Milena inveigled the usherette into allowing Honza into a film for grown-ups. Honza described their expeditions:

> When we went on an outing to the pictures in winter-time, the streets would already be dark when we came out of the cinema at six o'clock, the street lamps and neon signs would be lit and the sign above the Melantrich publishing house would be scribbling *Večerní České slovo* [*The Evening Czech Word*] in a line of light over and over again. Milena did not hurry me home, she knew that I loved the evening streets, just as she did. And if I had not understood something in the film we had just seen, we walked up and down Wenceslas Square from one

chestnut stall to another, warming our fingers on the hot chestnuts, while Milena patiently answered all my possible and impossible questions. Sometimes we went all the way home on foot, and carried on talking at home, because Milena never answered anything casually and there was always a great deal which I had to have explained . . .

Sometimes she could not answer me. There were things which she could never comprehend, and could never explain even to herself. When we came across something like that, she would speak about it with a quiet, burning anger, she never shrugged her shoulders in the resigned conviction that so the world goes, there's nothing to be done. She was incurable in her optimistic belief that the world could be arranged in such a way to suit everyone. At least, in those days she was incurable.

Her optimism was to be sorely tested. The year 1938 began with continuing tension across the continent. In February, Hitler made a notorious speech declaring himself protector of the ten million Germans living outside Germany (in other words in Austria and Czechoslovakia). Nazi influence on the Austrian government grew. In an effort to stave off Hitler's expansionist intentions, Chancellor Schuschnigg called a plebiscite on the country's links with Germany at short notice in early March. Hitler responded by closing the border and deploying troops nearby. Schuschnigg gave in and cancelled the plebiscite. But Hitler merely increased his demands, and his allies in Austria seized power. On 12 March 1938 German troops crossed into Austria. They met no resistance, and indeed some welcome from those Austrians who believed in a greater German living space. The Anschluss, or annexation, was achieved with hardly a murmur of protest from other European powers. Hitler, and the Czechs, knew that Czechoslovakia was next; the main concern of the British and French was how to stop the inevitable confrontation igniting a wider European war.

Milena could do little but watch events across the border, and record how they affected life in Czechoslovakia. Not long after the Anschluss she wrote an article showing how dangerous and insidious were the processes that could tear a society apart, and how civilised people could turn against each other and against outsiders. She saw it reflected in the way some of her more nationalist Czech friends found her friendship with German Jewish émigrés unwelcome, as well as more broadly throughout Czech society.

Munich

In quieter – and quiet – times, different people lived quietly next to each other and didn't worry much about politics. Politics didn't inflame them, it hardly seemed to concern them, it was something which happened somewhere else. Today, politics has entered the domain of ordinary people, their two-roomed flats with kitchens and all modern conveniences, it settles over the table with its crocheted table-cloth, it pours out of the radio which used to sing songs. Today, Mr Novotný is above all a Czech. And his good neighbour, Mr Kohn, is a Jew. And the son of the tenant Keller is a very tall, very athletic youth who wears white Bavarian stockings – in the middle of Smíchov, where there's not a mountain to be seen. And Mr Svoboda, the tailor in the basement, is a Social Democrat. Down in the basement there are also two emigrants, German socialists, living without work, without papers. And all the tenants in the house – Czechs, Germans, Jews – are sheepishly a little offended by their presence.

If these emigrants had become like blacks in America, this was even truer of the Jews. 'How many Jewish blacks are there today? In the Third Reich perhaps half a million. In Vienna and Austria perhaps 300,000. In Hungary Jews live as half-blacks, they can live and work, they have civic rights, but they are still bound by laws of quotas.' In this and other articles she described the growing persecution of Europe's Jews, ghettoed, marked out, banished to concentration camps, despised.

The wandering Jew had been joined by the wandering German and Austrian émigré. The Czechs were consequently unsettled.

In Vinohrady, Smíchov, Karlín, Holešovice and other suburbs a quiet wave of mutual tension rolls from person to person. A dangerous wave from faraway Germany, a foreign land. In little pubs people sit, deliberating. What will England do, how will France behave, what does Hitler intend? The truth is these are very pressing and important questions, lying on the skin of us all as tightly as a shirt, it is impossible not to think about them. But above all we need to know: what will we ourselves do? Not on a great international scale, but just on a private scale, whose radius is three and a half streets, the way home to a two-room flat with kitchen.

There was as yet no answer, as Czechs continued to feel like passive spectators of a game which would affect their future but in which they could not participate. After the Anschluss, many German democrats in the Sudetenland panicked, dissolved their political parties and, seeing which way the wind was blowing, joined Henlein;

the Czech government lost its German coalition partners. President Eduard Beneš (who had succeeded Masaryk) and his government had begun to respond to Henlein with negotiations and the promise of a clearer policy on minorities. But too late. By now reconciliation was impossible; Henlein had become a pawn in Hitler's grand scheme to force the Czechs into a confrontation. He instructed Henlein to make demands which would be unacceptable to the Czechs. On 24 April, Henlein issued his 'Karlsbad Declaration', calling for wide-reaching autonomy, and aligning himself clearly with National Socialism. When Milena visited Karlsbad, an elegant spa town called Karlovy Vary in Czech, a few weeks later, she found it almost empty of guests. 'The whole region, whose economic disaster is incalculable, is paying the bill for Henlein's April speech. . . . First of all the owners of the spa hotels – and they are mostly Henleinists. And then the whole region – they are also mostly Henleinists. . . . It seems that the only person who has not paid a penny for the huge damage caused by Henlein's speech is Henlein himself.'

Then in May, events threatened to turn the confrontation into a conflagration. Local elections planned for three Sundays in late May and June raised the political temperature, as Sudeten German leaders campaigned for the end of Czech domination and a return to the German fatherland. Rumours of a German invasion spread, and the Czech government received intelligence reports of German troop movements near the border. On 20 May, just before the first vote, President Beneš ordered a partial mobilisation, to the pride and relief of many Czechs. In the end, the reports of German activity proved unfounded and the Czech troops were demobilised. But the May crisis, as it was known, gave many Czechs the feeling that they had stood up to the Germans. In the end, the elections passed off peacefully, but Henlein's party won 90 per cent of the vote. The Czech government tried more negotiations, but in vain. President Beneš was not to know that in late May Hitler told his staff, 'It is my unalterable decision to smash Czechoslovakia by military action in the near future.' Nor did many Czechs realise the level of political support in Britain for Sudeten autonomy as part of a broader appeasement of Hitler to avoid war. Instead, they congratulated themselves that their bravery and readiness to defend themselves had had an effect.

Milena shared in the general relief. Peroutka had sent her to the Sudetenland, to towns like Liberec near the northern border, to report on the May election campaign, and ask the questions all Czechs were asking: in particular, could the Austrian Anschluss be repeated? For now, the optimism which Honza had identified in Milena endured, and she wrote two long articles, published at the end of May and the beginning of June, entitled 'There will be no Anschluss'.

She had certainly found in the Sudetenland much to disturb her. She visited impressive local sports facilities, the breeding ground of the militaristic youth culture which made up Henlein's power base. The Czech government might proscribe certain German associations and newspapers, but it could not ban Hitler worship nor the hope of invasion. However, Milena believed, the mobilisation of Friday 20 May had been effective.

> The army came. In the night, in long impressive ranks, in exemplary peace and quiet, long columns of vehicles rumbled across Liberec square. The army came – but it was Czech. From the centre of the country a flood of soldiers streamed towards the border with extraordinary order and discipline. A knot of people stood on the square, talking excitedly. By the Saturday afternoon there was not a white sock to be seen, and people who on Friday evening still raised their arm in greeting now wore Czech emblems in their buttonholes. Our soldiers came, and believe me, they came just in time. They came and showed all the heroic Czechs and Germans who spent the summer in the borderland speaking out against fascism that they did not speak out in vain, that they are not in a vacuum as it sometimes seems to them.

She described how many democrats had felt too intimidated to stand up to the Henleinists. Everyone was watched: 'In a little town – and in the north most towns are small – not even a mouse can hide.' The election campaign centred on the notion of a 'good German'; anyone else risked losing their job. In an industrial region which had been particuarly hit by the recession of the early 1930s, the Henleinists preyed on economic insecurity. Milena reported how after the Austrian Anschluss, Czech capital had fled the region, construction had ceased, and the ensuing economic hardship had added to the vulnerability of those most in need of support, the democrats.

Her criticism was not reserved for the Henleinists. Even at this sensitive moment, she was brave enough to point out the Czech government's own failings. The current crisis could be blamed on three things: the Anschluss, the organisational skills of the Henleinists, but also: 'Our simple inability to match Nazi propaganda with democratic propaganda.' The Germans tuned into radio stations they could understand – German ones from across the border. 'And as an antidote we provided half an hour of German broadcasting, mostly dull and indigestible.'

The second part of her article continued the argument, and described the implacable conflict between democrat and Henleinist in the area which had led to a damaging boycott.

> A man perhaps works in a factory, he is German but a Social Democrat – and his wife walks the streets of the little town pursued by scornful glances. The children point at her, the shopkeepers serve her unwillingly and sullenly, the priest does not return her greeting. . . . At lunchtime the children return from school: 'Mummy, you are not a German woman. Daddy is an enemy of the nation.' The family sits silently through lunch in deep misery. The man's courage is defeated by pressure at the factory.

It was particularly hard for the Jews. 'In the border town of Aš I spoke to a doctor. He has been in the region for twenty years, there is no one far and wide whom he has not once attended. Today people avoid him, they lower their eyes if they have to greet him, pass by on the other side of the street. He has almost no patients.'

It was a 'grave failing' of the Czechs that they had not built a coalition with democratic Germans. Cooperation would have been possible with 'those Germans who are not like other Germans'. 'Ordinary people are very grateful when they hear a Czech speak German. They emerge from their closed world and, nine times out of ten, wave their hand with a kindly smile which says: you are a Czech and I am German, let me be and I will let you be in peace. . . . The fact that these Germans love their language – and I don't see why we should not accept this – means that they are German, not that they are inevitably Nazi.'

In the elections, Milena argued, a united democratic bloc of Czechs and Germans, would in many districts have had a chance of defeating the Henleinists; instead that vote was split. And yet the mobilisation had shown how fragile the Nazi mood was. 'It seems to me that the kind of people who belonged to the Henleinist Germans have courage only when they stand together and when they shout. As soon as they disperse into individuals their courage is lost.'

The only consolation was that the mobilisation had shown the Henleinists that their hope of another Anschluss would not be permitted. 'The one possibility they do not have is exactly the one they so want: a repeat of Austria, a repeat of bloodless occupation, a repeat of the march of the Sieg Heil, concentration camps, the expulsion of people from the nation and the state, posters declaring that Jews are not welcome here. Simply, the possibility of Anschluss.'

Milena continued to cling to the belief that Czech defiance could deter German aggression. But despite this patriotic view the censors found much to quarrel with in her reports from the Sudetenland, and both articles appeared with great white gaps. She responded by challenging the censors who had complained that she was too critical of the government – it was not criticism but the truth. It was the German fascists who should be censored, she wrote in another article, not her. 'In reality, it seems that someone who works ardently in defiance of growing German fascism in Czechoslovakia is allowed to say less than Czechoslovak German fascists. I am pointing this out to Mr Censor because I am a little ashamed of what we are not allowed to say today.' She went on to write that as the effect of the mobilisation was wearing off, white socks were again visible on the streets of Sudeten villages, and the press and radio were still failing to counter Henlein's propaganda.

The censors let all this stand.

President Beneš's Statute on Nationalities in July failed to satisfy the Sudetens. The summer seemed suspended in a quieter but still apprehensive limbo, and Milena's conviction that there would be no Anschluss wavered. Émigré and Jewish friends began to make plans to leave. Willi Schlamm was reluctant, but Milena took every opportunity to persuade him and Steffi to go before it was too late. In July, Milena, Evžen and Honza went for a summer holiday in the Bohemian countryside south-east of Prague, and Milena knew that she might not see the Schlamms again. The village of Vojnův Městec, where they were staying, was 'a poor village in sedate countryside'; Milena's little family enjoyed expeditions to the ancient town of Žďár and to Žumberk castle. Milena found local villagers ready to fight, almost eager for another mobilisation, confident of outside help.

But part of her mind was back in Prague, as she thought of the prospect of losing the companionship of Willi. She was preoccupied with what had become an intense and sometimes difficult relationship. Milena was upset that Willi had not been able to see her before she left on holiday. She wrote to him that she had gone for a long walk to cheer herself up; her leg still troubled her but did not stop her resuming the habit of her childhood walks with her father. She told Willi that he should not be frightened by their friendship; he sometimes seemed nervous about any physical contact, yet was hurt by her realism about their relationship.

> You accept that I love you, that I care about your love, but when I saw that you didn't love me you say I became 'less nice'. There's some justice in that. I love you a great deal. I don't know exactly how. I only know I love you very much. But the precondition of this love was the certainty that you don't love me.... Had I believed that it was possible that you could love me as well, I would have fled to the ends of the earth. How you want to explain that is one thing, but it is true; I've only needed your friendship. Anything else would have been less. Only in this way was it possible to speak calmly to you, to feel always happy with you.

She invited Willi and Steffi to visit her rural retreat. But the Schlamms were on the verge of leaving and Steffi had said goodbye in Prague. Willi, however, did find a way to see her again, and they said their farewells at the train station at Německý Brod (now Havlíčkův Brod) at the very end of July.

Shortly afterwards she returned to Prague, and the *Přítomnost* office. Peroutka was away on holiday and Milena and a colleague were in charge. Prague felt empty. She wrote to Willi in Brussels and told him it felt very strange that he had left. She mentioned that she might try to visit, although she would have to arrange a passport and had no money for such a journey, what with Honza's clothes and school books to buy. She gave him advice about places to see in Belgium, recalling her trip in 1931. 'Go and look at Bruges, it's a quiet, sad and magical town, almost unreal. And go to the seaside. Belgium has the most beautiful sea in Europe. And if you have time, go to Ypres and above all look at the graves of the soldiers from the war. Don't tell me that you don't have to go – on the contrary, everyone should go and look.'

She wrote again a couple of days later. 'Already it is better, Willi.' She was more settled back into work and the pleasures of Prague. 'In the afternoon Honza and I swam from Mánes to the Bellevue. You were not there.' There was one consolation. 'I begin to see the good side of your departure: letters. I can still write everything to you even if I will never see you again. Absolutely everything. And I can write to you twenty times a day that I love you and no one can do anything about it! Wonderful!' This effusiveness was a safe indulgence against the background of her more muted, but more fundamental, partnership with Evžen.

The atmosphere in Prague was again nervous. The British Prime Minister, Neville Chamberlain, had sent Lord Runciman, a former Cabinet Minister, to try to 'mediate' between the Czechs and Sudeten Germans. Czechs were beginning to be aware of British and French ambivalence about their treaty obligations, and their desire to appease Hitler. 'There is a terrible depression over Prague,' Milena wrote to Willi. 'In the beginning people were full of spirit, but that is now beginning to fade. German broadcasts roar terrifying things, and in return we whisper popular songs.' Work was oppressively busy with Peroutka away. 'Be glad that you have gone. Nothing good can happen here. Only bad, evil things.' She asked him to phone her on her forty-second birthday, 10 August 1938, and to send an article about Jewish jokes.

She wrote to Willi almost every other day, in an echo of her correspondence with Kafka. The relationship was different; she was now the older one, and although she shared true sympathy and intellectual compatibility with both men, the terrible bonds and dark fear of her relationship with Kafka were replaced by a more flirtatious (if possessive) affection for Willi. But Milena's letters to Willi can help us imagine what her letters to Kafka might have been like, equally impetuous, warm, demanding, playful, sentimental. As she had once foretold, these love letters were often typed rather than handwritten. She missed him. 'It hurts and hurts, it doesn't stop for a moment, it doesn't slacken at all, there's no escape, every second must be endured and still it hurts.'

Without Willi's company Prague felt lonelier. She had nothing in common with the 'Stalinists' at the Metro café; Peroutka and his friends did not go out much; Jaromír was poor and drinking too much. And Evžen was busy, reporting on events in Slovakia, or off at political meetings. He missed Willi too, she wrote. Thoughts of a visit were fading; she did not have the money and it was far too sensitive a time to be away. Meanwhile, she was assiduous in helping Willi and Steffi arrange more permanent emigration. She applied her charm and persuasiveness to the French authorities in Prague to get him a French visa. In return she asked him ceaselessly for articles.

Their frequent correspondence soon posed Milena with the same dilemma as with Kafka: what language to write in? 'If I write in

Czech I have the impression that you don't understand me, and if I write in German I have the impression that I don't write what I want.' And again: 'In Czech I'm sentimental, sad and terribly truth-loving. In German I am a sober, brief and good-humoured person. So which one do you like best?' She fluctuated, sometimes switching from language to language within one letter.

The mood of uncertainty and even apathy in Prague continued. Milena felt like 'an old woman, who would like to run and who has a sick body and who, despite all her efforts, has some bitterness'. After the Anschluss people had been greedy for news; now they had lost interest. 'It's not courage, but tiredness, horrible, despairing, gnawing fatigue.' This was 'the new form of German "diplomacy"', the psychological wearing down of people.

The mood contaminated her relationship with Evžen, and Milena felt some distance between them. His anti-fascism took a different form from hers and to her incomprehension he drew closer to the Communist Party again. He and Milena no longer shared the same world, and without common purpose the lack of passion between them (as well as Milena's interest in other men) was perhaps more noticeable. 'I have the impression that he is searching for something,' Milena wrote to Willi. 'He's very sensitive and sad. He can't find land.'

In another letter she wrote:

> We hear a lot about the danger of war – we no longer consider whether it's a real or imagined danger. . . . Altogether, one doesn't know what is happening. Lord Runciman is fishing and hunting. That's the only thing one knows. It's always a big worry finding the right weekend for him – not too German, not too Czech, with a lot of fish, a lot of stags, a castle and a bit of nobility in the background. . . . This year is a mousetrap. One way or another we will be defeated. I don't see any way out. . . . I'm not pessimistic in the long run. But nothing that happens in the short term will be good for us. Peace can probably only be maintained if Czechoslovakia is sacrificed. Or the peace will not be kept and then, too. Czechoslovakia will die . . .
>
> If I look at Honza I'm sometimes desperate. If I look at other children I'm sometimes tired of life. In the cinema there's an advertisement for gas masks for children. I can't tell you how frightened the tastelessness of this advert makes me. One will die without knowing what one has died of.

But there was no relaxation of the tension, and war now seemed inevitable. All summer, the British and French had been urging

Munich

President Beneš to come to a settlement with the Sudeten Germans and give them some sort of autonomy, perhaps offering a plebiscite. President Beneš was now aware what reluctant allies the French and British were, but he still had hopes of his alliance with the Soviet Union (pledged to come to Czechoslovakia's support if France engaged on her behalf, as surely she must under her treaty obligations in the event of German aggression). Intelligence reports in August told of a German call-up and on 12 September Hitler addressed a rally in Nuremberg, whipping up feeling against 'that monstrous formation Czechoslovakia'. Clashes in the Sudetenland followed, with nearly thirty deaths, and the Czech government declared martial law in some districts.

Milena wrote to Willi the day after the Nuremberg rally. 'We all live in huge disruption, we sleep with our eyes half-shut, we hardly sleep at all. . . . I feel that terrible days lie ahead, before war comes. Already in the shops you can't get sugar, fat, bacon, jam. Everything is sold out. Prices have risen enormously.' She was thinking of going on another reporting trip to the north again, leaving Evžen and Honza in Prague. She told Willi that she had little admiration for President Beneš, but 'what a burden that man carries'. Honza was missing Steffi. As for Milena: 'I went to the Bellevue, Willi. There was no cake.'

Then, as in May, the crisis seemed to abate. Henlein fled to Germany, and the Czechs once again congratulated themselves on having managed the situation. But beyond their borders a fatal series of events was being set in train.

The British government had been disturbed by the Nuremberg rally and the Sudetenland clashes. Still fearful of being dragged into a war, Chamberlain decided to do something he had been considering for a while: go and talk to Hitler in person. The two men met at Hitler's mountain house at Berchtesgaden on 15 September 1938 and in essence agreed that the Germans had a right to Sudeten areas where more than half the population was German. The British and French then pressured the Czech government to agree. While the Czech government deliberated, Milena wrote to Willi about the Berchtesgaden meeting and told him what the Czechs understood to be the outcome, that there had been talk of a plebiscite and a hand-over of territory to be monitored by some sort of international police force. This, she said, would be the end.

Prague began to fill up with people fleeing from the border area

175

and Milena was increasingly busy at the paper, trying to keep abreast of events. Her letters to Willi became hurried notes. Milena was well placed to find out what the Czech government was planning to do. Her Aunt Růžena was a good friend of Hana Benešová, the president's wife. On 20 September, Hana told Růžena about the dilemma facing the government and what it was likely to do. Růžena told Milena. Milena told Evžen, and also Julius Fučík, with whom she was in contact again after his return from the Soviet Union. Next day, Milena's information was proved correct; the Czech government, fearing that the French would not stand by them and that without the French the Russians would do nothing, was prepared to give in. In the early hours of the morning, as an autumn mist lay over the city, the Czech government succumbed to French and British pressure to concede parts of the Sudetenland.

On 21 September Beneš issued a communiqué. 'The Czechoslovak government, forced by circumstances, yielding to unheard-of pressure and drawing the consequences from the communication of the French and British governments ... accepts the Anglo-French proposals with feelings of pain.'

Milena described the mood: 'On Wednesday – 21 September – in the morning hours, news began to steal around Prague: we are alone. The government has decided to withdraw from the Sudetenland. . . . People stood stock-still with clenched hearts, astounded, their deepest faith shattered. Alone? It was so unbelievable that we didn't believe it.' By the evening, when the rumours were confirmed by a radio broadcast, the streets filled with people. 'They came in working clothes, women holding children by the hand, men from offices, factories, from home. It was not yet a demonstration. It was a pilgrimage. A pilgrimage of the despairing, tormented and shaken.'

Milena wrote an article urging Czechs to stand firm and conduct themselves with dignity. They did. On the 22nd, there was a larger, but still peaceful, demonstration on Národní třída by Czechs stunned not to be given the chance to defend their country. On the same day, Chamberlain left London for another meeting with Hitler, this time in Godesberg, to tell him the good news.

But for Hitler the Berchtesgaden deal was no longer enough. He wanted Czech withdrawal and German occupation of the Sudetenland by 1 October, with no mention of a plebiscite. German troops were now massing on the border. Chamberlain in effect agreed; it was no longer a question of whether the annexation would happen, but how to manage it, and this was largely up to the Czechs. He returned to London and with some reluctance the British and French cabinets consented to back the Godesberg agreement as a means to avoid war. Chamberlain told the nation in a broadcast: 'How horrible, fantastic, incredible it is that we should be digging trenches and trying on gas masks here because of a quarrel in a faraway country between people of whom we know nothing.' Another meeting with Hitler was planned for 29 September in Munich.

Back in Prague, the tension in the city had eased, through sheer exhaustion. 'A dull, tired calm fell on the town. The city centre appeared like normal. The knots of people disappeared,' wrote Milena. But on the night of the 23rd, the government, alarmed by German troop movements called a general mobilisation. Milena wrote: 'At that moment a load fell from the hearts of everyone. Like a fresh stream of air, a new force arose. Hardly had the last word of the mobilisation rung out than people were already running out onto the streets. Some without coats, some in work clothes. Men with little suitcases, accompanied by women hastily dressed. . . . We are not a nation which goes excitedly to war. There was, however, a remarkable readiness, relief, enthusiasm, everyone smiled but no one sang.' As the mobilisation took effect, those left behind in the city hunted out black paper to cover windows ready for the blackout, and sat and listened out for planes. 'We wait.'

But just a few days later, all was over. On 29 September in Munich, a meeting of Britain, France, Germany and Italy (without Czechoslovakia) gave formal approval to what had already been conceded at Godesberg: 1 October was set as the date for the start of Germany's occupation of the Sudetenland.

The Czechs were devastated. President Beneš decided that Czech defiance was pointless without the support of his treaty partners. The mobilisation was, for a second time, recalled, and the elaborate (and to the Germans worrying) fortifications in the Sudetenland were abandoned. When German troops crossed the border on 1 October, about a third of Czech territory was lost; President Beneš resigned a few days later. The Czechs' sense of betrayal, by a Europe to which they felt they belonged, was absolute.

11

War

I do not belong to those people who are slaves to fine words like truth, justice, morality. Not because I would not stand up for what they represent, the expression of truths which ring out as the only real coinage in the world. But because whoever has eyes to see and ears to hear has always heard these words from the mouths of the powerful at the very moment when they oppress the powerless. Too much injustice has been done in the name of truth and humanity in recent years.

Milena's response to Munich, beyond anger, was to keep writing and keep her readers abreast of developments. A week after Munich, she wrote an account of the immediate events. A week after that, she gave a more thorough picture in an article entitled 'The Month of September'. In her diary of the 'dramatic and painful month' she selected the main events, political speeches and newspaper editorials from Europe's capitals. She juxtaposed fine words and shameful deeds and included the cries of men like Winston Churchill against appeasement. She finished with a rhetorical appeal to her readers. 'Each day something ends and each day something begins. The 30th September 1938 saw not only an end to the integrity of Czechoslovakia but the start of a new struggle for our freedom ... and in this struggle we must all work with all our strength.'

Milena knew that the implications of Munich and the German seizure of Czech lands, quite apart from the implications for European security, were broad. Slovakia (whose clerico-fascist leaders were close to Germany) and the impoverished Sub-Carpathian region further to the east saw in the fractures of Munich their own chance. Both regions declared autonomy and Milena predicted that as a result Czechs from these areas would pour into the Czech lands, adding to the refugees from Germany and elsewhere. The Czech economy, which had lost more than a third of its industrial potential and half of its coalfields with the Sudetenland, would be further burdened.

War

As the autumn progressed, Milena was proved right; tens of thousands of people poured in from the Sudetenland, Slovakia and Ruthenia. She appealed to her readers to show sympathy. If Czechoslovakia had fought, there would have been war dead. Instead, she wrote, there are war wounded, 'some thousands fallen . . . but these fallen live. Living people want to eat.'

Milena also called for help from beyond Czech borders. Charitable collections in France and Britain had raised some money to help. 'Perhaps we should say thank you. I'm sorry, I cannot. I don't think any of us who lived through these days, nights and weeks can. We were silent when they took our wealth, our mountains, woods, valleys, our mines – the work of twenty years. Why should our generation feel humble gratitude?' The charity of soup kitchens was not needed, for no one was starving. 'The problem is how to move people who are caught between two horrors, the horror of concentration camps in the Third Reich and the horror of unemployment in an impoverished land. . . . Czechoslovakia could be a transit point for refugees. But how can it be a transit point when all the borders are hermetically sealed?' She called on France and Britain to open their borders to refugees and help fund their departure. 'This is the least of your responsibilities, given the small price you paid for peace.'

While Milena exerted herself on behalf of anonymous refugees, she was also concerned about Evžen. She began to enquire how to get him out of the country. For it was clear that Prague might soon become very uncomfortable for a Jew, a Slovak and a Communist. Munich brought no relief from Hitler's attentions. He frequently sent for the new foreign minister, the conservative František Chvalkovský, and demanded that Czech policy be brought into line with German. The Czech government duly complied. The Communist Party was banned on 20 October and dissolved a week later. Klement Gottwald and other Communist leaders left for Moscow. The Czech fascists, by contrast, felt more self-confident; a National Socialist party was allowed and the ban on anti-semitic agitation was revoked. In November, President Beneš's empty post was filled by Dr Emil Hácha, an elderly conservative judge. His colleagues were men who believed, some more honourably than others, in peaceful coexistence with Germany. A country betrayed by appeasers was now led by appeasers, and Milena and Evžen watched nervously.

One tangible effect on Milena's life was an increase in press censorship. Milena knew that everything she wrote was monitored, that 'between the journalist and reader there is not only paper, but also the censor.' She recommended new ways of reading the newspapers, with a clever analysis of the classified advertisements. These told the real story. There were advertisements for summer houses and even shops and businesses in the border region, offers of service from professionals and craftsmen newly arrived in Prague, and small ads promising visas for America, Honduras, Australia.

Prices were rising and jobs scarce. Milena met the unemployed on the streets of Prague and in labour queues. She described how young and old men applied for work camps, which at least gave them a wage even if they had to leave their families. Another consequence of increasing unemployment was that married women were being sacked and 'returned to their normal calling'. Milena's blood boiled. 'How exalted it sounds! But what is it, this natural calling of women? Their physiological function? Can a physiological function be a calling? . . . There were times when we spoke about the emancipation of women, about the rights of women and the struggle to achieve them. Those times are gone.'

At the *Přítomnost* offices, Milena was busier than ever. Several of the staff had left, and Milena took on greater editorial responsibilities as well as writing her own articles. She wrote notes to Willi, fretting that she had not had a letter from him, and asking for articles about French foreign policy, his assessment of the political situation or topics like 'Why socialism always fails at the crucial moment. Not Marxism or bolshevism but socialism.' Somehow the pages of the paper had to be filled.

She missed Willi and Steffi but at least they were safe. Other friends met a sadder fate. One day, a few weeks after Munich, she was called to a Prague hospital where Rudolf Thomas, editor of the German paper the *Prager Tagblatt*, and his wife Greta, had been taken after poisoning themselves. Rudolf Thomas had been a good friend, a good talker and companion in Prague café life. Once, when Milena tried to entice him to go for a walk in the woods, he interrupted her: 'You know what, why don't you go and take photographs of the woods and bring the snaps to the café!'

Milena was greatly shaken by the death of Thomas and his wife. She wrote to Willi: 'They did it with dignity. You see, if you really want it, it happens very quickly, quietly and almost happily . . . there's something seductive about it, even for me. Not because of unhappiness. But because of a terrible tiredness. Tiredness about the future.' She told Willi she was worried about another of their friends and found pretexts to visit him to try to talk him out of his suicidal mood. But as someone who had herself tried to commit suicide as a young woman, she felt she had no right to criticise. She understood that for some people suicide might represent a kind of freedom from the half life which was all that was possible in those dark days.

As winter settled in, Milena felt more and more depressed. Everyone's morale was deteriorating. Her only consolation was her work. She acknowledged to Willi that Peroutka, after a lazy summer, had rallied and was striving to keep *Přítomnost* going. All the staff agreed to take a pay cut. 'It's desperately difficult. We haven't got enough information to write about or enough people. Any article from you is a great help.' She told Willi that she missed him. 'Sometimes I see you on the street and when I get closer it's not you. One day I followed a tram in a taxi because I was so sure you were there. You on a tram! How could I have been so silly!'

Christmas approached. Milena wrote her usual seasonal fare about children's toys, but this time as a fable for the times. 'Perhaps you are tired from the last months, exhausted by what's happened, almost crushed to death by the organised cruelty which has replaced liberalism. Perhaps you have moments when it seems that everything beautiful has vanished from our world. Children's toys can give you new hope.'

But it was a struggle. Milena left Honza and Evžen for a few days and resumed her travels around the country, this time going to the new border area with Germany. Her friend from the refugee organisation, Mařka Šmolková, had told a meeting of the League of Nations that it was impossible for the Czechs to handle any more refugees. Milena's own travels confirmed this and she realised that for the first time since the First World War there was a No Man's Land in Europe.

Today there is a No Man's Land just a stone's throw from the village. At some places along the German and Czech border – my God, what a border it is, a piece of wire in a field, a barrier across a road, a rope from tree to tree, a pathetic border, a child could kick it away – there is a strip of land which belongs to nobody. When the Czech soldiers departed, German recruits brought Jews deported from the occupied area. Then some refugee Jews returned from the remnants of Czechoslovakia, some because they heard rumours, some from fear for their property, others from fear for their loved ones who had stayed in the confiscated territory. They got through the barbed wire of Czechoslovakia. They did not get through the barbed wire of Germany. And then they could no longer get back across the Czechoslovak wire. The barbed wire of 1938 is firm and impenetrable.

She described the conditions in No Man's Land for the refugees, a father putting his children to sleep in holes in the ground covered with straw, a woman giving birth in a field, an old blind man. They survived because local people helped them with clothes, food and even tents. Eventually, as Milena had argued was necessary, guarantees from third countries meant that many of these refugees were allowed into the Czech lands on their way to western Europe or America.

Back in Prague, Christmas came and went cheerlessly. Domestic life was hard, since there was little money, no maid and food was becoming scarce. What semblance of family life Milena, Evžen and Honza had ever had was constantly interrupted by the flow of refugees and political dissidents whom Milena allowed to take refuge in her small flat. Milena and Evžen were both too busy to spend much time together but, despite their differences, he remained a gentle friendly presence in her life.

'Christmas was really awful,' Milena wrote to Willi. Jaromír was ill again, and Riva had come to stay, penniless, 'almost like a frightened bird'. Willi and Steffi sent Christmas letters, and Honza replied to Steffi: 'Have you got snow? We had lots but it's already melting. We have a new radio. I got lots of books for Christmas.' The radio was no doubt part treat, part necessity. Milena turned to the music stations as distraction and consolation after work, but the radio was also a vital source of news from foreign stations and offered some contact with a world beyond the claustrophobic Czech republic. Honza later wrote: 'She would keep tuning from station to station far into the night, and whether it was music or speech or only the hiss of a channel no longer broadcasting, she would not turn it off. . . . At least in this way, she could travel the world.'

The worst blow was the death of Karel Čapek on Christmas Day itself. It was a personal loss for Milena; she had known him as a young girl, and then again as a mature journalist. In her Communist phase she had considered him the worst kind of bourgeois intellectual. But in more recent years she had come to regard him as a heroic exponent of the liberal values of Masaryk's First Republic, a Czech patriot 'with a considered, subtle hierarchy of moral values, a firm world order in his heart and in his thoughts'. His death, at his house by a lake in the countryside outside Prague, officially from pneumonia, was more than a personal sadness. It seemed to symbolise the death of Czechoslovakia. Milena wrote a long obituary for *Přítomnost*:

> The year 1938 was like a flood which shifted boulders that had until then seemed so firm. He felt blow after blow after blow. The loss of French friendship, the loss of faith in the 'Marseillaise' – that hymn to democratic freedom – the loss of mountains and borders, a paralysed country, the restricted power of the poet. . . . Too much devastation for the heart of a man whose living art was to build, to construct, to work. . . . He was too modest and shy a man to die of a broken heart. So he died of pneumonia.

Milena had to comfort Peroutka, saddened by the loss of his great friend. But Čapek's death touched the general public too, and on the day of his funeral people flocked to pay their respects. 'It's not only love for Čapek,' Milena wrote to Willi, 'it's more, it's a demonstration, a confession. It's quite spontaneous and just as overwhelming as it was when Masaryk died. . . . It's so tiny this country. Yet it's simply amazing how much good happens here.' But these displays of Czech pride only made the Czech government nervous and infuriated the watchful Germans. The atmosphere of repression continued, and Milena's worries for Evžen increased. But, she told Willi, she saw her own fate quite differently from that of the Jews: 'The Jews really must get away from here. But I am not going away.'

Not all her articles were about the immediate political situation. In February she turned again to the plight of young working women, and the fact that 'emancipation' did not always bring freedom. Much of the work available to young women, in the factory or office, was drudgery. 'Work – followed by food and sleep so as to be able to go to work again – doesn't leave much room for joy.' They remained dependent on young men for invitations to a film or a dance, and therefore dependent on their looks. Milena listed the prices of cologne, lip rouge, face cream, the economics of beauty. She described the weekend courtship ritual on Wenceslas Square. 'They walk with slow steps in two streams – up the left side and down the right – exposed in the clear light of unloving sunshine. . . . They are almost all lifeless, thin-blooded girls with bad complexions, cheeks smudged with vermilion and cream, with sunken faces slapped with powder. They have masks rather than faces.'

Their desire to love and to be loved was 'like a bacillus', a disease which might cost them their decency and therefore their eligibility for marriage. 'The social conditions in which these girls develop cannot create what we need; good, healthy and natural women, excellent mothers and wise grandmothers.' This is classic Milena – sympathetic, a little snobbish, combining her outrage at individual cases with a broader analysis of the social reasons behind their plight.

But Milena could not distract herself or her readers from their main preoccupation for long. The months after Munich were, according to one observer, 'very, very sad. It was as if in a well-lit room one light after another was extinguished.' Milena wrote a tribute (which was perhaps an exhortation in disguise) to the courage of her countryfolk, their 'patient tenacity', as well as to their common sense and anti-authoritarianism. All they had left of free national expression was the Czech language. 'We Czechs cling to our language not only with national pride, national consciousness and national defiance, but because there have been whole decades when it is the only thing we truly own, the only expression of our thinking, our traditions, our way of life.'

She had nothing against the German language in itself, but she was appalled by the language of Hitler and in particular his notion of a German 'living-space' and a secondary role for the Czechs as a geographical bridge eastwards.

> I am a Czech and therefore I have a good ear for music. I hear words clearly and I know precisely what they mean. Space [*prostor*] – that is the sky, the air, clouds, something wide, vague, extensive. We, however, live on this clod of land, extracting a living from it. We have lived here for centuries, from father to son. We live here. We do not create a 'living-space'. . . . In my opinion, we do not constitute a bridge between Germans and Slavs. We – today's Czechs – constitute a bridge between the Czechs of yesterday and the Czechs of tomorrow.

This article was her most defiant statement of Czech pride yet, as she struggled to redefine an identity for her readers under the new conditions.

Such defiance was understandable but in vain. Munich had been only a temporary restraint on Hitler's ambitions; even a smaller Czechoslovakia remained an 'abscess'. If his longer-term plan to take

Poland was to be fulfilled, the irritating abscess must be dealt with. Hitler encouraged the Slovaks to declare full independence, and as March passed he made plans for a military occupation of the Czech lands of Bohemia and Moravia.

As Hitler prepared to pluck the fruits left unprotected by western appeasement, Milena made clear that she blamed the east as well. She had, she acknowledged in an article on 8 March, written enough about Munich and the traitors of western Europe. Russia and their Communist supporters in Prague were traitors too. She mocked the inappropriate bravado of the Communist newspaper *Rudé právo* which, until its closure in autumn 1938, had after each fresh disaster printed futile slogans such as 'Workers rise up!' or 'The workers will not stand for it!' 'How to explain that in the last six years the Communist press has strayed from reality like a landscape drawing by someone who is colour-blind?' There was no tangible help from Moscow, in the form of offers of asylum for refugees or security guarantees.

Milena was right that no useful help would come from outside. When the Slovak fascists, abetted by Hitler, proclaimed independence on 14 March 1939, Hitler used this as his pretext to move: if Czechoslovakia could not even keep itself in one piece, he had no option but to impose stability on the region. Munich was irrelevant. (Chamberlain too would explain that he had always regarded the Munich border guarantees as transitory and that with Slovak independence, albeit as a client state of Germany, any moral obligation to Czechoslovakia had ceased to exist.)

President Hácha and Foreign Minister Chvalkovský asked for an audience with Hitler. On 14 March they left for Berlin. But it was the fate of Bohemia, not Slovakia, that was on the agenda. In the small hours of 15 March, Hitler informed the president that he had given orders for the German army to enter Bohemia and Moravia. Any opposition would be met by the bombing of Prague. President Hácha had no choice. He telephoned Prague and gave instructions that the Czech army must not resist the invasion. Hitler forced him to sign a declaration saying that 'he confidently placed the fate of the Czech people in the hands of the Führer and of the German Reich.'

As the president capitulated in Berlin, and as the tanks and troops rolled through the snowy darkness across Bohemia, Milena woke early in Prague and turned on the radio. This is how she described the invasion and the days that followed.

Kafka, Love and Courage

How do the greatest events come upon us? Suddenly and unexpectedly. But when they do happen we always find we are not surprised. Everyone always has some presentiment, some idea of what is coming, which is drowned out by reason, willpower, hope, fear, work and the bustle of ordinary life . . .

On Tuesday at four o'clock in the morning, when the telephone rang, when friends and acquaintances phoned, when Czech radio began to broadcast, the town beneath our windows looked the same as any other night. The pattern of lights was the same, the crossroads made the same cross. Except that, from three o'clock, lights gradually came on. At the neighbours' opposite, below, above, then along the whole street. We stood at the window and said to ourselves, they know. We woke people up with a phone call: Do you know? Yes, they replied. A troubled dawn over the roofs, a pale moon behind the clouds, faces drawn with sleeplessness, a cup of hot coffee and the regular voice of the radio. This is how the most important things happen, silently and unexpectedly . . .

As always, when great events happen, Czechs behave excellently. We should thank Czech radio for the brief reports it broadcast patiently and regularly: Keep calm. Go to work. Send your children to school. At half-past seven in the morning, the usual procession formed of children on their way to school. Factory workers and clerks went to work as usual. The trams were full as usual. The only difference was the people. They stood in silence. There were no knots of people talking in the streets. No one raised their head from their desk in the office. . . . At 8.35 on 15 March 1939 the Reichstag army arrived on Národní třída. The people streamed along the pavements as usual. No one looked up or turned their head. German citizens of Prague welcomed the Reichstag soldiers.

The German soldiers even behaved decently. It is extraordinary how everything changes when something breaks up into its constituent parts, when individual people stand face to face. On Wenceslas Square, a Czech girl met a group of German soldiers. And because it was already the second day, because our nerves were all a little frayed, and because it is only on the second day that we understand better and think more, she burst into tears. And then something amazing happened. A German soldier came up to her, a simple, ordinary soldier and said, 'Aber Fräulein, wir können doch nichts dafür . . .' ['It is not our fault . . .'] He said it as if he was soothing a little child. He had a German face, a little freckled, with reddish hair, and a German uniform. Otherwise nothing distinguished him from a young Czech recruit, a simple man devoted to his country.

War

Not all Czechs behaved with dignity.

I was talking with a German, a National Socialist of course. He spoke for a long time and very thoughtfully about the Czech situation and about the advantages and disadvantages he himself could see. . . . He asked me rather warily, 'How do you explain that so many Czechs come up to us and say Heil Hitler?'

Czechs? Surely there is some mistake. There isn't. They come to our office, they raise their right hand and say Heil Hitler. Why? I could tell you about a writer who cares desperately that his plays are shown on the Berlin stage immediately. I could tell you about many people who do more than they have to, in feverish haste. You know, every German understands national pride and national spirit. Humiliating behaviour only provokes in today's German a wry smile, believe me.

In two days the face of the town has changed beyond recognition. . . . Men in uniforms drive along the streets in vehicles we have never seen before. They drive hither and thither, they always know what they have to do, they behave absolutely decisively and methodically. They buy maps of Prague and French and English books. Knots of soldiers walk along the streets, they stand in front of shop windows, they stare, they talk. Meanwhile, not a single cog stopped, not a single pen, not a single machine.

On Old Town Square is the Tomb of the Unknown Soldier. Today, nothing can be seen of it except a huge heap of snowdrops. What is this incredible force, which secretly directs people's steps, bringing crowds of Prague citizens here? Everyone lays a bunch of snowdrops on the little tomb with its great memory. People stand around and tears stream down their faces. Not only women and children, but even men, who are not used to tears. And again it is somehow wonderfully Czech. It is not fear at all, it is not grief, it is not despair, it is not wounded feelings, it is only sadness. This sadness must find some outlet, several hundred eyes must overflow . . .

At the back of the crowd I saw a passing German soldier stand and salute. He looked into the eyes red with weeping, into the teardrops on the snowy mountain of snowdrops, he saw people cry who were crying because he is here. And he saluted. Probably he understood why we are sad. Glancing back at him I thought about the Great Illusion: will we ever really live alongside each other – German, Czech, French, Russian, British – without hurting each other, without having to hate each other, without doing each other injustice? Will the empires ever really understand each other as individual people understand each other? Will the borders between countries ever come down, as they come down between people? How wonderful it would be to live to see that day!

But as Milena dreamed, a harsher reality was being imposed on the Czechs. Hitler arrived by special train in Prague on the evening after the invasion; the next day he declared Bohemia and Moravia a German protectorate, a part of Greater Germany. There was no response from the western powers. Hácha remained in nominal power, but a Reich Protector, Baron von Neurath, was appointed and he had ultimate control. The civil service was left in place but German appointees were added, and German troops and Gestapo officers appeared on the streets. (The Czech army was largely disbanded.) Germany rapidly took control of the economy, in time appropriating banks, factories – in particular the arms industry, which would become crucial to the German war effort – and Jewish-run firms. Czech societies and organisations such as Sokol were banned, and many towns brought in harsh anti-semitic regulations restricting Jewish freedom of movement. Street signs were replaced by signs in German as well as Czech and the Germans even insisted that everyone should start to drive on the right. First Republic Czechoslovakia had driven on the left, as in Britain. There were remarkably few traffic accidents.

The disingenuous German message was that Czechs need have nothing to fear. They remained autonomous, but were now properly within the German sphere. German propaganda worked to convince Czechs that while they were a distinct people, they had no real history of their own. Anything heroic or strong in their past, such as their mediaeval and renaissance history, in fact stemmed from the German presence and influence. Bohemia was and always had been German.

Milena shared her occupied nation's stunned grief. But, she told her readers, there would have been no point in resisting the Germans. 'It would have been a suicidal gesture. Perhaps it is beautiful to die in vain. Perhaps it is beautiful to shed blood in a heroic gesture for your country. I don't even think it would be that difficult. But we must do something quite different. We must live. We must save every man we have, every sinew, all our strength. Every one of us must defend our living language, our national selfhood and its expression.' The new situation demanded a new consciousness.

German propaganda must be resisted by the conscious nurturing of nationhood. Political events were making a fervent patriot of Milena.

This was a risky stance to take. The Gestapo had come prepared with a list of intellectuals, left-wingers and Jews to be rounded up. German refugees were sent to concentration camps. Within a few days several hundred communists were interrogated, though most were freed with a warning. Peroutka was arrested and Milena took over the editorship of *Přítomnost*. When Peroutka was released a couple of weeks later she kept the position and Peroutka remained in the background.

The arrests and intimidation increased Milena's fears for Evžen. She had burnt papers, photographs and letters which might incriminate either of them as too left-wing or anti-German. But this was not enough. Evžen must go. She asked Willi (who was now with Steffi in America) to help. 'Evžen must leave, and quickly. . . . It's urgent . . . I just don't know if we'll succeed in getting him away.' Friends were also suggesting that she leave. 'But we can't all three of us go at the same time. Anyway it's unnecessary, because nothing is happening to me here, and I've still got a lot to do for the time being. I can't tell how long I still have left to work here. In any case, it's much more time than Evžen has. And anyway nothing worse will happen to me than losing my income. But he is under immediate threat – of a different fate.'

Through her contacts with refugee organisations Milena became acquainted with a group of British men and women working in Prague as teachers, who were involved in helping people leave the country. Through them she met a young man called Joachim von Zedtwitz, a German count with anarchist leanings who also wanted to help the refugees. Milena's flat was used as a halfway house for Czech soldiers and airmen who wanted to go via Poland to France, where a Czech unit was gathering in preparation for the war which everyone expected, and, increasingly, for Jews. The people who gathered in the flat would not always know each other's names, since secrecy was vital. But they included several important journalists such as Rudolf Keller, of the *Prager Tagblatt*. Zedtwitz would collect the refugees in his soft-topped Aero two-seater sports car and drive them to the Polish border, where other resistance workers would pass them on. Jochi, as Milena came to call him, was perfect for such work. The Germans would never suspect this dashing, blue-eyed figure, with a swastika badge under his lapel to be flashed when convenient. He and Milena became good friends. She enjoyed the company of the elegant and energetic young man, and he admired her as a dedicated and politically astute woman: 'At that time,' he later said, 'Milena looked like Churchill. She had the same bulging forehead, the same prodigious intelligence in her eyes, the same asymmetrical mouth drawn in at the corners, the same look of determination. Her resemblance to Churchill is no accident; their looks reflected the same political genius.'

Evžen, Milena decided, should use this escape route at once. Evžen wanted Milena and Honza, now ten, to go with him; Milena assured him they would follow a few days later, and one morning she and Honza waved Evžen's big bearlike figure off in Jochi's car. Honza later wrote: 'And all at once, as soon as they had vanished from sight, the full horror of the previous days sank in. The flat was dead, Milena and I dropped everything and fled into the street, away from the flat, which was suddenly so empty and whose walls felt as if they were closing in on us.'

Later in April, Milena heard that Evžen had reached Poland safely and was on his way to England. Willi and Steffi wrote offering to help if he needed papers for America. Milena wrote to thank them and said: 'When he left, I suddenly discovered that I still love him. . . . For a long time I thought it wasn't true. . . . Evžen went round the corner, I saw him from the window, how he vanished; that corner is still here, sometimes I think that I could just run down there and find him.'

She tried to communicate with him, and sent a message via Eduard Goldstücker, a Communist intellectual who had first met Milena when he was a young student and had sold her some photographs for *Tvorba* in the early 1930s. Although he knew Milena's lack of sympathy for the Communist cause now, he came to visit her in June and she gave him a message for Evžen about how he could contact her. For a while they were able to correspond, and she wrote to him about her fund-raising efforts to pay off his debts and save for future emergencies and about how she and Honza were getting on.

She reassured him that she would leave too. But there was much to be done in Prague, both helping refugees and keeping *Přítomnost* going. She spent long hours at the offices in Národní třída, in her uniform blue dress or suit, chivvying people to deliver articles, editing them, planning coverage. As if arguing out her own feelings about whether or not to leave, she wrote an article about the temptations of running away from difficult situations. People, she declared, must learn the art of 'standing still', of facing reality and holding firm. The Czechs would only survive by standing together. She recalled her father's bravery in the face of the Austrian demonstrators when she was a child, and the audience in the theatre during the First World War, standing to attention for the Czech national song. In her articles she told parables for her readers; she was also weaving herself a new version of her life as a daughter of the Czech nation. The political crisis brought her closer to her father. They had talked on the telephone on the morning of 15 March, and Dr Jesenský had shown concern for Evžen, grudgingly accepting his place in his daughter and grand-daughter's lives. Shortly before Evžen's departure he gave him some money.

The importance of defining a strong Czech identity grew as German propaganda intensified. One area of argument was the Czech language. The German occupiers declared German an official language along with Czech, but the Czechs refused to concede that German was the superior language. The German press in Prague took this as a gross insult, until in August 1939 a new decree gave German precedence over Czech. The German policy towards Czech culture was a subtle one. Folk culture was accepted and even encouraged, as long as it was presented as the quaint ways of a small people subservient to a larger one. What could not be tolerated was any claim by Czech culture to take an equal place on the European stage.

Against this background, Milena's championship of Czech language and culture was defiant. But her growing identification with the Czech nation sometimes strayed into sentimentality. She wrote a tribute to Czech women, caring for their families in these hard times. Their task now, Milena wrote, was to keep the Czech flame alive.

> Our mothers return to the task of our grandmothers. I see my grandmother before me and will never forget her. She looked like Božena Němcová's Babička, as all our grandmothers did. . . . Little things become great symbols. And since it is women who wield the little things in their hands, they also rule over the great symbols. Czech songs and Czech books. Czech hospitality. Czech language and customs. Czech Christmas eggs, Czech gardens, Czech homes, Czech songs and the good-hearted spirit of the Czech people. All these little things lie in the hands of Czech women.

There is no suggestion, however, that Milena saw such a role for herself. She was too busy with other work to sing folksongs to Honza or bake Czech cakes.

For as well as working at *Přítomnost*, Milena was also in contact with people trying to organise an underground, uncensored press. A diverse group, including writers and publishers, began to produce a cyclostyled publication, *V Boj* (*To the fight!*), based at the house of Major Škalda in Budečská street in Vinohrady. Milena became involved in helping distribute *V Boj*, whose few hundred copies came out every week or so. Occasionally she wrote articles. The magazine, on thin paper with a sketch or cartoon on the cover, included translations of articles from foreign papers, analysis about the likelihood of war, and rousing articles to encourage its readers. Milena was also involved in the broader resistance, collecting information from her journalistic and old Communist contacts. (Although the Communists pursued their own activities, there were some links.) Even if there was little direct action for the resistance to take, it was vital to show Czechs and the exiled Czech leadership that the networks were in existence and ready for when the time came.

This work enmeshed Milena deeper in Prague. She knew that she was running risks, and that her home and office might be searched. (Kafka's letters to her would then be at risk. She gave them to her friend Willy Haas, who had returned from Berlin earlier in the 1930s but was now planning to leave again. He was one of the few people with whom Milena talked about Kafka and the old days, as they went for walks around Prague. He was as interested as she to have and protect the letters; in the end he left them with relatives in Prague until after the war, when he eventually edited and published them.) But Milena could not think of leaving Prague. There were always others who needed the escape route more or who needed her help. She took in her friends, the journalist and translator Stanislav Budín, his wife Hana (an architect who had taught Jaromír) and their children for a couple of months, until they were able to get papers to leave. 'She refused to take us to the station,' Stanislav wrote, 'but said goodbye at home, with tears in her eyes.' He had always regarded her as a loyal friend, and once out of the country he tried to repay her, making efforts to get papers so that she could join them in South America. Another contact was doing the same in Oslo, and Evžen of course in London. He still believed she would come.

But she knew by now that she would not. One incident at the time illustrates her state of mind. Some weeks after the occupation, she agreed to have coffee with a young lawyer acquaintance, Libuše Vokrová. They met at the café next door to the *Přítomnost* office. The red plush seats, the mirrors and discreet lighting called for a relaxed bustle of customers. Instead the café was almost empty, except for a few German soldiers in the far corner. Milena, imposing as ever in an austere suit, and Libuše, a small, neat woman, were far from relaxed.

Libuše went straight to the point. Through her connections with one of the resistance groups she had met an English woman ('a Gainsborough portrait') who was in a position to provide visas to Britain for Czechs in danger if Libuše could get hold of their papers within twenty-four hours. Libuše's group had a list of those they considered most at risk. Milena was not on it, but Libuše, who admired Milena's work, had sought her out.

As Libuše Vokrová recalled the encounter, to her amazement Milena refused the offer of escape. Somewhat sternly she said, 'How should I leave my place, now, when I *am Přítomnost*? Who else would do it?' Libuše argued (rightly as it turned out) that the German censors might not allow *Přítomnost* to be published much longer. She also said that Milena would be of just as much use working for the Czechoslovak cause in London. But she also appealed to Milena as one mother to another. Shouldn't Milena be thinking of Honza? Milena was adamant that *Přítomnost*, her work and her country were the most important thing. Hours later Libuše was on her way out of Czechoslovakia.

Perhaps as a necessary defence, Milena became increasingly scornful of people who left with what she saw as no real cause. She described meeting a doctor, blonde, well-dressed, who told Milena she was determined to leave with her family since there was nothing to look forward to in Prague. Milena protested: 'And where does she want to go with these children? ... In a few Sundays this blonde creature will join the crowd of people who gather at the consulates, carrying their best suitcases and first-class boat tickets, to leave for somewhere where they will live more comfortably ... these are the people who were "by chance" in London in May, and "by chance" again in September.'

By contrast there was Franta Slezák, a villager whom she met in his garden at Slaný outside Prague.

What are you doing, I asked. Well, I have to collect the potatoes and the rye. It was a cold spring, but they've come up nicely, by some miracle. I have to cut down two old apple trees in the orchard and plant new ones. ... Well, I say, and how do you cope with the

Germans? What do you mean, they go their way, I go mine, he said quietly. I have my fields, hens and geese, the children go to school and the farm is in debt. That's me. And you're not afraid? What would I be afraid of? ... And, he continued with that wonderful Czech humour: Anyway, a man dies only once, and if he dies a little early, so he's dead for a little longer.

This 'natural courage' was, like 'the art of standing still', to be found in a picture of traditional Czech life. It was not just for the German censors that Milena suggested that there was no need to be afraid of the Germans. It was her own necessary conviction if she was to stay, shoring up her courage with a timeless image of Czech resilience.

She needed all her strength. The atmosphere in Prague was debilitating. A Czech soldier wrote: 'You never hear any good news. Every day brings something bad, and every new thing is always worse. You are permanently living in anxiety, permanently afraid of what the next day will bring. ... There is no possibility of personal relaxation.'

Milena certainly knew no relaxation. *Přítomnost* was under surveillance by the Germans, and Milena was regularly called in for interrogation by the chief German censor, Wolfram von Wolmar. These sparring partners shared a strange kind of mutual respect for each other's intelligence and persistence as they faced each other across von Wolmar's desk in the Petschek Palace, an imposing former bank building off Wenceslas Square which the Gestapo had taken over. Milena found von Wolmar always courteous, however stern his warnings.

One way round the censor's sensitivities was to confront them head on. In one article Milena described yet again the Munich betrayal of Czechoslovakia, a little country only as big as 'a coin in the palm of Europe'. But to those for whom it was home, she wrote, it was 'a magic land', and it had been a hard blow not to be able to defend it. Surely, she wrote, German readers should be able 'to understand this pain better than anyone else, for the Germans are a nation of soldiers.'

The subtext of her articles at this time was a search for an ideal kind of Czech nationalism, quite different from the dangerous nationalism of Nazi Germany. Her articles formed a continuing discussion between herself and her readers (and the censor). What did it mean to be a 'good Czech'; how to be a proper patriot without becoming a bitter chauvinist? She explored this theme in an article entitled 'Am I above all a Czech?' A reader had commented that he liked her articles because she seemed 'above everything' to be a Czech. But for Milena nation could not be enough. The French had been a glorious nation; now, after the Munich crisis, they had lost the world's respect. 'I am of course a Czech, but above all I try to be a decent person.'

This article provoked many letters. One reader wrote that she was belittling her nationhood. The times were not right, he said, for a cold analysis of the concepts of nation and humanity; 'Now the fire must blaze, the brave heart must pound, eyes must shine: I am Czech and I will remain so for ever!' But for Milena this credo could never be an end, only a beginning: 'I demand something more: that we fill the concept of our Czechness with the most honest, most beautiful and most pure content.'

Her demand was necessarily vague; there could be no call to direct action against the Germans. What Milena was trying all the time to encourage was an attitude of self-respect. In another article she wrote that there was no point wilting in the shadow of the Germans. 'We have got into the habit of whispering, instead of speaking aloud.' The danger was that 'the buzzing reaches even the Germans, and is unacceptable to their ears. Because they don't understand what we whisper, they can only imagine. And because they don't understand why we whisper, they become irritated.' She urged Czechs to speak freely, and not to retreat into black humour, the resort of the powerless.

> However much I love the Czech sense of humour, there are days when it's good to have less humour rather than more. Jews of course have the best and the deepest jokes. Out of the agony of their terrible fate stream jokes dripping with blood. There are Czech jokes which have the same philosophical depth and hopeless irony as Jewish ones. But I cannot laugh when I hear them, although I find them remarkable. I would not wish my nation this fatal mental brittleness which breeds such ironic scepticism.

Her message was not only for her readers. She wanted the remnants of Czech power in the country not to whisper either. Milena acknowledged the difficulties for the all-party National Assembly which the Germans allowed to be established, in having to keep both the Reich Protector and the Czech people happy. But she served notice that although the people had not been able to vote for the National Assembly Czechs expected it to stand up for their interests.

Czech society was inevitably becoming polarised, between those determined to defy the Germans and those who felt that the best way to survive was by compliance. Many people such as Czech civil servants or workers in the Škoda arms factory knew that their well-being depended on collaboration. But even here resistance was possible for those who dared. Documents and new regulations could be slowed up, and some of the shells produced for Škoda developed imperceptible faults which made them of little use on the battlefield. Then there were the girls who refused to dance with German soldiers at Saturday night dances, shopkeepers who refused to serve Germans or were at best icily polite, or people who refused to take trams now that they had German as well as Czech signs on them. Attendance at Czech concerts and plays was higher than ever. And then there were people like Milena. On one level preaching dignified co-existence. On another working for the underground resistance, preparing people and networks should the time come for real action against the Germans.

Milena's flat became a kind of salon for non-collaborators, including the young. She described the scene. 'In front of me is a group of young people. They sit in my garret, drinking tea and chatting. . . . They put me to shame. They know much more than I know. . . . They are straightforward and unpretentious, not blinded by any party dogma. They are serious, simple, independent, clever and therefore very beautiful.'

Was one of the group Lumír Čivrný? While working as a tutor for Honza he became very close to Milena. He admired her independence, her hard work, her bravery, her emotional openness; she was a woman of depth. Later, he understood that her emotional and practical generosity to others was in part a way of acting out what she would have liked in return. 'At night, when she was on the edge of exhaustion, she would pick up the telephone and ring anyone she thought might be feeling dejected, and listen and offer consolation and encouragement through the darkness. As if she herself had a bottomless supply of strength. In reality she thirsted for consolation and encouragement. But she did not know how to ask for it; she hid her longing for compassionate tenderness in irony and sarcasm.' Milena in turn liked the young man's intelligence and enthusiasm. With Evžen away and the departure of many other friends, including

War

Ernst Pollak, she needed companionship. After her youthful relationships with much older men the friendship of young men like Lumír and Joachim made her feel attractive and needed, and brought her affection without too much risk of exposure.

She enjoyed talking to Lumír, and arguing with him about culture and politics. He wrote poetry and still had the idealism of youth; he was fervently socialist. She told him that beyond Hitler lay another, equally dangerous threat, tyranny from the left. 'She could see further than anyone else at the time. I could not follow.' The friendship and affection of the young Čivrný brought her much warmth.

Her other source of strength in these weeks was the belief that she was doing something important. All her youthful longings and desire for love were submerged, through willpower, in the task at hand. *Přítomnost*, including her articles, was eagerly read. Before, she had been unusual but not alone as a prominent woman journalist. Now, as the editor of one of the few remaining publications, she was unique. She knew that this left her exposed. As the pressure from the Germans on the paper increased, she wrote, in what would prove to be one of her last articles, her own manifesto.

> On 15 March, the Czech journalist was given a new task. . . . The Czech journalist has in his hands living Czech words and in front of him a piece of white paper. A year ago, a Czech journalist was, compared with a soldier, more or less a private person. This has changed. For the piece of white paper, and the Czech words, are the material with which our generation will fight for the development and consciousness of our nation. In the whirl of political events and in the forging of political values, the Czech journalist stands as the only intermediary between events and people . . .
>
> Although I have not spoken to every individual, I know quite clearly that we all feel the same. In this situation it is not possible to feel any different. Anyone who did has already left, leaving their white piece of paper blank. We who stayed have set to work.

In a message for the censors she wrote that Czech journalists were not preaching an anti-German message. She wanted to help ease tension between Germans and Czechs, so that they could live together tactfully and calmly. But it was a fine line to walk, encouraging the Czechs without exasperating the Germans. She used various tricks. Sometimes a direct appeal to the censors, sometimes (despite her earlier earnest plea for a serious rather than a comic approach) a joke. In June she went too far. In an article about the need to provide jobs for demobilised Czech soldiers, she praised German military might. 'Czech soldiers pass by under a window and the pavement rings a little. But only one German soldier has to pass by a café for the glasses to shake and plaster to fall from the ceiling.' She also quoted a parody of a German soldiers' song, from Bertolt Brecht's *Threepenny Opera*. This passed the ordinary censors but not the alert eye of von Wolmar. Milena was summoned, played innocent – 'She had never doubted that it was a German soldiers' song, because it sounded so very soldierly and so very German' – and eventually provoked the exasperated von Wolmar to throw her out of his office. She later told Margarete Buber-Neumann that she was 'proud of having made this disciplined, cultivated German lose his self-control'. Milena's youthful streak of deviousness and duplicity lived on in her ruthless and sometimes manipulative determination to keep the paper going.

But there was a price to pay: the increasing watchfulness of the censors. In July, Milena wrote an article about the economic consequences of the German occupation. It would be her last. She described the restrictions on labour rights, the removal of the right to strike, the slow but sure appropriation of Czech labour for the German cause. It was not easy to know precisely what was happening because there were no statistics on unemployment or even on the shrunken country's population. But many workers were now choosing or being forced to work in Germany, because that was where the jobs were. This, Milena chastised, was a betrayal. Everyone who leaves 'takes a piece of our culture, a piece of our thinking, a piece of our national being, a piece of our skills. Even a big stone can crumble and be worn away by raindrops – and we are not a big stone.' Czechs would only survive if enough remained to retain a critical mass. The government must do what it could to provide jobs at home, and she recalled her father's talk of the building of the National Theatre and the contribution everyone made; that spirit was needed again.

She had created a language of heroism and national sacrifice which may in part have helped her stand firm herself. But it was too much for the Germans. Her passport was taken away, and the interrogations increased. She wrote to Evžen about the atmosphere in Prague: 'We are alive, but we don't know how. We are all waiting for something but we don't know what. Something is in the air but we don't know what.' Evžen wrote to the Schlamms: 'It's as if she's confined. She's continually interrogated. . . . At the beginning of this month she went through some bad days. Sometimes she didn't come home at all. She had to promise that she wouldn't leave the country.' She was banned from writing, and in August the paper was banned entirely. (On 1 September, Peroutka was arrested and taken to Buchenwald concentration camp where he remained until the end of the war.)

Without the paper to keep her in Prague, Milena sought refuge out of the city. She had sent Honza to a summer holiday camp at Medlov in western Moravia in July. In August she and other friends, including Jaromír and Riva, went to join the children. The camp consisted of wooden huts gathered around a lake in the woods. By day everyone swam and walked and read, respite from the endless talk of impending war. In the evening, everyone gathered in the communal building around a big open fire. There were games and songs and charades, and sometimes a wildness among the adults which the children hardly understood. 'Milena swung from mood to mood,' Honza later wrote. 'Or more precisely she was in all moods at once. She sparkled with wit and venom, she was witty and wildly happy and at the same time deathly sad; at night she would go for a swim, tearing along despite her lameness, and then letting the water carry her as if she was drowning.'

On 23 August their holiday was interrupted by news of Hitler and Stalin's Nazi-Soviet Pact. The Soviet Union wanted more time to arm, while Hitler wanted to make safe his eastern flank. The news was a terrible betrayal for those who looked to the Soviet Union to help defeat Germany in the case of war. And then came the news on 1 September that Germany had invaded Poland. The group returned to Prague; Milena knew that war was now inevitable. On 3 September, Britain and France, honouring their pledge to Poland as they had not to the Czechs, declared war on Germany. The Second World War had begun.

Any chance of escape for Milena through Poland had now gone. In London, Evžen knew that Milena would not be able to join him. Friends from the time chastised themselves long afterwards that they had not made Milena go earlier, but in truth she did not want to. There are perhaps two main reasons why she stayed. First, the growing patriotism which made leaving seem like a betrayal of her country. She knew that she could be useful (this alone was a seductive argument for someone uncertain of her place in the world), and beneath the sometimes excessive rhetoric of her articles lies a real and considered patriotism. She believed that Czechs were by and large a decent, cultivated people with their own precious traditions, who did not deserve to be wiped out. Her sentimentality did not blind her to the fact that patriotism by itself is not enough, nor that there were many Czechs who were colluding, passively or not, with the Germans. But she now identified herself with her people, and she could not leave them.

The other reason was Prague itself. Milena had known exile and it had made her homesick. Since her return from Vienna life had not been easy, but one source of sustenance had been the city itself. She knew it inside out, she had lived in several of its corners, her journalism had taken her to others. She had watched the trees turn on Petřín Hill and the ice floes drift on the Vltava too many times. Prague had given her work, it had given her a kind of home with Evžen and Honza, and in the end it had given her back her relationship with her father. She had spent too much of her life not feeling at home to feel easy at throwing away any precious sense of belonging.

She also seems to have adopted a reckless defiance that nothing would happen to her. Close friends knew that she feared for her own safety, that the interrogations had made her sleepless and nerve-wracked, but in front of many people, and certainly in front of Honza, she insisted that she would be safe. As her article from 1925 about the bravery of Captain Scott suggested, the sources of courage are mysterious, buried deep in the heart.

In some ways the war was a relief. At least the allies were now engaged, and there was hope that the Germans would be defeated. But the rapid German victory over the Polish army was not encouraging. To Milena and others involved in the resistance struggle it seemed more important than ever to keep Czech hopes and dignity alive. From London, where Beneš was organising a government in exile, came the message that there was to be no open resistance. Milena continued to contribute to the underground, and there were plans for her to start another publication in case *V Boj* was closed down.

The Germans were pursuing a carrot and stick approach. Rationing was introduced on 1 October which was more generous than in the Reich. The workers were to be kept well fed and productive. But if the Czechs were to be reduced to a slave class of the Reich, the intellectuals, regarded as the fount of Czech nationalism, must be dealt with.

As Czech independence day on 28 October approached, Milena and her colleagues in the underground considered what to do. In the end it was decided to encourage an expression of Czech pride. The Czech government appealed for calm and Czech police were deployed to keep control. In Prague demonstrators gathered in the city centre wearing Czechoslovak colours in their buttonholes. But soon German SS officers and soldiers appeared and began to harass the demonstrators. Then they opened fire. Czech restraint vanished, German notices were torn down, the windows of German schools smashed, Germans set upon. In the shooting a student, Jan Opletal, was wounded. He died of his wounds a few days later. More demonstrations followed, which the Germans used as an excuse to act against the students. On the night of 16 November hundreds of students and teachers were arrested, and nine of them were summarily shot. Hitler shortly afterwards ordered all Czech universities and schools closed.

It was in this atmosphere of heightened German watchfulness that Milena made a terrible mistake.

On 11 November 1939, Milena sent Honza on a resistance errand, as she often did. Even though when she telephoned ahead to Major Škalda's house, a strange voice answered, she packed the child off and told her to say that she had come to collect some books. Who would suspect the child, with her short hair, trousers and sweater like a boy? She was supposed to collect the latest issue of *V Boj*, but if anything did not seem right she should ask to use the telephone as if she had forgotten what books she wanted. It was a Saturday, Lumír was visiting, and back in Kouřimská, Milena and he waited.

When Honza got to the apartment in Budečská street the door was opened by the Gestapo. Honza said what she had been told to. But instead of letting her use the phone, the officers insisted on taking her home to Mummy. The helpless Honza led them to Kouřimská. The officers searched the flat, took away some letters and papers, but mercifully never found the copies of *V Boj* hidden in the linen chest. They arrested Milena and Lumír. Milena told Honza to go to their friends the Mayers, whose daughter had recently gone to England, and stay there until she returned home. Poor Honza, far too capable and mature for her age, burnt the copies of *V Boj*, packed a few things, scooped her kitten into a bag, and took a tram to the Mayers.

Milena had arranged to see Joachim von Zedtwitz for lunch a few days later. But she never came. Zedtwitz too was detained. 'At the interrogation I was only asked about Milena. The Gestapo knew nothing about our escape work.'

12

Imprisonment

Milena was taken to Pankrác Prison, Prague's main gaol which stands on a slight hill to the south of the city. The prison, built a few years before Milena was born, consisted (and still does) of red-tiled four-storey blocks with few traces of architectural adornment. There is some art nouveau patterning over the doorway through which Milena would have entered and a small wooden clocktower better suited to a gingerbread house than a prison. But once inside, these concessions to the outside world are forgotten. Milena entered a realm of long corridors and endless clanging gates.

The Gestapo took over the former solitary confinement wing for its special use, preserving some of the tiny cells as they were, in other cases knocking two or three together to make a larger cell, perhaps five by ten yards, to hold several women. Each had a bare wooden floor, a lavatory in one corner and a small high window. The cell Milena was put in housed more than a dozen women, all political prisoners, and in a strange way it became home, offering friendship and even comfort after interrogations.

The prisoners were brought coffee and bread in the morning, perhaps some potatoes with a scrap of meat for lunch and another small meal in the evening. The bread, dark and rich, was well-regarded by the prisoners. Sometimes the German women guards relaxed the rules and allowed visitors to bring presents of food.

Unlike the regular criminals in the prison, the political prisoners were not allowed to work. They were taken outside to the prison yard for an hour's exercise every morning. The women walked in two circles, the younger, fitter ones on the outside, the older, weaker ones (including Milena) inside. They passed the remaining long hours in the cells talking, telling stories or discussing the fragments of news about their families and political developments which filtered in from outside. Sometimes a student would try to recall her lectures and give

Imprisonment

the others a talk on biology or Czech history. In the evenings they sang, which Milena enjoyed.

But this routine was frequently broken. Every day at least one of the women would be called for interrogation, and Milena was often taken in the prison van with other prisoners and armed guards to the Petschek Palace, known as 'Pečkárna'. She would arrive back at the cell exhausted, battered and sometimes bloodied from her interrogation as the Gestapo tried to wring incriminating information from her. She kept her silence; she was determined to protect others and anyway she believed she had little to tell them which they did not already know.

The waiting room at Pečkárna, where prisoners had to sit facing a blank white wall until they were called, was nicknamed 'the cinema'. One day in late January, more than two months after her arrest, Milena noticed Lumír Čivrný in the cinema. He had been released after his detention with Milena but was brought in for interrogation once again in the round-ups of students that persisted after November's persecution. Lumír watched how, in a moment, Milena approached a Czech woman who was working as an orderly in the room, grabbed her mop and headscarf and began sweeping the room, limping her way towards him, smiling and graceful. When she reached him, she leant over and whispered, 'You were our tutor and nothing else. Do you understand? That and nothing else.' He took her encouraging smile to the torture room, and was soon released.

Inside the prison too she was considerate and brave. Prison could not quell her need to be loved, or her determination to help others. Some of the younger prisoners knew of her from her journalism. One, Marie Chaloupecká, noticed her during the exercise hour. She smiled and even dared to greet her heroine. A guard pulled Marie out of the circle, slapped her and had her moved to another cell which exercised at a different time. Milena was clearly touched, because over the next few days she smuggled notes to Marie, via the prisoners who delivered the meals. 'My pretty dark-haired girl,' Milena wrote. 'I was very happy to see you because you are young, and can smile and are full of life. I have a little daughter and I hope she will laugh like you. I hope you and I will meet after the war in the evening with Jana or friends. Don't be sad, you must keep your humour.' Other notes also referred to Honza, and Marie believed that Milena saw her as a substitute daughter. Milena did not hide her remorse about the situation she had inflicted on Honza.

Occasionally, Milena was able to smuggle messages out of the prison, hidden in the bundle of linen which she handed over for friends to collect and wash every Thursday. They included a letter for Honza: 'I want only to say, be calm and happy, that I am healthy, and I look forward greatly to seeing you.' She entrusted her to the Mayers and to Jaromír and Dr Jesenský's care.

> Grandfather is wonderful, Honza, and behaves beautifully to me and to you, and everything that he asks from you is only for your good and for your future well-being. . . . My dear, imagine that we will again be together in some little room, if we can't have the old one, don't cry, we'll have another, we'll always find somewhere beautiful together, we'll spend the evening together and chat, I'll tell you so much and you'll tell me everything about yourself, more than to your best friend, you'll tell me everything, my sweet, golden girl. Honza, please, write to me more often than is allowed, I will always get a letter from my child. . . . Honza, you wrote to me once that you will love me until I am old – remember? Already, I am old, my dearest. An old mummy, who has nothing else but you, but that is a great deal. I am very rich, Honza, and happy that I have you.'

Her concern about Honza is clear in a note to a friend, Rokyta Illnerová, scribbled on a piece of fabric. Rokyta was a Jewish journalist whom Milena had known for some years and who was a near neighbour in Vinohrady. She had helped to distribute *V Boj*. Milena wrote that she was healthy but worried about Honza. She knew the Mayers were doing their best, but Honza was a difficult child. She asked Rokyta to keep an eye on her. 'I don't have any idea how long this will last. It seems that they think I am hiding something, but I really cannot say anything, since I know nothing and I keep telling them. Eventually they must themselves realise that I know nothing. There's talk of an amnesty on 15 March [1940], but there was that sort of rumour before Christmas too. As long as I am in Prague, there's hope that I will come home.'

Her friends shared this hope. In London, Evžen tried to establish Milena's fate. Dr Jesenský had telephoned him with news of Milena's arrest, but since then he had heard little. In March 1940 he wrote to the Schlamms that she was still in prison, but that he was doing his best to get her released and to arrange money and papers for her to leave Czechoslovakia. A Bolivian visa was one possibility. In April he wrote again, saying he had had news that Milena had been freed. He still believed this in July. By the following spring he was writing: 'In the last few months I haven't had any direct reports. . . . At the moment there's no hope for her to be able to leave the country. . . . I'm not really worried.'

Evžen was sadly misinformed. In spring 1940 Milena had left Pankrác, but she was taken to a prison in Dresden for trial by the Reich. She waited for weeks, suffering from dental problems and a skin infection as well as rheumatism. The German authorities offered her a legal representative since German was not her first language. She refused the offer and prepared her own defence. She faced several charges of resistance and treachery against the Protectorate, but was acquitted of most of them for lack of evidence. Eventually, in the late summer, the court decreed that she be returned to Prague. Milena assumed she would be released.

But the Gestapo was reluctant to let her go, confident that she was a nationalist, a resistance worker and a trouble-maker. She was returned to a different cell in Pankrác. Her fellow prisoners were struck by her emaciated frailty, but also by her dignity and the way she held her head erect. She had lost a lot of weight in Dresden and her skin was loose on her body. Her swollen joints were in pain, several of her teeth had gone, and she had digestive problems. New prisoners to the cell were usually allotted the worst sleeping places, by the lavatory. But a young Communist and nurse, Hana Housková, gave up her place.

Hana was impressed by Milena's unbroken bearing, her insistence on retaining the forms of civilised behaviour and her uncowed journalistic curiosity. She would greet the guards politely in the morning and even conduct long discussions with them about German history and relations between Germans and Czechs. Most responded in kind. If not, Milena stood her ground. Once when a guard handled her roughly she said, 'Get your hands off me.' When the other prisoners expressed their surprise at her behaviour, Milena would respond with what Hana described as her 'Mona Lisa smile'.

Milena's charisma and the respect she earned saved her from ostracism by the young Communist prisoners in her cell. But they would not accept her Trotskyite views. When she talked to them about the Moscow trials, one woman recited the defence, 'When forests are felled, splinters fly.' Milena replied, 'It was not splinters, it was people.' She did not talk much about her personal life or her past, but she could not help pouring out the remorse she felt at deserting Honza.

One day in October 1940 she was called out of her cell and, to her surprise, taken to receive her father and Honza. Honza later wrote: 'I couldn't recognise her ... This gaunt figure with its shoulder-length hair, prominent cheek-bones and huge blue eyes more closely resembled the "little Milena" her father had once known than the Milena I remembered, but even he did not recognise her at first as she came towards us. It was only because of her stiff-kneed walk that I knew it was her.' Honza was now living with Dr Jesenský, since the Mayers had left the country. The little girl thought to please her mother by telling her she was refusing to learn German at school. But Milena smiled and told her that on the contrary German was a lovely language and could not be held responsible for the people who spoke it. When the guard took her father and Honza away, Milena wept.

Although her fellow prisoners told her she should be cheered by the visit, Milena was sure it was a bad sign, that it had been a parting. She seemed at last to have lost spirit and to exist in a limbo. Hana noticed that Milena's hair, an extraordinary barometer of her state, became lifeless. 'When everything was peaceful her hair was velvety, smooth, waving lovingly about her face. When her spirit suffered, her hair became tangled, and hung about her head as if it did not belong to her.'

Milena was proved right. She would not see her father or daughter again. One morning, at the end of October, her name was called for the transport. All the prisoners knew that this meant transport to a concentration camp, and Milena had heard enough from the refugees whose stories she had told in *Přítomnost*, as well as rumours spread in Dresden and in Prague, to have some idea what this meant. She packed her toothbrush, toothpaste, the glycerine soap she was allowed for her peeling hands, and a cape she had been given in a recent Thursday parcel. There were tears as she said goodbye. The authorities had decided she should be sent to Ravensbrück concentration camp for 're-education'.

Ravensbrück women's camp was established by the Germans in 1939, fifty miles north of Berlin at Furstenburg. It was used at first to corral undesirable Germans, Austrians and gypsies. After 1939 came Poles and Czechs and in time it became the main receptacle for female political prisoners from all over Europe, resistance workers, radio operators, socialists and Communists, women who harboured Jews, and some Jews themselves. The camp lay in a hollow near the bleak marshland which surrounded Furstenburg Lake, among scattered trees which were just visible to the inmates from behind the high stone wall. There were two rows of eight wooden barrack buildings known as blocks, each with two dormitory rooms for about a hundred women, a washroom and a private room and office for the guard. Around each block was a small flowerbed with grass and trees, where no one was allowed to walk. In between the blocks was a large clear space for walking and roll-calls; at the end were the administration offices, the kitchen, the infirmary and a small concrete prison known as the bunker. Later, more blocks were built, but this is how the camp was organised when Milena arrived.

She was deposited with other prisoners at Furstenburg railway station two miles from the camp. Guards and SS officers beat and harried them into rows of five and marched them to the camp. Here Milena was given a grey-blue striped dress with a red triangle patched on to show that she was a political prisoner and her prisoner number stitched on the sleeve. (Milena's number was 4714; her friends nicknamed her 4711 after the cologne.) She also received an apron and rough jacket, and wooden clogs for her feet. Her wavy hair was shorn and she was given a scarf to wear. In a way she was lucky to arrive in the early days of the camp. For now, underwear was changed weekly and dresses monthly. Later, when the camp became more crowded, the women were not .given changes of underwear and dresses for months, and prisoners who arrived in summer ended up wearing thin dresses through the cold winters. Milena was also given a towel and bed coverings, a mug, plate, bowl and cutlery. These too became luxuries; spoons later became as precious as bread.

The new prisoners were received by one of the senior camp guards, informed about the prison rules and punishments, and warned against fraternisation with the guards.

The women were organised partly by category (political, Jewish, 'asocial') and partly by nationality. Milena was assigned to Block 1. This block was for the most serious political prisoners and was less crowded and more gently run than some of the other blocks. As well as a German guard, each block had a 'block leader' chosen from among the prisoners, whose responsiblity it was to keep the block tidy and her charges disciplined. Some block leaders used their post to curry favour and privileges from the Germans. Others used it to protect the prisoners and make life as bearable as possible, sending letters for them, finding extra food or arranging less gruelling work.

Milena's block leader was a sympathetic Social Democrat from Vienna called Roza Jochmann.

Milena soon knew the camp routine. The women were woken at five o'clock in winter, half-past four in summer. They had three quarters of an hour to wash, dress, make their bed and eat breakfast of ersatz coffee and perhaps bread. A siren called them to roll-call, where twice a day they stood to attention in rows of five in front of their block, for up to two hours. Lunch of soup or vegetables came at noon, and a similar meal before bed at eight o'clock. Each prisoner received a few ounces of bread a day. At the weekend there might be some salami or margarine.

The only unregulated time came on Sunday afternoons, when the women were allowed to meet and talk or walk around the camp. If the SS officer in the guard room was in a good mood he might play classical music over the loudspeaker system. The prisoners were allowed to receive occasional letters.

One stroke of good fortune was that, partly because of her education and medical background and partly because of her frailty, Milena was put to work in the office of the camp infirmary. This was a much easier life than the hard labour of stone-breaking or road-building inflicted on stronger prisoners, or even than cutting down trees in the forest or working in the camp kitchen garden. Other women became cheap labour for nearby factories. There was a textile factory making soldiers' and prisoners' uniforms: later, arms manufacturers built factories near the camp, exploiting its captive population to produce field phones, submarine and rocket parts. Working inside the camp, in the kitchen, laundry or infirmary, was regarded as the lightest load and offered the best opportunity to manipulate the camp system to steal extra food or simply to keep warm.

Milena soon made the acquaintance of other prisoners in her block and beyond. She heard from a German woman about another prisoner whose fate interested her, Margarete Buber-Neumann, who had arrived from the Soviet Union. One day, she introduced herself to the slightly younger Margarete, as 'Milena from Prague'. In snatched conversations and longer Sunday afternoon discussions, the two women talked and were soon close friends. Margarete had been married to Heinz Neumann, a German Communist leader. In 1937 they had fled to Moscow but because of their Troyskyite leanings were soon arrested. Heinz was executed and Margarete sentenced to forced labour in the Karaganda camp in Kazakhstan. In 1940, the

Imprisonment

Soviet Union agreed with Germany to return German prisoners; Margarete was handed over to the German authorities, who promptly sent her to Ravensbrück.

She was an intelligent, independent-minded woman, although perhaps less immediately forceful than Milena. They were not unalike; Margarete too had broad cheekbones, arched brows and a good mouth, if less full than Milena's. Margarete was immediately struck by Milena's height and poise and found her full of energy and emotion, although she noticed that her face was already 'prison-grey' and her rheumatism continued to plague her.

The two women shared a loathing of Soviet Communism, and Milena was eager to hear Margarete's first-hand reports of hardship and injustice in the Soviet Union, which confirmed all she had suspected in Prague before the war. They compared the Soviet and Nazi systems, and Milena suggested to Margarete that when they left the camp they should collaborate on a book about the two great tyrannies: 'The age of the concentration camp'. Margarete found Milena open-minded, with no anti-German prejudice as such. She thought her command of the German language excellent.

But their views laid Milena and Margarete open to charges of Trotskyism and treachery from Communist women in the camp. There were many Communist prisoners in Ravensbrück and they recreated some of the party organisation and discipline they had known in freedom. They held discussion groups and disseminated Communist ideas; they were not pleased to find Milena and Margarete countering their message with anti-Communist attitudes. One of the leading Communists in the camp was Jožka Jabůrková, the Communist journalist whom Milena had known before the war. There is no doubt that she had been a dedicated campaigner for working-class women, and was a source of strength and encouragement for many women in the camp. But she was also a fervent believer in party discipline, and, according to Margarete, she and other senior Czech Communists in the camp told Milena that she would have to make a choice, between acceptance among the Czech community and her friendship with Margarete. Milena chose friendship. (Jabůrková died in the camp in 1942.)

Milena found the antipathy of the women hard to bear, but the Czech Communists did not spurn her completely. One young doctor, Zdena Nedvědová admired Milena's courage and warmth, and her support for younger prisoners. She later cared for Milena when she was ill in the camp, and after the war she came to realise that Milena's political views had been prophetic. But at the time she accepted that to believe Milena and Margarete meant betraying one's faith in the USSR.

Other women valued Milena's friendship. Her strength of character enriched the poverty of camp life, and she drew on all her inner resources to keep up her own spirits and rally others. Her friends included Tomy Kleinerová, an old acquaintance from Prague who had worked at the YMCA. Despite Tomy's bad hip, which gave her much pain, she had a robust sense of humour and a good supply of jokes; she and Milena shared a pallet in Block 1 when the blocks became more crowded. Then there was a dancer from Prague called Nina Jirsíková, and later the young nurse from Pankrác, Hana Housková, who arrived in 1942. As in Pankrác the women were ingenious about avoiding boredom. They gave lectures and started history or political groups, held sing-songs and concerts, taught each other languages, made playing cards, crafted jewellery out of buttons. As long as her health allowed, Milena was an important figure in the camp's intellectual life.

But her main source of succour was her friendship with Margarete. They spent as much time as possible together, talking about their past lives, creating an oasis of intimacy in the harsh camp. Margarete described Milena as 'a scarecrow with a lovely face', Milena thought Margarete looked like a 'blue village Madonna' in her blue prison dress. They spent hours fantasising about a future life in freedom, the clothes they would buy, the places they would visit. Milena dreamed of drinking coffee in one of her favourite Prague cafés or simply sitting somewhere in a field under a tree with the sun shining. The only real elements of individuality and beauty in the camp were the tiniest things; in the infirmary office where she worked, Milena kept flowers, a glass button in the box with her pencils, a photograph of Prague and a mountain landscape.

Margarete had huge admiration for Milena's courage, her refusal to be cowed by the camp authorities. She would stand not quite straight at roll-call, or take her scarf off and wave at Margarete across the camp. On dark winter evenings, Milena would take Margarete's arm as they walked among the blocks; tiny gestures but, under the camp's harsh rules, true defiance. 'Under these circumstances,' Margarete wrote, 'the feeling that one was necessary to another human being was a source of supreme happiness, made life worth living, and gave one the strength to survive.'

As their friendship developed, Milena took greater risks. Margarete was block leader of the Jehovah's Witnesses' block and thus had use of the guardroom. Margarete described how Milena would visit her there in the afternoon with the excuse of running infirmary errands. She even risked coming after dark, and the two women would spend the whole night talking by the stove. Milena also tried to teach Margarete Czech. On Sunday afternoons sometimes, they would sneak into the doctor's consulting room in the infirmary. 'Her way of speaking, of moving, of holding her head; with every gesture, she said, "I am a free woman."'

Margarete was not only impressed by Milena's courage and intelligence; she was drawn to the deeper undercurrents of emotion, the hidden sorrows and 'aura of mystery'. The two women shared the feeling of being outsiders, not only in the camp but in their previous lives. Milena would also talk, as she had in Pankrác, of her enormous sadness about Honza. At times she felt that her whole life was meaningless. She wondered if she had really achieved anything through her journalism and regretted not having written a book. (Friends had often encouraged her to write a book, but she had never found the time. Perhaps this was wise; the critic F. X. Šalda once told her, 'Woman, you are an excellent journalist, but God defend you from the temptation to write a novel.') Now, Milena told Margarete, 'The age of poetry was over, there could be no excuse for writing anything but disciplined prose.' She was also mournful about her personal life. 'I seem to have been fated to love weak men,' she said. 'None of them really took care of me and protected me. It's not good for a woman to be too independent. Men don't like it for very long, and that even goes for weak men. After a while, they find themselves another woman, a delicate little thing, who sits on the sofa with her hands in her lap and looks up at them admiringly.'

Milena's lifelong search to be loved and needed informed her new friendship. Once Margarete brought Milena a piece of her bread. Milena rejected it. Margarete wrote that Milena explained that 'the mere thought of accepting bread from me made her miserable, because in our friendship she always wanted to be the giver. She wanted to help me and care for me. When I told her I had a family, a mother and brothers and sisters, she seemed disappointed. She wanted me to be all alone in the world, wholly dependent on her care and help. To her, friendship meant doing everything, sacrificing everything for another.' Later, Milena would have to let Margarete reverse the roles.

But Milena's melancholy strain did not submerge her. She resisted the depression and passivity which were the worst enemies of the women in the camp. Her friendship with Margarete was one defence. It offered an alternative universe, a place of freedom within the confines of the camp. Such passionate friendships were not uncommon in Ravensbrück, although they were not without risk. If the guards discovered overt lesbian behaviour the culprits were punished with severe flogging. Mostly the women subsumed their erotic longings in intense friendships, long conversations about past love affairs and dreams of freedom. Margarete described how sometimes she was mesmerised by the whispered singing and secret dancing of gypsy women in the camp.

The unusually hot summer of 1941 brought news of the German invasion of Russia. This raised the hopes of Communists in the camp that with the end of the Hitler–Stalin pact the Soviets would now contribute to the defeat of Germany and the liberation of the camps. Milena's anti-Communist views seemed even more treacherous. There was news too of a tougher policy towards the Czechs. The Protectorate regime had not destroyed the Czech spirit; resistance and sabotage were on the increase and, as the war intensified, Germany needed complete control. A new Reich Protector was appointed in September 1941, Reinhard Heydrich, an SS officer who became known as the Butcher of Prague. He had a number of senior Czechs arrested and executed, police and SS activity was increased, Jews were made to wear yellow stars, the country was cowed. In London, President Beneš finally denounced the Czech government in Prague who, he had come to believe, only served to give some legitimacy to the brutal German regime.

There was no sign of a German defeat. More women kept arriving in the camp, from Russia, Ukraine, France, Belgium, Holland, charting the progress of the war. New blocks were built to house the new arrivals, but still conditions deteriorated. In October 1941, another of Milena's Prague acquaintances arrived at the camp, Anna Kvapilová, a music librarian. She described how Milena did what she could for new arrivals. 'Milena stood at the doorway of the infirmary where they took us for examination. She wore the blue camp dress with the unnecessary apron and said with a smile, "Welcome girls"

Imprisonment

... She was strong and optimistic.' Anna wrote stories and observations about life in the camp and made a collection of songs which she insisted on keeping in hiding; she made a special book of Czech poems for Milena.

In the summer of 1942, a large number of Czech women arrived from the village of Lidice not far from Prague. They had all been arrested as part of German reprisals for the assassination of Reich Protector Heydrich in May 1942 by Czech resistance workers parachuted in from Britain. It was the most conspicuous and daredevil act of the resistance, but the consequences were cruel. Lidice, which the Germans believed had in some way helped the assassins, was made an example of and razed to the ground. The women were arrested, the men shot. When the women arrived in Ravensbrück, they brought news to Milena of the state of the German occupation of Prague, the ever-tightening martial law and economic exploitation of her country, the slow bleeding and demoralisation of a nation.

Conditions in the camp were becoming harsher too. As the war progressed, and the German war machine was driven harder and harder, those in command strove to retain discipline. New commanders in Ravensbrück tackled the overcrowding by herding more women into the dormitories, three hundred together in blocks designed for a hundred. When in the summer of 1942 Margarete was relieved from her duties as block leader because of insubordination by the Jehovah's Witnesses and moved to Block 1, she, Milena and Tomy all shared a bed. The camp commander also created a network of camp spies from among the women themselves to help keep order. Punishments were meted out freely, including brutal solitary confinement in the camp prison, the bunker. Another solution was simply to dispose of excess women. In the autumn of 1942 the whole Jewish block was deported to Auschwitz. Other undesirables, such as the infirm, were given lethal injections.

The infirmary was one of the most perverse and hellish parts of the camp, and Milena did what she could to lessen the nightmare. The doctors had begun to use the camp inmates as guinea-pigs in medical experiments. One, Dr Sonntag, preferred to use women he regarded as dross – criminals and 'asocials' such as prostitutes or women who had cohabited with 'foreigners'. Women with venereal disease were particularly dispensable. Milena had to process the venereal disease tests and she falsified as many as she could to try to save at least some women. The victims were used for experiments in amputation, sterilisation and transplant techniques.

In the winter of 1942, one of Miiena's gestures of defiance nearly backfired. She forged a TB certificate for a frail friend to exempt her from work. Then came orders that all the infirm, asthmatics, mental defectives and cripples were to be removed to another camp. Milena saw the first shipment of women being dragged and hauled and dumped into trucks. Next day the trucks returned with a mound of miscellaneous clothes marked with the numbers of the prisoners who had been taken away. There were also false teeth and spectacles. The camp authorities had simply disposed of the dregs of the camp. Milena realised what was happening, quickly made out another TB certificate for her friend giving her a clean bill of health, and arranged her speedy discharge from the infirmary.

From now on, Milena and Margarete had no illusions about the scale of the inhumanity being exercised in the camp (even if they had no knowledge of Hitler's concept of a 'final solution'). After the removal of the Jews and the infirm, they had to listen to the sound of prisoners being summarily shot, especially many Poles. It was more important than ever to remain healthy and safe from the doctors' attentions.

In the autumn of 1942, Milena had her first bad attack of inflammation of the kidney. She lay in the infirmary with a high fever, terrified of being given a fatal injection. Her friends stole flowers from the camp garden to cheer her up. Fortunately, Milena soon recovered, but she knew that the illness remained with her. She was severely depressed. 'She often complained that she had lost her capacity for spontaneous feeling, that her feelings had lost their freshness, become mere copies, memories of authentic feelings she had once had,' wrote Margarete.

In October 1942, Margarete was given a job as secretary in the office of a senior SS officer in the camp, Frau Langefeld, who was comparatively well-regarded by the prisoners as someone who disapproved of the worst cruelties of the camp and rarely showed violence towards the inmates. Milena kept Margarete informed about the extent of experiments in the infirmary. Dr Sonntag had left, but a woman doctor, Dr Oberhauser, and others were turning healthy women into cripples with their amputation experiments, and killing others during experiments with painkillers. Pregnant women who arrived in the camp had their babies aborted. Milena saw new coffins almost every morning in the infirmary yard. There was worse. Milena discovered that one of the doctors, Dr Rolf Rosenthal, was having an affair with one of the nurses. They would meet in the infirmary at night, administer lethal doses of the barbiturate Evipan to gypsies, Jews and others, and extract any gold from their teeth to be sold for their own profit. Milena persuaded Margarete to talk to Frau Lange-feld about these abuses. Frau Langefeld was horrified, but did nothing until she learnt about the summary killings of some Polish nationalists whom she admired. But when she made her report it led to her own removal from duties, and Margarete's detention in the bunker, in a tiny cold dark cell with scant food.

Margarete was distraught at being separated from Milena and unable to care for her; Milena had been much weakened by her illness. Milena in turn was worried about Margarete. She begged and begged one of the Jehovah's Witness orderlies to smuggle in messages and parcels. A stern lecture on Christian charity was eventually effective, and the woman smuggled in a little package of sugar and buns which Milena had obtained. But after a few such missions, the orderly pleaded with Margarete to send Milena a message asking her to stop; it was too dangerous for all concerned.

Then Milena took an even greater risk. About three weeks into Margarete's confinement, she went to the chief Gestapo officer in the camp, Commander Ramdor. According to Margarete, Milena told him what was happening in the infirmary in the knowledge that however sadistic he might be, he could not allow a camp official to make personal profit out of violence. She appealed to him as a German who surely understood the importance of friendship to let her see Margar-ete. Her audacity coupled with her charm worked. Ramdor let her visit Margarete and Dr Rosenthal and the nurse were arrested. Margarete was released shortly afterwards and had to be taken straight to the infirmary to recover her strength. She idolised Milena more than ever.

The mood in the camp changed yet again as 1943 progressed. The German army had been massively defeated in the long battle of Stalingrad in the winter of 1942–43, and during the year there were more indications that German power was ebbing. News bulletins were no longer broadcast through the camp, and among the prisoners there was new hope of freedom. Milena was the camp Cassandra, warning that if Stalin were victorious the West would forgive him his crimes and hand him central Europe. She argued that National

Socialism and Communism were as bad as each other, and painted a bleak picture of Europe under Soviet domination. The Communist leaders in the camp warned Milena and Margarete that when the Russians came they would be shot or sent to Siberia for their treachery. Milena said often to Margarete: 'If ever I get out of here alive, I don't suppose for one moment I shall be able to return to Prague. But where should I go?' Even Margarete thought this was too pessimistic.

Their friendship was as intense as ever. They once quarrelled about the interpretation of a postcard of an expressionist landscape. Milena, in a rage, tore the card up; Margarete burst into tears. 'Milena said sadly, "It's awful to see someone you love crying. It makes me think of last farewells, of my tears in cold railroad stations . . . the end of love . . . Please, don't ever cry again." . . . But what could have made her so angry? "All of a sudden," she said, "I had the impression that we had become like other people, who keep talking at cross-purposes as though there were a wall between them, I felt that nothing either of us said could reach the other's heart." '

Once, as they walked in the camp in autumn 1943, Milena talked about her daughter and the letters she received. ' "I really know nothing about Honza," said Milena sadly. "If only she would tell me the colour of her dress or whether she's started to wear silk stockings, or what she does on some particular day. If she'd only stop telling me that she goes to school and likes to play the piano." ' Milena worried about Honza, knowing that she was a difficult child, capable of running away from her grandfather. In the monthly letters they were allowed to exchange, Dr Jesenský wrote to Milena about 'the little pagan', but with affection. 'My father's love for his own flesh and blood had a strange way of expressing itself, but it can't be helped,' Milena told Margarete.

Milena tried hard to keep her spirits up, but her health was getting worse. Margarete did what she could to find Milena extra food or arrange rest for her. She was often exempted from roll-call. Camp life was increasingly uncomfortable. There were now several thousand women in a camp designed for about 1,500. The only advantage of the chaos was that it became easier to protect women from death or deportation by simply hiding them from the authorities.

Milena was forty-seven on 10 August 1943. She was in great pain from rheumatism and kidney inflammation, and her friends arranged a party to cheer her up. Margarete, Anna Kvapilová, Tomy Kleinerová, Nina Jirsíková the dancer and other Czechs were there. Milena received embroidered handkerchiefs, a cloth heart with her name on it, a figurine made out of a toothbrush and flowers. She was moved to tears by the sincere friendship of these women, in some ways the most unconditional she had known.

The winter of 1943 was hard. The prisoners knew that Hitler was under increasing pressure and would lose the war, but had no idea when. Milena grew worse day by day, with aching pains in her back and stomach. She made herself take her place at her desk in the infirmary, but collapsed more and more frequently. With all optimism gone, she would remark that she would never see Prague again. Eventually she decided to consult one of the doctors. Dr Rosenthal had left, to be replaced by Dr Percy Treite. Although he was involved in the camp programme of experimentation and forced sterilisations, he was more humane than some of the other doctors. He let suitably qualified prisoners (including Hana Houskova and Dr Zdena Nedvĕdová) work in the infirmary and care for their own. He told Milena that he had studied in Prague and even attended her father's lectures. When she told him about her illness he investigated, and said the only hope was to remove the infected kidney. (Hana Housková and Dr Zdena Nedvĕdová believed that Milena's condition was caused or exacerbated by a return of gonorrheal illness.) In the spring of 1944 Milena decided to take the risk. Dr Treite operated and then allowed Dr Nedvĕdová to administer a series of blood transfusions from a Polish girl who worked in the kitchens and was thus better nourished than other prisoners. All went well. Milena and her friends believed she would get better and her energy and capacity for life began to return. Her friends visited her in the infirmary to chat or play cards with a tiny pack hand-made by another Czech prisoner, Vĕra Papoušková. Prisoners had since the end of 1942 been allowed to receive parcels from home. Milena's father sent her some postcards of sketches of Prague, and Milena spent hours showing them to Margarete, describing the city and her favourite haunts. She yearned desperately for news of her father and daughter, and to go home. She also talked about Honza to a Czech friend, Jiřina Svobodová, whom she had known in the *Národní listy* days and who also had a little daughter. Milena dreamt of a great reunion for both mothers and daughters after the war.

But the remission was short. She weakened again and in April it was clear that the other kidney was infected. According to Hana

Kafka, Love and Courage

Housková and Dr Nedvědová, Dr Treite administered another blood transfusion without consulting them, several days after the original daily series. Antibodies had developed and Milena rejected the blood. She rapidly worsened. Margarete believed that Milena knew what was coming. ' "Look at the colour of my feet," she said. "Those are the feet of a dying woman. And the hands!" She held out her hands. "The lines are disappearing. That's what happens just before the end." '

In the middle of May she received an unexpected parcel from Joachim von Zedtwitz, who she had believed dead. He had been arrested shortly after her, but released in 1943. In cooperation with Dr Jesenský he had tried to arrange a pardon for Milena, but in vain. Milena was overjoyed to hear that he was alive.

A day or two later, Milena began to slip in and out of consciousness. In the early hours of 17 May 1944, a quiet, cloudy Wednesday, she died. Her friends washed her body and laid some flowers on her corpse. Dr Treite declared that she had died of uncertain cause, and, unusually, wrote to Dr Jesenský, inviting him to come to collect Milena's ashes. But Dr Jesenský was too devastated by the news to travel.

Back in 1921, Milena had had a strange dream which she wrote about in *Tribuna*. Its imagery proved strangely prophetic of what lay ahead both in Central Europe and for her. She dreamt that she was far from home, and that her land had been smitten by catastrophe, such as war or plague; everyone was driven to flight.

> Endless trains, one behind the other, left the station for the world, all completely full. Panic overtook everyone, no one wanted to be last. People fought for a seat with their life. Between me and the platform were vast crowds of people and there was no hope that I would force my way through. Despair overtook me.
>
> 'I am young, I cannot die,' I shouted . . .
>
> Then someone tapped my shoulder. When I turned round, an unknown man put a ticket in my hand and said: 'With this ticket you can go anywhere. It will get you a passage through borders and a place on the train. Don't be afraid, and be brave. Now, go, go, it's time . . .'
>
> As the train left, catastrophe began. The ground caved in, and the world changed into a network of railway tracks . . .
>
> Finally the tracks stopped at a border.
>
> 'Disembark for passport control,' bellowed the desperate guard . . .
>
> I extracted my ticket. It was folded over twenty times. I unfolded

Imprisonment

it. The customs officer, impatiently shifting from one foot to the other, reached out his palm, having already decided that he would not let me through. I looked inside. It said: 'Sentenced to death.'

Icy perspiration broke out on my forehead. My heart stopped beating ... I said to the officer, in desperate appeal: 'Perhaps it's just a password so that I can more easily get to the other side of the world.'

Milena was forty-seven when she died in Ravensbrück. Her ashes were sprinkled on Lake Furstenberg, as was routine.

Afterword

After the war, Milena's reputation was toyed with and eventually scorned by those who saw her as a symbol of all that must be eradicated in Communist Czechoslovakia. In the immediate aftermath, before the Communists took over in 1948, some of those who had known Milena in Ravensbrück wrote articles about her last days, and testified to her courage in the camp and her status as a celebrated pre-war journalist. But in time these were obliterated by other, less flattering, accounts. Gusta Fučíková, the wife of Julius Fučík, who had good reason to resent Milena given her intimacy with her husband, and who was herself sent to Ravensbrück for the last two years of the war, pointed out what she saw as Milena's betrayal of the Communist Party. She described Milena's influence on 'weaker and less conscious anti-fascist prisoners, how she weakened the struggle and how she woke despair in many women.' Julius Fučík had himself been arrested by the Germans in 1942 and executed the following year. After the Communist Party took power in Czechoslovakia, Fučík was portrayed as a Communist martyr and his wife as an honoured widow; her account therefore carried weight, and in the careful rewriting of history by the Communists an official picture of Milena appeared as an anti-communist and a decadent bourgeoise. Stories about drug-taking and shop-lifting, as well as her relationship with Kafka, the individualist and Jew, were enough to damn her. As the rest of Europe was coming to know Kafka as a genius (*Letters to Milena* was published in the early 1950s), in Czechoslovakia both Kafka and Milena were non-people.

This changed with the more reform-minded Communism of the 1960s. In 1963 a conference was held on Kafka which included discussion of Milena. And in 1966 Professor Eduard Goldstücker wrote an article arguing for an honest appraisal of her: she was neither the idealised muse of Kafka nor the demon of the Communists, but

an important, complex figure in twentieth-century Czech history.
And Milena's daughter's book was published in haste just before the
Soviet tanks arrived to crush the Prague Spring in 1968.

But after the reimposition of hardline Communism Milena was
once again *persona non grata*. Margarete Buber-Neumann and Jaroslava Vondráčková wrote about her, and others, notably Marie Jirásková, continued to collect material about her. Some of this material
was published abroad but it was not available in Czech, or only to a
very few. It is only now, after the collapse of Communism in 1989,
that Milena's life and work can truly be recovered.

This is too late for most of those who were close to Milena.

Her father, devastated by her death, died in 1947. His was a long
and distinguished career as a professor of dentistry. Even as an old
man, he continued practising his profession and skating on the frozen
Vltava. His sixtieth birthday in 1930 had been marked by notices in
the newspapers and his death was met by professional and personal
tributes.

Ernst Pollak, who married again, died in London in 1947. Jaromír
Krejcar too left Prague with Riva during the war, and died in London
in 1949.

Evžen Klinger returned to Prague after the war. He was imprisoned
from 1949 to 1956 and then worked in the Ministry of Culture and in
other posts. He died in Prague in 1982.

Staša Jílovská worked in the Ministry of Information after the war
and had a successful career as a respected translator. She died in
Prague in 1955.

Margarete Buber-Neumann survived Ravensbrück and after the
war lived in West Germany where she wrote several books, including
Milena. She died in November 1989, just a few days before the fall of
the Berlin Wall and Prague's Velvet Revolution.

Jaroslava Vondráčková continued her textile work and built up a
collection of material about Milena's life. She died in Prague in 1986.

The saddest fate was Honza's. After her mother's death, Honza
lived with her grandfather and then, after his death when she was in
her late teens, she largely brought herself up. Her inheritance was
soon squandered. Milena's friends tried to help her as much as they
could, but as the daughter of an undesirable she remained on the
margins of society. Her personal life was precarious. She married four
times and had five children, but her instability as well as the
authorities' hostility led to their being taken into care. Like her

mother, she had a period of drug addiction and spent a year in prison. She only ever had menial jobs, but she was involved in Prague's artistic underground and several of her short stories were published. She inherited some of her mother's brilliance and her account of Milena's life, although inevitably flawed, is powerfully written. Her later years were more tranquil, but she died in a car crash in 1981, aged 53.

One of the few people still alive to have known Milena well is Joachim von Zedtwitz, now living in Switzerland. His testimony and other documentary evidence prepared by Marie Jirásková was presented to the Yad Vashem commission in Jerusalem in 1994, and in spring 1995 Milena was honoured posthumously as a righteous gentile for her work in helping Jews escape from Prague in 1939.

This is one very proper form of recognition. Milena realised, when many others did not, the true level of risk for Jews in Hitler's Europe. But her work helping Jews was a part of her efforts on behalf of all those she regarded as persecuted. While she could not save the whole Czech nation from Hitler's clutches, she did all she could to keep her compatriots' spirits up and assert her nation's right to fair treatment by other European countries, long after that right had been trampled on.

This defiance was the considered position of the sometimes sombre-looking middle-aged woman whose face emerges from the last photographs. It is a strong face and, despite its heaviness, still beautiful in the gentleness of the mouth and tilt of the nose. As if, after all the misfortunes of the 1930s, Milena had emerged to a place where no pride, no self-consciousness, no diffidence – nor even any bonds of love – could hold her back. So that, despite the apparent decline from the serene (but sometimes melancholy) beauty of the photographs from Milena's early twenties, the woman in the later photograph appears to have won a confidence her younger self never knew. If the young Milena was impelled to act by her beauty and energy and dreams, the older Milena was freed to act by the mature realisation that none of these was a guarantee of happiness.

What unites the two images, what united the two Milenas, was her refusal to abide by what convention or other people demanded of her. The single thing that emerges from all the testimonies of those who knew her, whether briefly or intimately, is the force of her personality. It was not always a benign force. She could be demanding, elusive, manipulative, and to those who did not know her, sometimes aloof. But to those who knew her well, or were prepared to look beyond her failings, she was enormously charismatic, generous, loyal and brave; above all she was blessed with a rich, astute intelligence. She poured this intelligence, and the emotions with which it was intertwined, into her relationship with Kafka and into the final, courageous years of her work as a journalist. Kafka once described Milena, brilliantly, as 'a miraculous, violated, inviolable creature', and the years that followed her relationship with him made this an even truer description.

Theirs were two very different lives whose paths intersected briefly and fatefully, at a certain time and, above all, in a certain place. Kafka once wrote, in a letter to a friend which Milena could not have seen, of the 'claws' of Prague: 'Prague doesn't let go . . . You have to submit or else.' Milena felt something similar: 'Perhaps everyone loves their home town, in time appreciating the security of their origins, their cradle . . . their mark, which is sometimes a gift, sometimes a burden. But does anyone from any other town love it as we love Prague? Anywhere else lies somehow lightly on the spirit and the heart, for it is not a burden. But love for Prague is fateful, it will not go away, and in one shape or form it lasts for ever.' Milena deserves to be remembered as so much more than Kafka's Milena. Perhaps, better said, and as she herself said, as 'Milena from Prague'.

Notes

Main Sources

LM   *Letters to Milena*, Franz Kafka, ed. Willy Haas, trans. Tani and James Stern, Penguin edition, London 1983

DK   *The Diaries of Franz Kafka 1910–1923*, ed. Max Brod, Penguin edition, London 1972

JV   *Kolem Mileny Jesenské*, Jaroslava Vondráčková, Prague 1991

M B-N   *Milena*, Margarete Buber-Neumann, London 1990

JC   *Adresát Milena Jesenská*, Jana Černá, Prague 1991

Fond JV   Archive of documents and manuscripts belonging to Jaroslava Vondráčková, deposited at the Museum of Czech Literature at Strahov, Prague after her death.

Svěd.   'Deset adres Mileny Jesenské', Jaroslava Vondráčková, in *Svědectví* quarterly magazine, 1987 pp. 888-930.

LS   Unpublished letters from Milena to Willi and Stefanie (Steffi) Schlamm

Tr   Article by Milena in *Tribuna* newspaper

NL   Article by Milena in *Národní listy* newspaper

Pr   Article by Milena in *Přítomnost* magazine

LN   Article by Milena in *Lidové noviny* newspaper

HCR   *A History of the Czechoslovak Republic 1918–1948* eds. Victor S. Mamatey and Radomír Luža, Princeton 1973

Background sources for all chapters

JV, JC, M B-N
HCR
The Heart of Europe, J. P. Stern, Oxford 1992
Czechoslovakia in European History, S. Harrison Thomson, London 1965
Czechoslovakia at the Crossroads of European History, Jaroslav Krejčí, London 1990
City of Prague archive

Notes

Foreword

xii   Review
David Pryce-Jones reviewing *Kafka's Milena*, Jana Černa, trans. A. G.
Brain, London 1988, in *The Financial Times*, 20/2/1988

Chapter 1: Childhood

1   *Old Czech Legends*
by Alois Jirásek, trans. Marie K. Holeček, London 1992
1   'old but impoverished'
M B-N p. 18
2   'If only just a little something'
JV p. 80
2   Jesenius
M B-N p. 36 is mistaken. Cf. 'Kafkuji, Kafkuješ, Kafkujeme', Jaroslav
Dresler, *Svědectví*, 1964
3   mother's green eyes
'Maminko, bud' hezká' NL 19/4/25
3   'If my wife can't nurse'
JC 14
4   St Mikuláš and cinema
JV 10
4   'In those days'
'O umění zůstat stát' Pr 5/4/39
5   'When my mother took away'
'Cesta k jednoduchosti' NL 8/5/26
5   'Silly, kitsch picture'
LS 2/8/38
6   Background on Jews in Prague
The Nightmare of Reason, Ernst Pawel, London 1988
The World of Franz Kafka, ed. J. P. Stern, London 1980
Conversations with Lenka Reinerová, Prague
7   'Then came a Sunday'
'O umění zůstat stát' Pr 5/4/39
8   Dr Jesenský's career
Jan Jesenský, František Neuwirt, Prague 1948
8   Dr Jesenský's duel
'Rané české překlady z Franze Kafky', O. F. Babler in *Franz Kafka
Liblická Konference 1963*, Prague 1963
8   'a punishment of my childhood'

Notes

'Jaké hračky?' Tr 18/12/20

9   'he spanked her', 'threw her'
M B-N 19

9   grandmother's apartment
'Intimní světlo' NL 15/3/23

9   'And when someone said'
'Česká maminka' Pr 19/4/39

9   Hotel Prokop
'O "Prokopu" Špičáku' Tr 25/6/21

10   'trained monkey'
JC p. 28

10   'When I was small'
'Listy ze Zapadlé Lhoty – Les' NL 28/6/25

11   'I don't wonder at you'
JC 18

11   Minerva
První české dívčí gymnázium, sbornik ke 100. výroăbcí založeni 1890–1990
Prague 1990

13   'silent, dreaming, shy'
JV p. 12

13   'in a grey outfit'
'Milena Jesenská', Marie Tarantová, *Doba*, 19/5/46

13   'a black beard'
'A v potu tváře své chleb si dobývali budeš' Tr 19/6/21

13   'Scattered with heaps'
'Břicho měst' Tr 18/9/20

13   Jarmila Ambrožová
Conversation with Professor Eduard Goldstucker, Prague

14   Staša Procházková
Conversations with her daughters, Olga Housková in Prague and Staša
Fleischmann in Paris

15   Mother's illness
M B-N p. 23 (pernicious anaemia), JV in *Sved.* (leukemia)

15   'My mother never spanked me'
M B-N p. 16

15   'We weren't alone'
'O "Prokopu" Špičáku' Tr 25/6/21

17   Jiří Foustka
Unpublished memoir by Staša Fleischmann, 1983

17   'We were sitting'
'O "Prokopu" Špičáku' Tr 25/6/21

18   'War to us was simply'

Notes

from *Streitbares Leben*, Max Brod. Munich 1969, quoted in *The Nightmare of Reason*, Ernst Pawel, London 1988, p. 317

18 'adding to the beat'
'O všelijaké muzice' Tr 22/6/21

18 'I want to thank you'
První české dívčí gymnázium (see above), p. 87

18 crush on Albiná Honzáková
Letters from Milena to AH 1912–1914, in *Sved.*, p. 920. At one stage it seems that AH asked Milena to stop writing to her. As with Kafka later on, Milena was unable to obey.

Chapter 2: Freedom

20 long narrow skirts
'Milena Jesenská', Marie Tarantová, *Doba* 19/5/46

20 'Dívka z Minervy'
Conversation with Marie Chaloupecká, Prague

20 'On Sunday morning'
Josef Kodiček, quoted in M B-N p. 31

21 attend concerts unchaperoned
Marie Tarantová, *Doba* 19/5/46

21 'People came and gave'
'S "ubohým a holým" ' Pr 5/7/39

22 *Strakonický dudák*
'O všelijaké muzice' Tr 22/6/21

22 'free and open to ideas'
Max Brod, quoted in 'Kafka's Prague', F. W. Carter in *The World of Franz Kafka*, ed J. P. Stern, London 1980, p. 34

24 Max Brod
Život plný bojů, Max·Brod, Prague 1966

24 Franz Werfel
A Life Torn by History, Franz Werfel 1890–1945, Peter Stephan Jungk, trans. Anselm Hollo, London 1990

24 Café Arco
still situated at Hybernská 12

25 'He soon stood up'
JV p. 18

25 Ernst Pollak
JV, JC, M B-N
Veruntreute Geschichte, Milan Dubrovic, Vienna/Hamburg 1985
His surname is sometimes spelt with one *l*, but on his marriage certificates and letters he used two.

25 'Milena was sitting'

M B-N p. 42
26 'and then you will'
JV p. 18
26 Amalie Kreidlová
Letter to JV, quoted in notes in Fond JV
27 'short, slight'
Dubrovic, see above, p. 52
27 'heliotrope-coloured dress'
M B-N p. 45
28 'Always the same debts'
JV p. 20
28 'If I wish anything for you'
quoted in JV p. 22
29 'A democratic Europe'
Czechoslovakia in European History, S. Harrison Thomson, London
1965, p. 317
30 Veleslavín
Clinic archives
30 Ernst's letter to employees
Mýtus Milena, Marta Marková-Kotyková, Prague 1993, p. 27
30 'Psychiatry is a terrible thing'
Milena to Max Brod, Letter I, appendix to *Dopisy Mileně*, Franz Kafka,
Prague 1968
31 16 March 1918
Prague marriage register

Chapter 3: Vienna

32 'When I arrived'
Undated LS 1938 or 1939
32 Vienna
Austria 1918–1972, Elizabeth Barker, London 1973
Fin-de-Siècle Vienna, Carl E. Schorske, Cambridge 1981
35 'Our entire group was sitting'.
Gina Kaus, in *Hermann Broch: A Biography*, Paul Michael Lützeler,
trans. Janice Furness, London 1987, p. 45
36 'Milena had taught him'
M B-N p. 52
36 'She sometimes gave the impression'
from Willy Haas's afterword to *Briefe an Milena*, quoted in M B-N p. 52
36 Hermann Broch, Ea von Allesch
Hermann Broch: A Biography, see above; Afterword by Růzena Greben-
íčková in JV

Notes

37   Jarmila went to the airport
      Conversation with Lenka Reinerová
37   'round like the moon'
      'Moje přítelkyně' Tr 27/1/21
38   'not a café'
      quoted in *Hermann Broch*, see above
38   'What's up with Milena?'
      JV p. 30
38   Tried to leave Ernst
      LM p. 32
39   Classes
      LM p. 45
39   'erotic crisis'
      Mýtus Milena, see above, p. 30
40   'Milena needed immediate contact'
      JC p. 33
40   'Best to get under the quilt'
      'Vídeň' Tr 30/12/19
42   'There are all sorts'
      'Jak se ve Vídni lidé živí' Tr 27/1/20
43   'I know people'
      'Kino' Tr 15/1/20
44   'Carnival is something'
      'Masopust ve Vídni' Tr 22/2/20
45   'In the beginning'
      Masks of the Prophet: The Theatrical World of Karl Kraus, Kari Grimstad,
      Toronto 1982
45   'falling in love'
      Fin-de-Siècle Vienna, see above, p. 9

Chapter 4: Kafka

The quotations from Kafka's letters in this chapter can be found in LM,
pp. 17–63 unless otherwise specified. They are largely in sequential order
although I have taken into account the edition in German and Czech which
has re-ordered the letters and added material. Additions from *Dopisy Mileně*,
Franz Kafka, trans. Hana Žantovská, I have indicated.

46   Franz Kafka
      The Nightmare of Reason, Ernst Pawel, London 1988
      A Biography of Franz Kafka, Ronald Hayman, London 1981
      Kafka, Pietro Citati, trans. Raymond Rosenthal, London 1991
      The World of Franz Kafka, ed. J. P. Stern, London 1980
      Franz Kafka Liblická Konference 1963, Prague 1963

Notes

47 'The Stoker'
'Topíč', Franz Kafka, trans. Milena Jesenská, *Kmen* 22/4/20
49 Felice Bauer
Letters to Felice, Franz Kafka, eds. Erich Heller and Jurgen Born, trans. James Stern and Elizabeth Duckworth, London 1978
49 'No one has ever'
LM p. 108
50 heller
a small coin, LM p. 19, quoting Milena back to herself
51 'poor brain'
LM p. 28, quoting Milena
51 'this has offended me'
LM p. 39, quoting Milena
51 'I would be doing well'
Letter to Max Brod, *Letters to Friends, Family and Editors*, Franz Kafka, ed. John Calder, London 1978, p. 237
52 'What is it in human nature'
'V Pratru' Tr 20/5/20
53 'which has fallen into my lap'
LM p.37, quoting Milena
57 'I beg you, really beg, beg you'
Letter I to Max Brod, see above
59 'really quite fabulously beautiful'
LM p. 70
59 'The first was unsure'
LM p. 81
59 'For the four days'
Letter V to Max Brod, see above
60 'You once asked', 'It is therefore "samozřejmé"'
LM p. 109

Chapter 5: Love Letters

The quotations from Kafka's letters in this chapter can be found in LM pp. 64–179, unless otherwise specified. They are largely in sequential order (see note to Ch. 4).

62 Milena wondered
Dopisy Mileně, pp. 45,67
62 'fallen angel'
Dopisy Mileně, p. 81
62 'Yes, you're right'
LM p. 77, quoting Milena
63 'The history of my marriage'

Notes

Letter II to Max Brod 29/7/20, see above

64   drugs
cf. LM p. 138

65   Count Franz Xaver Schaffgotsch
Mýtus Milena, p. 89 passim

65   'What I would like best'
LM p. 87, quoting Milena

65   'When I lay for a week'
'Moje přítelkyně Tr 27/1/21

65   dark rings under Milena's eyes
LM p. 93

66   'little animals'
LM p. 116, quoting Milena

67   'not one calm second'
LM p. 174

67   *Letters from Prison*
'List Rosy Luxemburgové z vězení Soni Liebknechtové' Tr 26/8/20

67   'What a delight it is'
'Cestování' Tr 18/7/20

68   mediation of Kafka
Dopisy Mileně, pp. 169, 172

70   'Cafés with a quite special life'
'Kavárna' Tr 10/8/20

72   'perhaps the most noble'
'Moda a sport' Tr 5/9/20

72   'Life is dry, hand to mouth'
'Život v horách' Tr 19/9/20

73   'wide, greeny-blue Danube'
'Podunajsko – kraj Nibelungů' Tr 25/9/20

73   short pieces
'Franz Kafka z knihy prosy', trans. Milena Jesenská, *Kmen* 9/9/20. English translations of 'The Sudden Walk', 'Excursion into the Mountains', 'Bachelor's Ill Luck', 'The Tradesman', 'The Way Home' and 'Passers-by' are included in *Kafka The Complete Short Stories*, ed. Nahum N. Glatzer, London 1992

73   'A Report to an Academy'
'Zpráva pro Akademii', Franz Kafka, trans. Milena Jesenská Tr 26/9/20. An English translation can be found in *Kafka The Complete Short Stories*, see above

75   advertisement in *Neue Freie Presse*
reproduced in *Mýtus Milena*, see above, p. xvi; Kafka helped place the advertisement. Cf. *Dopisy Mileně*, p. 162

76   'In me is an unfulfilled dream'

Letter V to Max Brod, see above
77   'Are you saying'
    Letter III to Max Brod, see above
77   'Milena, do understand my age'
    LM p. 47
78   'With her refined sensuality'
    Rio Preisner, 'Franz Kafka and the Czechs', *Mosaic*, Winnipeg 1979, p. 133
78   'perhaps the one true love affair of his life'
    Pawel, p. 388, see above

Chapter 6: Postscripts

79   'It was terrible'
    Letter V to Max Brod, see above
79   'Look at the election posters', 'At the edge of the town'
    'Nová krása' Tr 31/10/20
81   'goodwill'
    'Novoroční přání' Tr 1/1/21
81   'Perhaps every town'
    'Tanec nad propastí' Tr 5/11/20
81   'Yes, yes, I agree'
    'Cibulička almužnou' Tr 9/12/20
82   'It must be brief'
    'Reklama' Tr 12/12/20
82   'A street is not'
    'Výkladní skřině' Tr 21/8/20
82   'authenticity'
    'Kyč' Tr 11/3/21
82   'a wide sofa'
    'Ruční práce' Tr 1/1/21
83   toys
    'Jaké hračky' Tr 18/12/20
83   'the decisive features'
    'Děti' Tr 9/1/21
83   not to write
    Letter to Max Brod, *Letters to Friends*, see above, p. 254
83   'I am at my wit's ends'
    Letter IV to Max Brod, see above
85   *Cesta* stories
    'Dva holoubci', Jules Laforgue, trans. Milena Jesenská, *Cesta*, vol III, 1921 no. 10

Notes

'Příběh jednoho zločinu', M. Gorky, trans. Milena Jesenská, *Cesta*, vol IV, 1922 nos. 16–19

85   Kafka's boyhood charity
      'Děti' Tr 9/1/21

85   'I know someone'
      'Tajemná vykoupení' Tr 25/2/21

85   'When I glimpsed you'
      'Všem drobným jarním kytičkám' Tr 26/3/21

86   'You are going to see Milena'
      quoted in *The Nightmare of Reason*, p. 416

86   'harder, terser'
      JV p. 61

86   Rosa Luxemburg
      Červen vol IV 1921, p. 27 passim

87   Devětsil
      Devětsil, The Czech Avant-Garde of the 1920s and 1930s, Oxford 1990, catalogue of Oxford Museum of Modern Art Exhibition

87   'The higher up near the roof'
      'Ti nahoře a ti dole' Tr 3/2/21

87   'I don't think that I could have'
      Letter VII to Max Brod, see above

87   'A whole chapter'
      'O "Prokopu" Špičáku' Tr 25/6/21

88   'In the morning the catastrophe'
      'Loučení, loučení' Tr 17/8/21

89   'You arrive one evening'
      'Okno' NL 27/9/21

90   'The letter-writer'
      Letter to Robert Klopstock, *Letters to Friends*, see above, p. 302

90   'After paying four calls'
      DK 15/10/21

90   'Always M. or not M.'
      DK 2/12/21

90   'M. is right'
      DK 18/1/22

90   'The two questions'
      DK 19/1/22

90   M. is right about me'
      DK 20/1/22

90   'the joy of merely talking'
      DK 4/2/22

Notes

91 'If M., for example'
    DK 29/1/22

91 'strangeness and enchantment'
    The Castle, Franz Kafka, trans. Willa and Edwin Muir, London 1992, p. 46

91 'From some sort of depression'
    'Vulgarní literatura' Tr 4/3/22

92 'Čička'
    'Slečná Čička' Tr 4/2/22

92 'M. was here'
    DK 8/5/22

92 'returns to Prague'
    'Výkladní skříně' Tr 21/8/20

92 'Cheerfulness is the first rule'
    'Vídeň', Tr 4/4/22

93 separate bedrooms
    Dubrovic, see above, p. 52

93 'If you say to someone'
    'Povrchní povídání o vážném předmětě' Tr 17/6/22

94 'quite white with powder'
    'Charlie Chaplin' NL 20/7/22

95 good summer
    LM p. 181

95 'Not long after'
    'Obyčejná historie o Kočičce Čičce' NL 5/10/22

95 Jiří Weil
    Fond JV

95 Paris or London
    'Paříž nebo Londýn' NL 5/11/22

96 Berlin
    'Der blaue Vogel' NL 15/12/22

96 'When that is a bit'
    Letter to Karel Scheinpflug 5/1/23 in Fond JV

96 'Will o'the Mill'
    'Will z mlýna', R. L. Stevenson, trans. Milena Jesenská, *Cesta* vol V,
    1923. The original can be found in *The Merry Men and Other Tales*,
    R. L. Stevenson, London 1924. It was first published in 1878.

96 'clear and crystalline'
    'Robert Louis Stevenson' NL 21/11/23

96 'There's no translation yet'
    Letter to Karel Scheinpflug 5/1/23 in Fond JV

97 'Translation'
    Letter to Karel Scheinpflug 4/2/23 in Fond JV

97 'I, who with pen in hand'

Notes

'Robert Louis Stevenson' NL 21/11/23
97 *The Master of Ballantrae*
Rytíř z Ballantrae, NL 21/11/23 passim
97 'The Devil at the Hearth'
'Ďábel u Krbu', NL 18/1/23

Chapter 7: Transition

100 'The Emancipation of Women'
'O té ženské emancipaci někdik poznámek velice zaostalých'
NL 17/2/23
101 Men were undoubtedly freer
'Mužóm do výbavy' NL 11/11/23
101 She advised men
'Pro muže, aby neřekli' NL 3/5/23
102 'Her eyes were blank'
M B-N p. 68
102 'in fact, an intercourse with ghosts'
LM p. 182
102 'to whom I perhaps enjoy writing most'
LM p. 184
102 'the opposing side'
LM p. 183
103 'Letters'
'Dopisy' NL 8/3/23
103 'I still often think', 'But at the moment'
LM p. 186
104 fashions in underwear
articles in NL, 28/1/23, 1/3/23, 29/3/23 and 7/6/23
104 'crystallinely chaste and pure'
'Amerika contra Německo' NL 7/4/23
105 'The Judgment'
'Soud', *Cesta*, vol V, 1923 p. 369. An English translation can be found
in *The Complete Short Stories*, see above p. 77
105 sensitive and impressive translator
'"The Judgment": A New Perspective', Hana Arie-Gaifman, *Cross Currents, A Yearbook of Central European Culture*, 1983, p. 159
105 Stories in *Cesta*
'Posedlý knihomol', Gustave Flaubert, Vol V, 1923, pp. 220, 241;
'Láska na první pohled', E. A. Poe, Vol V 1923, pp. 81, 103, 124; 'Žid',
Stendhal, Vol VII, 1925, pp. 292, 308
105 'Prague, my little golden town'
'Pólo před nábřežím' NL 10/6/23

Notes

106 'Cause or Effect'
'Příčina nebo účinek' NL 12/6/23

106 large debts
Mýtus Milena, p. 30

107 'The press blamed Georg Kaiser'
'Případ Jiřího Kaisera' NL 9/3/21

107 'a matt black car'
'V poledne na Příkopech' NL 9/3/23

107 'The whole world'
'Radosti do deseti korun' NL 11/8/23

108 'They all had slender'
'Kultura těla' NL 27/9/23

108 'the fairy-tale palaces'
'Srdce na zkušené' NL 23/10/23

108 lost suitcases
'Omnia Mea Mecum Porto' NL 13/3/24

108 'So far, things in Berlin'
LM p. 188

108 'full of excellent resolutions'
'Nepřítel' NL 28/9/23

109 'To close the door here'
'Srdce na zkušené' NL 23/10/23

109 'Men have a much easier time'
'Mužům do výbavy' NL 11/11/23

109 'How should a woman feel'
'Thema, které k módě nepatří' NL 22/11/23

110 'If I can wish you anything'
'Od člověka k člověku' NL 6/3/24

111 northern spring
'Sluníčku vstříc!' NL 6/3/24

112 Schaffgotsch's reliability
Mýtus Milena, p. 91

112 'I sat next to Kafka'
LS 8/8/39. Milena was prone to exaggerate and the story may have developed over time to a death-bed scene. But there seems little reason for her entirely to have made up the idea of a visit, especially given Schaffgotsch's separate reference.

112 Death of Kafka and obituaries
The Nightmare of Reason, p. 446 passim

112 'Dr Franz Kafka, the German writer'
'Franz Kafka' NL 6/6/24

114 attentive to Milena
M B-N p. 75

Notes

115 French underwear
'Moderní prádlo' NL 20/11/24
115 'In Praise of England'
'Chvála Anglie' NL 8/2/25
115 'With two women'
'Dva dopisy' NL 13/2/25
115 Divorce
Prague registry archives
116 her greatest love
Conversation with Staša Fleischmann in Paris
116 'A Great White Silence'
'Veliké, bílé mlčení' NL 3/6/25
116 *Milena's Recipes*
Mileniny Recepty, Prague 1925
116 *How To Bring Up Children*
Jak zacházeti s dětmi, Žena imprint, Topič, Prague 1925
116 *Peter Pan*
Petr Pan v Kensingtonském Parku, J. M. Barrie, trans. Jirka Malá, ed. Milena Jesenská, Prague 1925
117 *Peter Pan and Wendy*
Petr Pan a Wendy, Prague 1926 and 1927
117 'Letters from Arcadia'
'Listy ze Zapadlé Lhoty' NL 28/6/25, 9/7/25, 12/7/25, 16/7/25

Chapter 8: Prague

118 Poetism
Devětsil, see above, p. 19
120 'I don't like people'
'Stanovisko k módě' NL 7/5/25
120 fashion and architecture
'Novinky ze všech koutů světa sebrané' NL 10/4/24
120 Běla Friedländerová etc.
Fond JV
120 Milča Mayerová
Correspondence with Helen Lewis, a Jewish dancer from Prague and author of *A Time to Speak*, Belfast 1992
121 short bobs
'Především to mikádo' NL 10/9/25
121 'Being a journalist'
'Samostatná ženske zaměstnání' NL 12/7/25
121 'Where's Milena'
M B-N p. 82

Notes

121 His own divorce
Mýtus Milena, p. 91

121 'We perhaps do not see it'
'Pěšinkami všedního života I' NL 5/11/25

122 'Nowhere abroad does such a light'
'Světla nad Prahou' NL 4/2/26

122 'The town stopped being a fairy tale'
'Lokální patriotismus' NL 2/9/26

122 no paradise
'Malá strana s druhého hlediska' NL 11/3/26

122 'I imagine a language'
'Smysl pro geometričnost' NL 18/4/26

123 'When you enter a room'
'Ruská společenskost' NL 29/11/25

123 'Jesus Christ, what are you wearing'
JV p. 87

124 'the way to simplicity'
'Cesta k jednoduchosti' NL 8/5/26 and anthology of the same title, Prague 1926

125 Jaromír Krejcar
Devětsil, see above, Fond JV, his own articles in Prague newspapers and magazines, conversations with Staša Fleischmann in Paris

126 'The further development of Prague'
'Praha' NL 8/7/26

126 'modern people'
'Co je to vlastně: moderní človek' NL 11/7/26

127 Czech Communism
HCR, *Czechoslovakia at the Crossroads* see above. 'The Communist Party of Czechoslovakia and the Czech Resistance 1939–1945', Radomir Luza, *Slavic Review*, Stamford, Vol 28 no. 4 1969

128 Julius Fučík
Report from the Gallows, Julius Fučík, trans. and with a biographical note by Stephen Jolley, London 1951

128 'The journalist is interested'
'Role žurnalistiky v dnešním písemnictví' NL 7/11/26

129 'She fixed her eyes upon you'
JV p. 99

129 'I do not know how it is'
JV p. 90. The phrase 'once I thought I understood it' is unlikely to refer as far back as Milena's schoolgirl crush on Albina Honzáková. Perhaps it is a reference to the intensity of her friendship with Staša; Kafka in LM p. 84 describes Staša's gaze, as she looked at a photograph of Milena during a visit to him in Prague, as 'almost incomprehensibly

long and attentive, silent and serious'. But there is no evidence that the friendship, however intense, was sexual. It is more likely that Milena was referring to someone in Vienna, or even to Slávka herself.

130 'I think that the best person'
'Kletba výtečných vlastností', *Cesta k jednoduchosti*, Prague 1926

131 'Women, however'
'O primadonství', *Pestrý Týden*, 2/11/26

132 Civil wedding
Prague registry archives

132 'That day a piece of our life'
'Stěhovati se' NL 17/7/27

132 Prague's courtyards
'Pražské jarní dvorečky' NL 29/4/28

132 'Many thanks, Milena'
quoted in M B-N p. 87

133 'In that time'
'Vzpomínky na Julia Fučíka', Jiří Weil, *Lidová kultura*, II, 5/12/46

133 'beautiful blue eyes'
Letter to JV in Fond JV

133 *Člověk dělá šaty*
Topič, Prague 1927

133 *Šťastnou cestu*
Topič, Prague 1928

133 freedom of the road
'O cestovních kancelářích', 'Alespoň sen!', *Šť'astnou cestu*, pp. 75,84

133 'The Trench-coat'
Šťastnou cestu, p. 92

134 'Why is this land'
'Mezinárodní výstava Werkbundu "Die Wohnung" ve Stuttgartu' NL 23/10/27

135 'I could write pages'
'Jak si představujeme ideální školu' NL 11/9/27

135 the modern home
'O moderním bydlení' I and II, NL 5/2/28, 19/2/28

135 'unconsidered propaganda'
Staša Fleischmann memoir, see above

136 back on her feet
Conversation with Staša Fleischmann about letter from Milena to her mother in summer 1928

136 in bed all summer
JC p. 73

136 'the most beautiful corner of the world'
'O Šumavě a lidé které nosí' NL 8/7/28

136 'soon afterwards'
     M B-N p. 88
136 gonorrhea
     notes for draft article by JV in Fond JV
136 perhaps a Caesarian
     a Caesarian was certainly considered, according to Augusta Müllerová,
     an architect and colleague of Krejcar, in a letter to JV in Fond JV. But
     neither JC nor M B-N mention a Caesarian as having taken place.
136 'Milena spent the entire'
     JC p. 74

Chapter 9: Motherhood

137 'right knee'
     Some accounts have 'left knee' but Milena herself in the article
     'Očíslovaní lidé' NL 24/2/29 refers to her right knee
137 'that ladies' man'
     JV p. 101
137 'Rather than give you'
     JV p. 88
137 cosmetic surgery
     'Kosmetické operace' NL 11/11/28
137 'Again you must help me'
     Letter in Fond JV
138 advertisement
     ReD no. 10, 1928
139 'The pain was indescribable'
     M B-N p. 89
139 furnishings
     Letter in Fond JV
139 book of modern photography
     'Svět jest krásný ("Die Welt ist schön", Kurt Wolff, Verlag Munchen)'
     NL 20/1/29
139 'The two lads carried me'
     'Očíslovaní lidé' NL 24/2/29
139 'A man who stopped loving me'
     'Kdo je vinen' I and II, NL 3/3/29 and 10/3/29
140 'You are right that I'
     Letter in Fond JV, June 1929
141 'The café table marks'
     'Ženatý bohém' LN 29/7/29
142 'fragile glass'
     'Přátelé našich přátel' LN 11/8/29

Notes

142 'Between Jája and Honza'
Lásky holčičky půl druhého roku staré' LN 15/12/29

143 'Civilised Woman?'
'Civilisovaná žena?' LN 1/12/29 and reprinted in *Civilisovaná žena, Civilisierte Frau?*, Brno 1929, a collection of essays in Czech and German on the theme of 'Civilised Woman?'

144 distributing children
Fleischmann memoir, see above

144 Ma-Fa
JV p. 105

145 articles about drug abuse
Svěd., p. 909

145 'Life is terribly hard'
JV p. 106

145 holiday in Belgium
conversation with Staša Fleischmann and LS 2/8/38

145 Jája's perspective
JV p. 107

146 took everyone out for dinner
Stanislav Budín memoirs, *Jak to vlastně bylo*, Prague 1970

146 affair with Fučík
Conversation with Eduard Goldstücker

146 contact address
Rudé právo 24/7/32

146 Eisenstein films
Fleischmann memoir

147 'This is Julius Fučík'
Ibid.

147 Kurt Konrad
JV p. 116

147 'Dear Mr Kocourek'
'pomoc přijde odjinud' *Tvorba* 9/2/33

149 'Should I refuse', 'Human love'
'Kocourkovská generace' *Tvorba* 23/2/33 (includes Kocourek's reply and Milena's counter-response)

149 membership of Communist Party
JV believed Milena was in the party (JV p. 119) as did Buber-Neumann (M B-N p. 92). Jiří Žantovský, then a young Communist in Prague, believed she was not the joining sort (conversation in Prague). The then chair of the Vinohrady section told JV that she had not been able to expel Milena from the party in 1935 because she was not in the files as a member. But JV believes she could have been expelled earlier or

kept at a distance for 'conspiratorial reasons' (JV p. 119). What is not in doubt is Milena's close involvement with the party.

150 Rise of Hitler
A Concise History of Germany, Mary Fulbrook, Cambridge 1990

150 'Only a strong and united democracy'
'jakou frontu chceme?' *Tvorba* 23/3/33

151 'Is it possible to bring up a child'
'Je vůbec možno vychovati dobře dítě doma?' *Žijeme* 1932/33 p. 230

152 Krejcar in Moscow
'čtrnáct dní v moskvé' *Tvorba* 13/7/33

152 'It is a poor quarter'
'Vono to baroko je dobrý jen pro voko' *Svět práce* no. 2, 1933

153 manufacturer of slogans
M B-N p. 92

153 Bohumír Šmeral
JV p. 119

153 ' "If you can't keep quiet" '
Hast Du Auf Deutsche Geschossen, Grandpa?, Fritz Beer, Aufbau-Verlag, Berlin 1992, p. 262

154 'honest to the point of self-destruction'
Ibid. p. 260

154 Jožka Jabůrková
Reportáž o novinářce, Marta Pilná, Prague 1959

154 Evžen Klinger
Conversations with Staša Fleischmann in Paris, Eduard Goldstücker and Miroslav Galuška in Prague

155 Divorce
Prague registry archives

156 'Milena would literally weigh'
JC p. 86

156 'The "Dicodit jug" '
JC p. 84

157 'hopeless, stupid feeling'
JV p. 125

157 'With those kind of people'
Svěd. p. 925

Chapter 10: Munich

Background sources for Sudeten Germans and Munich crisis
HCR, *Czechoslovakia at the Crossroads*, see above; *The Parting of Ways*, London 1982, *Europe and the Czechs*, London 1938, and *A German Protectorate*, London

Notes

1942, all by Shiela Grant Duff; *Munich, Prologue to Tragedy*, John Wheeler-Bennett, London 1948, *Munich*, Robert Kee, London 1988

158 'It is a great shame'
   Mýtus Milena, p. 59
158 shabby clothes
   Conversations with Steffi Schlamm
160 Bohnice
   Svěd., p. 914
160 a beautiful Prague spring
   A Noble Combat The Letters of Shiela Grant Duff and Adam von Trott zu Solz 1932–1939, ed. Klemens von Klemperer, Oxford 1988
160 'There are workers and craftsmen'
   'Lidé na výspě' Pr 27/10/37
161 Mařka Šmolková
   M B-N p. 119 and 'V zemi nikoho' Pr 29/12/38
163 'Vienna in spring'
   'František Liliom, obchod smíšeným zbožím' Pr 15/12/37
163 'In Vinohrady in front'
   'Lidé v pohybu' Pr 29/12/37
163 'One night the park-keeper'
   JC p. 90
164 'I know how Milena was glad'
   Letter to JC 7/6/48 in Fond JV
165 Relationship with Schlamms
   Unpublished letters and conversations with Steffi Schlamm
165 Lumír Čivrný
   Conversations with Lumír Čivrný in Prague
165 'crystalline type of the New Woman'
   original Czech manuscript of Čivrný memoir published in *La Nouvelle Alternative*, No. 4, 1986, Paris
165 'When we went on an outing'
   JC p. 93
167 'In quieter – and quiet – times'
   'Soudce Lynch v Evropě' Pr 30/3/38
168 'The whole region'
   'Kolik stála Henleinova řeč v Karlových Varech?' Pr 22/6/38
169 'It is my unalterable decision'
   Munich, Prologue to Tragedy, p. 61
169 'There will be no Anschluss'
   'Anšlus nebude' I and II, Pr 25/2/38 and 1/6/38
171 'In reality, it seems'
   'Kolik stála Henleinova řeč', Pr 22/6/38

171 'a poor village'
'Česká vesnice 1938' Pr 10/8/38

172 'You accept that I love you'
LS undated, summer 1938

172 'Go and look at Bruges'
LS 2/8/38

172 'Already it is better'
LS early 8/1938

174 'If I write in Czech', 'I have the impression'
LS 18/8/38

174 'We hear a lot about the danger'
LS undated, 8 or 9/38

175 'that monstrous formation Czechoslovakia'
Munich, p. 149

175 'We all live in huge disruption'
LS 13/9/38

176 Milena's information
Extracts from Fučík's diary, *Tvorba* no. 36, 1948 and letter from Klinger to *Tvorba* no. 38, 1948

176 'The Czechoslovak government'
Munich, p. 170

176 'On Wednesday – 21 September'
'Průřez tří dnů' Pr 28/9/38

176 urging Czechs to stand firm
'Pověz, kam utíkáš – povím ti, kdo jsi' Pr 21/9/38

177 'How horrible, fantastic, incredible'
quoted in Kee (see above), p. 193

177 'A dull, tired calm'
'Průřez tří dnů' Pr 28/9/38

Chapter 11: War

178 'I do not belong'
'Nad naše síly' Pr 12/10/38

178 account of the immediate events
'Průřez tří dnů', Pr 28/9/38, drawn on in the previous chapter

178 'The Month of September'
'Měsíc září' Pr 5/10/38

179 'some thousands fallen'
'Nad naše síly' Pr 12/10/38

180 'between the journalist and reader'
'Denní zprávy na posledních stránkách' Pr 19/10/38

180 Milena met the unemployed

Notes

'Nezaměstnanost za prahem domácnosti' Pr 2/11/38

180 'returned to their natural calling'
'Vdané ženy z práce' Pr 9/11/38

180 'Why socialism always fails'
LS 2/11/38

180 'You know what, why don't you'
Čivrný memoir, see above

180 'they did it with dignity', 'It's desperately difficult'
LS 17/11/38

181 'Perhaps you are tired'
'Co dává doba dětem v hračkách' Pr 14/12/38

181 'Today there is No Man's Land'
'V zemi nikoho' Pr 29/12/38

182 'Christmas was really awful'
LS undated, Christmas 1938

182 'Have you got snow?'
Letter to Steffi Schlamm, undated, Christmas 1938

182 'She would keep tuning'
JC p. 96

183 'with a considered, subtle hierarchy
'Poslední dny Karla Čapka' Pr 11/1/39

183 'It's not only love for Čapek'
LS 1/39

183 'Work – followed by food'
'Podmínka přijetí; bud' hezká' Pr 8/2/39

184 'very, very sad'
Conversation with Eduard Goldstücker

184 'We Czechs cling to our language'
'Jak se stýkati s Čechy?' Pr 15/2/39

184 'an abscess'
HCR p. 302

185 'Workers rise up!'
'Dobrá rada nad zlato' Pr 8/3/39

185 'he confidently placed'
HCR p. 269

186 'How do the greatest events'
'Praha, ráno 15. března 1939' Pr 22/3/39

188 The protectorate
HCR, *The Killing of SS Obergruppenführer Reinhard Heydrich*, Callum MacDonald, London 1989, *A German Protectorate*, Shiela Grant Duff (see above), *It Happened in Czechoslovakia Inside a German Protectorate*, George Hronek, Prague/London, *The Czechs Under Nazi Rule*, Vojtech Mastny, Columbia NY, 1971

Notes

188 'It would have been a suicidal gesture'
   'O střízlivosti a gestu' Pr 29/3/39

189 'Evžen must leave'
   LS undated

189 English men and women
   Harold Stovin, Kenneth Ogier, Bill Henson and Mary Johns(t)on, cited
   in testament from Joachim von Zedtwitz to the Yad Vashem commission in Jerusalem

189 Joachim von Zedtwitz
   testament to Yad Vashem commission

190 'At that time'
   JC p. 106

190 'When he left'
   LS, late spring 1939

190 'standing still'
   'O umění zůstat stát' Pr 5/4/39

191 'Our mothers return to the task'
   'Česká maminka Pr 19/4/39

191 *V Boj*
   Military Museum archives in Prague, *Paměti II (1938–1945)*, Václav
   Černý pp. 150, 152

192 Kafka's letters
   Haas introduction to LM, 'Jak to bylo s Kafkovými dopisy Mileně',
   Alena Wagnerová, *Lidové noviny*, 31/7/93

192 'She refused to take us'
   Budín memoir in Fond JV

192 Libuše Vokrová
   Conversation in Prague

193 'And where does she want to go'
   'Co očekává Čech od Čecha?' Pr 3/5/39

194 'You never hear any good news'
   A German Protectorate, Shiela Grant Duff, p. 241

194 Wolfram von Wolmar
   A German Protectorate, p. 277

194 'a coin in the palm of Europe'
   'Co očekává Čech od Čecha?' Pr 3/5/39

194 'Am I above all a Czech?'
   'Jsem především Češka?' Pr 10/5/39

195 'Now the fire must blaze', 'I demand something more'
   Reader's letter and Milena's reply in 'Stačí být Čechem?'
   Pr 24/5/39

195 'We have got into the habit'
   'Promiňte, že nešeptám' Pr 24/5/39

Notes

195 National Assembly, 'In front of me'
'Lidé v Národním souručenství' Pr 31/5/39

196 'At night, when she was'
Čivrný memoir, see above

197 'On 15 March, the Czech journalist'
'Týká se nás všech' Pr 14/6/39

197 'Czech soldiers pass by'
'Soldaten wohnen auf den kanonen' Pr 21/6/39

198 'takes a piece of our culture'
'S "ubohým a holým"' Pr 5/7/39

198 'We are alive'
Mýtus Milena, p. 49

198 'It's as if she's confined'
Unpublished letter to Willi and Steffi Schlamm 21/8/39

199 'Milena swung from mood to mood'
JC p. 110

200 feared for her own safety
Božka Nováková in *Svěd.* p. 917

200 another publication
JV p. 144

201 the arrest
Čivrný conversation and memoir, JC p. 116

Chapter 12: Imprisonment

202 Pankrác prison
Prison archives, conversations with Marie Chaloupecká and Hana Housková in Prague, 'In the cell with Milena Jesenská', Hana Housková, *Listy* no. 4, 1992

203 'You were our tutor'
Čivrný memoir, see above

203 'My pretty dark-haired girl'
note to Marie Chaloupecká

204 'I want only to say'
Svěd. p. 920

204 'I don't have any idea'
transcript of note in Fond JV

205 'in the last few months'
Unpublished letters to Schlamms 21/3/40, 27/4/40 and 15/7/40

205 Dresden
M B-N p. 149, JV p. 147

205 'Mona Lisa smile', 'when forests are felled'
Hana Housková in *Listy*, see above

Notes

206 'I couldn't recognise her'
JC p. 118
206 'When everything was peaceful'
Housková in *Listy*, see above
206 Ravensbrück
M B-N, *Under Two Dictators*, Margarete Buber, London 1949, *Ravens-brück*, Dagmar Hájková et al., Prague 1963, *The Holocaust*, Martin Gilbert, London 1987, *Women in the Resistance and in the Holocaust*, ed. Vera Laska, Westport Connecticut, 1983
208 'Milena from Prague'
M B-N p. 1
209 'Milena chose friendship'
M B-N p. 10
209 Zdena Nedvědová
JV p. 153
210 Tomy Kleinerová
JV p. 150, M B-N p. 176
210 'a scarecrow'
Under Two Dictators, see above p. 238
210 'Under these circumstances'
M B-N p. 156
211 'Her way of speaking'
M B-N p. 150
211 'aura of mystery'
M B-N p. 39
211 'Woman, you are an excellent journalist'
Budín memoir in Fond JV
211 'the age of poetry was over
M B-N p. 159
211 'I seem to have been fated'
M B-N p. 82
211 'the mere thought of accepting bread'
M B-N p. 8
212 'Milena stood at the doorway'
'Za Milenou', Anna Kvapilová, *Svobodné noviny*, 18/5/46
213 Assassination of Heydrich
The Killing of SS Obergruppenführer Reinhard Heydrich
213 lethal injections
Women in the Resistance and in the Holocaust, p. 221
214 TB certificate
M B-N p. 167
214 'She often complained'
M B-N p. 177

Notes

216 Frau Langefeld
M B-N p. 179 passim

216 'If ever I get out of here'
Under Two Dictators, p. 240

216 'Milena said sadly'
M B-N p. 175

216 'I really know nothing about Honza'
M B-N p. 197

217 Dr Percy Treite
Ravensbrück (see above), M B-N p. 201, 'Poslední dny Mileny Jesenské', Hana Housková in collaboration with Zdena Nedvědová, *Tvorba* 10/91

217 diagnosis and care
'Poslední dny Mileny Jesenské', see above

217 Jiřina Svobodová
Svěd. p. 923

218 'Look at the colour of my feet'
M B-N p. 203

218 'Endless trains'
'Sen' Tr 14/6/21

219 as was routine
92,000 Jews and non-Jews died in Ravensbrück. 23,000 women, Jews and non-Jews, were liberated by the Red Army on 20 April 1945. *The Holocaust* (see above) p. 805

Afterword

220 'weaker and less conscious'
'Jak by se nemělo kritizovat', Gusta Fučíková, *Kulturní tvorba*, 21/11/ 63

220 Goldstücker article
'À propos Milena Jesenská', Eduard Goldstücker, *Literární noviny*, 1966

223 'miraculous, violated, unviolable creature' LM p. 128

223 'claws'
Letter to Oskar Pollak, 20/12/02

223 'Perhaps everyone loves'
'Světla nad Prahou' NL 4/2/26

Index

Index

Index

Index

Index